# State, School, and Politics

# State, School, and Politics

## Research Directions

Michael W. Kirst
Stanford University

**Lexington Books**
D.C. Heath and Company
Lexington, Massachusetts
Toronto          London

pg.

# Table of Contents

# Foreword

This volume is a particularly appropriate introduction to the Lexington Books series on the politics of education. It presents a variety of views on what needs to be done, as well as the limits on that necessity, if the disciplines of political science and educational administration are to collaborate. This series is dedicated to encouraging a reunion of the two after a long and fruitless separation.

Scholars of school and state have been partners through much of western civilization, as Heinz Eulau reminds us later in this book, because their interactive effects could not be dissected. The purposes of the state could not ignore the instrument of the school if its ends were to be achieved. In turn, the objectives of the school, particularly the moral ones, could not be met if they ran against those of the state. If, in classical definition the school has the task of transmitting the cultural heritage and if part of that heritage deals with approved forms and policies of the state, the two institutions are inseparable in fact as well as theory. That intimacy is even greater than that of state and Church. The latter achieved a tenuous separation at times—in the Holy Roman Empire or modern democracies—but little of this has been known in the relationship of school and state.

Yet, in this century in America, political scientists have turned from the school as a proper focus—one of many—for their study. Educational specialists, both scholars in universities and administrators in districts, developed and sustained the belief that it was separate from, and should be immune to politics. Why this came to be has been set forth in Thomas Eliot's seminal essay in 1959 and commented upon, usually critically, in the decade or more following. The separation, though, was more one of belief than of fact. As these essays are aware, the political qualities of schooling have been, and remain, considerable.

That awareness, and its policy consequences, are conceptualizations which illuminate this book and others in the series. The criteria for the following volumes are few. The focus is upon American schools that are public and precollegiate, although some comparative analyses with other nations will be encouraged. The substance of each study will be an empirical base beyond that of the case study; preference is given to macroanalysis and comparative analysis, whatever the special topic. There are too many case studies in this field set in uncomparable designs permitting no generalization about other places and times. Further, the conceptual and theoretical constructs which guide the research must be explicit but presented with a minimum of jargon. Finally, the conclusions must meet the "So what?" criterion, i.e., what are the policy implications of such scholarship? This is designed to move scholars to think about the effect of their learning upon the policy world and those who work in it. These volumes are not restricted to political scientists or to educational administration scholars alone. The Siamese twin nature of the subject just does not permit such compartmentalization, as the present volume clearly demonstrates.

Such works are directed to the growing interest in politics of education instruction in undergraduate and graduate work in education and political science, to the increasingly politicized constituents of local schools, to those schools' administrators who increasingly face a political world, and to policy-makers at state and national levels who need knowledge about schools but must answer Herbert Spencer's question, "What knowledge is of most worth?" By drawing upon a diversity of disciplines, basing findings upon a sufficiently wide data base, and expressing all this in clear language directed to specific recommendations, we hope this series will contribute to answering Spencer's question.

It will be obvious that such a task is not easy from the essays that follow. The conflict represented there may depress those who want scholars to hand them agreed resolutions, possibly on graven tablets. But such conflict is a source of enrichening, a sign of intellectual ferment from which others will learn and seek verification. As such, it represents the diversity confronting the policy-maker. If wisdom commences with the knowledge that one does not know, but must learn, then the field of politics of education stands as a challenge for scholars to learn and as a hope for policy-makers to benefit. The challenge and hope provide this field excitement in the decade to come and a forum where discipline and relevance can meet.

FREDERICK M. WIRT

# Preface

This volume is an outgrowth of a Research Workshop on the Politics of Elementary and Secondary Education. Conferees were selected from the following aspects of the relationship between politics and education.

—the interaction of political and educational institutions, i.e., the ways in which the politics of community, state, and nation affect the operation of educational institutions.
—the political analysis of educational institutions, including processes of bargaining and decision making, and models of governance.
—the contribution of education to the development of political institutions and behavior, including patterns of political socialization and recruitment.

Some of the participants had worked extensively in one of these areas, and others had completed research that could be related to education and politics, thereby providing new insights.

A list of participants follows:

Joel S. Berke
Syracuse University
   Research Corporation
723 University Avenue
Syracuse, New York

Daniel Elazar
Department of Political Science
Temple University
Philadelphia, Pa.

Herbert Jacob
Department of Political Science
Northwestern University
Evanston, Illinois

Edgar Litt
College of Liberal Arts and Sciences
University of Connecticut
Storrs, Connecticut

George Lanoue
Columbia Teachers College
New York, New York

Stephen K. Bailey
Department of Political Science
Syracuse University
Syracuse, New York

Patrick Crecine
Department of Political Science
University of Michigan
Ann Arbor, Michigan

Laurence Iannaccone
Ontario Institute for Studies
   in Education
102 Bloor Street West
Toronto, Ontario
Canada

Michael Lipsky
Department of Political Science
MIT
Cambridge, Massachusetts

Norton Long
University of Missouri
St. Louis, Missouri

Kenneth Prewitt
Department of Political Science
University of Chicago
Chicago, Illinois

Ira Sharkansky
Department of Political Science
University of Wisconsin
Madison, Wisconsin

Sheldon Wolin
Department of Political Science
University of California
Santa Cruz, California

David Minar
Department of Political Science
Northwestern University
Evanston, Illinois

Harmon L. Zeigler
Department of Political Science
University of Oregon
Eugene, Oregon

Hendrik Gideonese
Bureau of Research
U.S. Office of Education
Washington, D.C.

Edward Greenberg
Department of Political Science
Stanford University
Stanford, California

Hans Weiler
Departments of Education and
   Political Science
Stanford University
Stanford, California

Paul E. Peterson
Department of Education
University of Chicago
Chicago, Illinois

Robert H. Salisbury
Department of Political Science
Washington University
St. Louis, Missouri

Frederick M. Wirt
School of Education
University of California
Berkeley, California

John Meyer
Department of Sociology
Stanford University
Stanford, California

Heinz Eulau
Department of Political Science
Stanford University
Stanford, California

H. Thomas James, Conference Chairman
The Spencer Foundation
Chicago, Illinois

Michael W. Kirst, Conference Director
School of Education
Stanford University
Stanford, California

David Grossman, Research Associate
School of Education
Stanford University
Stanford, California

Ideally, the conference could have mapped the conceptual boundaries of the whole research field of politics and education and, then, derived an explicit ranking of research topical priorities. The lack of theory from either political science or education to guide our efforts, however, impeded such an outcome. A sound way to rank research priorities is through the contribution of a proposed study to an overall theoretical structure—but we have no such theoretical structure. Recent conferences in political science were not fruitful in finding priorities for research in that entire discipline because of the same problem.[a]

Given limits on the state of the art, the preconference papers were designed around the following charge: "If you were to study something that would contribute the most to this field, what would you study and how would you do it." Two of the participants (Eulau and James) were asked to prepare opening presentations on the boundaries and intersect between education and politics. Through this procedure the conference could begin with several specific research proposals and then could proceed to explore linkages, gaps, and sequencing. This approach proved to be useful in that the papers fell into four distinct clusters with each cluster representing considerable internal similarity in orientation.

## The Four Research Focus Areas and Participants

**Cluster I**: New goals and objectives for educational institutions: stress on normative analysis of public policy alternatives and reexamination of prior assumptions upon which research is based (Bailey, Greenberg, Minar, Salisbury, Wolin, and Eulau).

**Cluster II**: The political education of youth: New directions in research on political socialization including cross-cultural studies (Hess, Litt, Meyer, Prewitt, Weiler, and Jacob).

**Cluster III**: An analysis of the governance of educational institutions: Especially issues of power, role, and decision-making (Gideonese, Elazar, Iannacone, La Noue, Lipsky, Peterson, Zeigler, Wirt, Kirst).

**Cluster IV**: The study of input-output-feedback relationships in educational policy-making—includes analysis of the distribution of financial inputs and their relationship to outputs (Berke, Crecine, James, Long, Sharkansky).

After initial discussions, Cluster IV disbanded and redistributed its membership among the other three. Consequently, the viewpoints of this cluster were integrated with the other groups. The organization of this book follows the cluster concept with each section organized around a discussion cluster.

[a]Heinz Eulau and James C. March, *Political Science* (Englewood Cliffs, N.J.: Prentice Hall, 1969).

The objective of the conference papers was to elicit new ideas and specific research projects. Consequently, the papers selected for this volume comprise a variety of writing styles. Some of the authors chose to use an extensive bibliography of prior research in their area of interest before proposing a new direction. Others decided to begin with the idea that interested them and develop this in detail, with less attention to an exhaustive bibliography of the general area of concern. It was the director's intention that there would be no uniform format for the papers so that their focus would be on the proposed research directions without constraints imposed by a specified style of presentation.

# Acknowledgments

This volume is based on a Conference sponsored by the Committee on Basic Research in Education (COBRE) which is part of the Division of Behavioral Sciences in the National Research Council. The Committee on Basic Research in Education is sponsored jointly by the National Academy of Sciences and the National Academy of Education. Each of the papers was prepared for the research workshop held by the Committee on Basic Research in Education which is supported in this endeavor through a contract between the National Academy of Sciences and the U.S. Department of Health, Education and Welfare, Office of Education. Sherman Ross, the Executive Secretary of COBRE, and his staff associate, Barbara Meeker, deserve special acknowledgment for their contributions in organizing the research workshop. Financial support from COBRE is also gratefully acknowledged by the editor for his analysis of the conference discussion that appears near the end of this volume. David Grossman, a Stanford graduate student, assisted the editor in the entire effort with special contributions in political socialization and normative theory.

H. Thomas James, president of the Spencer Foundation and a member of COBRE, was the moving force behind the idea of a conference in education and politics. He saw the potential of exploring the intersect between these fields and served as conference chairman. The editor hopes this volume will fulfill some of his hopes for the outcome of the conference.

# Background: The COBRE Conference

At the request of the U.S. Office of Education, the National Academy of Sciences (NAS), jointly with the National Academy of Education (NAE) established the Committee on Basic Research in Education (COBRE) in 1968 to support the conduct of research of a fundamental character in education.

This Committee is currently composed of a group of distinguished scientists, with Patrick Suppes (Stanford University) as chairman, and James S. Coleman (The Johns Hopkins University) as vice chairman, and includes the following members: John B. Carroll (Educational Testing Service), Ernest W. Caspari (University of Rochester), Bruce K. Eckland (University of North Carolina), Robert M. Gagné (Florida State University), Wayne H. Holtzman (The Hogg Foundation for Mental Health, University of Texas), H. Thomas James (The Spencer Foundation), Arthur W. Melton (University of Michigan), Julius B. Richmond, M.D. (Harvard Medical School), A. Kimball Romney (University of California at Irvine), Edgar H. Schein (Massachusetts Institute of Technology), and Theodore W. Schultz (University of Chicago). The program is administered by the Division of Behavioral Sciences of the National Research Council. Henry David, Executive Secretary of the Division, is the Project Director.

Also serving on the Committee in earlier years were: R. Taylor Cole (Duke University), Lawrence A. Cremin (Teachers College, Columbia University), John I. Goodlad (University of California at Los Angeles), Louis Hartz (Harvard University), and Fritz Machlup (Princeton University). In its first two years of life, COBRE developed a project grant support program in the behavioral sciences in support of basic research on problems relevant to education. The selected projects were funded by the Office of Education. For its third year, a special small grant program directed toward recent doctoral recipients was established. The purposes of the grant program were to support research which will contribute to fundamental knowledge, and will deepen understanding of the critical problems in educational theory, policy and practice. In this effort, the behavioral sciences include anthropology, economics, geography, linguistic political science, psychology, and sociology, and also the relevant areas of the biological sciences, engineering, history, philosophy, and other sciences.

A second phase of third year activity was a series of eight research workshops. These workshops were invitational, informal, fifteen to twenty participants and ran from five to ten days. Each workshop was directed by a member of COBRE, and their general goals were to identify significant researchable questions in the area, to define regions or groups of research efforts, and to identify individual scientific contributors.

This book is derived from such a workshop held at Stanford University in September 1970 under the direction of H. Thomas James and Michael W. Kirst. The workshop was convened under the title of "Politics of Elementary and Secondary Education," and concentrated on the contributions of political scientists. Specific, advance contributions were commissioned, and Dr. Kirst prepared a summary and overview of the workshop. This book, with changes and additions, is a derivative of this process.

COBRE, the NAS and NAE, and the sponsors, the U.S. Office of Education, hope that *State, School, and Politics: Research Directions* will contribute to a richer and sharper development of political science research contributions to the problems of education. We thank the participants and the contributors, the director, and the editor, for their efforts.

Sherman Ross
Executive Secretary
Committee on Basic Research in Education

Division of Behavioral Sciences
National Academy of Sciences-National Research Council
Washington, D.C. 20418

# Introduction

The politics of education is a new and still largely uncharted area of research concentration. As recently as 1959, Thomas H. Eliot presented the need for a beginning of research in this field in the *American Political Science Review.* In 1969, the American Educational Research Association had enough interested members to form a special interest group concerned with the proper scope, methods, and objects of inquiry.

Neither of the parent disciplines—political science or education—has provided clear concepts or ready-made, tried and tested, methods for study of educational politics and policy formulation. The reform of school administration in the early 1900s sought to divorce education from overt political conflict. This reform tended to remove incentives for scientific research that questioned the tenet that politics and education do not mix and deflect concern from the intersect of politics and education. Students of the government of education usually paid their way by seeking answers to questions of urgent interest or importance to school administrators (particularly how to raise more money). Studies dealt largely with internal and stable aspects of educational institutions and practices, delimited in scope to specific program areas, educational levels, states or localities, and so on. Moreover, the value educators attached to isolation of their activities from general government may, to a large degree, explain the absence of research directed to the comparison of public school systems with other social institutions having education-related goals.

A number of environmental influences in the last decade have brought about a significant change in research preoccupations. Funds from USOE and private foundations stimulated work by a variety of social scientists from other disciplines. Legislators began to ask for more precise evaluations of the results of formal schooling before assenting to the open-ended cost estimates of schoolmen. Far-reaching proposals to change the traditional relationships among the three levels of educational government were widely discussed across the country by such scholars as Conant, Gardner, and Heller. At the local level, parents, teachers, minority groups, and students have gone into action to redistribute political influence previously held by professionals. Research focused on curriculum change, school desegregation, community involvement, etc., raised questions about political structures and processes that would impede or encourage educational change.

Lindblom has described public policy-making as marked by "complexity and apparent disorder," a statement equally applicable to the present study of educational politics. Research still tends to deal with a single level of government, with a restricted set of variables or a small number of units studied in depth. Recent studies have highlighted different components of the educational-political system, but the units of analysis are not yet numerous or broadly enough defined to be fully representative; and the research designs are not sufficiently similar to provide the basis for amassing cumulative or comparative findings. We have little insight into the functioning of political processes over time or the relationship between the various federal levels and branches of educational government. Efforts to study the effects of school bureaucracies on policy formulation and implementation have lagged. Political socialization research has been limited by a model which conceptualized socialization as the transmission of belief systems and behavior patterns from adults to pre-adults. The bibliographic essay by Professor Wirt at the end of this volume is a comprehensive documentation of prior work in this field and the above issues.

In sum, little agreement exists about priorities or theory to guide research. Political norms in education policy-making have not been seriously considered. As was the case in the early discovery of America, a variety of explorers have staked out and laid claim to sections of unsettled terrain. Little attention has been given to the development of conceptual or normative frameworks; rather concepts and constructs previously put forward by various social scientists have been adopted, and imported models have tended to suggest rather than control the research design. Research designs using survey techniques and multiple regression have tended to mask political variables. Case studies have limited usefulness for building generalizations. Political systems analysis has been used as window dressing but has yet to prove rewarding as a method for studying the politics of education. The political aspects of the future of American education have been largely unexplored.

The embryonic state of the art (as detailed in Wirt's essay) is an ample justification for a book on education and politics. This unexplored area could avoid the unrecognized value assumptions and methodological pitfalls of prior political studies. But the papers highlight another compelling reason for the focus of this volume. At a time when public agencies of all types are undergoing extreme stress and a crisis of confidence, public education is, perhaps, experiencing more of these pressures than the average public enterprise. The administrative reforms from 1890-1920 established a relationship between the general governments at all levels and the school which persisted in the main until the 1960s. This relationship embodied substantial covert interactions between the state and the school that were rarely recognized or discussed overtly. These reforms also emphasized internal public education governance pattern that included at its core the primacy of a central civil service bureaucracy and the professional educator.

Issel concluded that the 1890-1920 reforms:

... stripped the ward school boards of power, left them intact only as boards of visitors, and placed the control of the schools in the hands of cosmopolitan and efficiency minded upper class businessmen and professionals, whose legislative decisions would be carried out by dispassionate, university trained, educational experts according to the impersonal criteria of bureaucratic social organization.[a]

[a]William H. Issel, "Modernization in Philadelphia School Reform, 1882-1905." *The Pennsylvania Magazine of History and Bibliography*, Vol. XCIV, No. 3 (July 1970), pp. 381-82.

This turn-of-the-century movement swept away the spoils system for teaching jobs, governance by subcommittees of ward-based school boards, and the decentralized school management.

The reforms also fostered the myth that eduation and politics could be kept separate. At the same time our national heritage of "local control of education" restricted the federal role and deflected interest in exploring the intersect between national political forces and local education policy. Today, however, we see the same slogans of the 1890-1920 era (accountability, community control, eliminate red tape, revamp curriculum) being used to: (1) increase the overt intersection of education and politics, (2) break down the central administrative structure of American schools, and (3) restrict the power of school professionals and bureaucrats. Students, community groups, and teachers are expanding their influence and employing collective political action.

In short, recent reform in school governance is a growing force that runs counter to the 1890-1920 theme of separating education and politics. Even teacher negotiations that fix school policy in collective bargaining contracts are increasingly moving into the political arena of general government, particularly the mayor's office. The cost-revenue squeeze at the local level is moving the base of tax support to the state and federal level, but bringing with the dollars increased control from state and federal politicians. These politicians are answerable to different constituents than the educator's professional association.

Heinz Eulau's introductory paper places this general issue of the intersect of politics and education in the broad context that it is treated within this book. Western political philosophy has exhibited dualistic thinking about the state-school relationship which centers around the basic query: should the state shape the school's function and purpose or should the school shape and guide the states'. In the terminology of the scholar in analyzing the state and school, which is the independent and which the dependent variable? The Greek tradition believed schooling shaped the citizen to fulfill himself in terms of the interests of the *polis* (state), and the latter assured that the former does that job well. Eulau has termed this the "utopian scent"—that education can create the perfect political order. This Greek viewpoint assumed that education was subordinate to, indeed the servant of, political order.

This Greek tradition in which a good society was created by integration of all institutions and values has echoes today. School critics on the right insist that teacher, student, and curriculum should uphold the ends of national government and accept patriotic and generalized presentation of history. Society can be preserved if the school supports the state. Meanwhile, growing movement on the left calls for the school to be reformed because of its dominance by false values which produce a conformist and corrupt population. The school creates and reinforces that "establishment" which has dominant influence in all of American life.

Eulau contends, however, it is unlikely that the state can be only what the school lets it be. It would be hard to find, he observes, "a political order in the real world which, even if we could agree on its being close to perfection has been created out of or by an educational system." If the school is the dependent variable then political problems are not basically traceable to the school but to the state.

# Introductory Essay — Political Science and Education: The Long View and the Short

HEINZ EULAU

Some years ago, reviewing the contemporary state of political science, I noted that "political scientists are riding off in many directions, evidently on the assumption that if you don't know where you are going, any road will take you there."[1] I am very glad, therefore, that we—both students of politics and students of education—have this opportunity to consider the relationship between our respective disciplines and to explore common ground before we rush off our separate ways doing all kinds of things we should not be doing and neglecting things that we should attend to.

No political scientist who has ever smelt the scent of Utopia can escape a fascination with education, and for once, I think, we are not riding off because something is fad or fashion. To believe otherwise would be taking a very short view indeed. And if one were only to take the short view, one would deprive onself of the sustained efforts made through the centuries by political philosophers to understand the relationship between politics and education.

But if one took only the long view, the result would be stultifying because one would inevitably come to the conclusion of *toujours la même chose*. If the short view is short, the long view, paradoxically, is even shorter. I propose to tread in-between, partly because by education and inclination I have a historical bent of mind, partly because by trained incapacity I cannot ignore the shape of things as they are. Happily, history has always meant to me the study of how things have come to be what they are, so that I have always succeeded in eluding the comfortable assumption either that the past is full of infinite wisdom or that present trends will continue indefinitely into the future.

Let me begin, therefore, at the beginning. The trouble is, of course, that political scientists not only may not know where they are going but also may be disagreed on where they come from. As I wrote at the earlier occasion, "whether one prefers to trace political science back to Plato and Aristotle, or to the more empirically-minded Machiavelli, or to the establishment of independent academic departments of political science in the late nineteenth century, or to Charles Merriam's *New Aspects of Politics* (1925), is largely a matter of taste."[2] Fortunately, the challenge of this opportunity leads me to amend the statement. Where one begins is perhaps not a matter of taste after all but dictated by what one is interested in. And if one is interested in politics and education, one better begin with Plato and go from there.

What makes Plato so pregnant with meaning today is the current impasse over

1

the relationship between the educational system and the political order. There are those who, because they believe that education is dominated in any case by something they call the military-industrial-political complex, would make the schools staging areas of reform or revolution. And there are those who, because they mistake their establishment views and values for universal verities, would rather throttle education or choke it to death than have it sullied by political reality. Both sides, I suggest, might find it profitable to read Plato. For Plato's *Republic*, it seems to me, represents this myopic view of the relationship between politics and education; in fact, it is *the* educational institution. There is simply no difference between the state of the Republic and its educational system. They are the same because they have the same goal—the well-being of the state. Education is not an end but the means by which human nature can be shaped in the right direction to produce the harmonious state. As the virtuous citizen can only fulfill himself in the *polis*, the state must see to it that training of the young is consonant with the welfare of the state. If the educational system is good, almost any improvement is possible in the political order.

There are two things to be derived by implication from this mini-presentation of Plato on education. First, there is the utopian scent—education can create the perfect political order. And second, because the image of the political order is perfect, at least in the beholder's mind, education can be nothing but the handmaiden of politics. Both presumptions, I daresay, are still very much with us—in whatever guise. They explain, I think, both the optimism and dogmatism of all those, whether of the Right, Center or Left, who believe that if something is wrong with the social and political order, all that is needed to rectify things is more education, better education and morally right education. But, as I said, these are only presumptions, and a presumption is, by definition, a conclusion that is not based on evidence.

Let me put it differently. I know of no political order in the real world which, even if we could agree on its being close to perfection, has been created out of or by an educational system. If anything, the relationship between politics and education, it seems to me, is the other way around. If the political order is sound, stable, legitimate, just or whatever other criterion of "goodness" one wishes to apply, education and all that is implied by education, such as the creation of new knowledge or the transmission of traditional knowledge, flourishes. If the political order is in trouble, education is in trouble. If we were to follow Plato or, for that matter, Aristotle who believed that education is prior to politics, we would have to conclude that our public troubles—the war in Vietnam, poverty in the ghettos, pollution of the life space, and so on—are due to our educational system. Of course, John Dewey and Dr. Benjamin Spock have been blamed; but I seriously doubt that we can take such scapegoating seriously. On the contrary, therefore, if we find our educational system wanting, I think we should try to look at the public order rather than, as we have done so much in education, contemplate our navels as if the outside world did not exist.

Perhaps I am overstating the anticlassical view somewhat, but I do so only because I sense the spell of Plato and Aristotle is still so very much with us, even though it is camouflaged these days in the rhetoric of Herbert Marcuse or the aphorisms of Chairman Mao, on the Left, and the "public philosophy" of Walter Lippmann or the homilies of Max Rafferty, on the Right. But if we assume that it is the political process and the condition of political affairs that make education what it is, I think we find ourselves at the interstices of polity and educational system where political science as a theoretical science and education as an applied science can truly meet on empirical ground.

Let me state all this more formally. I think we have to think of politics, broadly conceived as including both government and societal happenings, as the independent variable and of education as the dependent variable. Now, what bothers me about most of the recent research in political science that deals with education or education-related topics like socialization or attitude formation is that it has been largely cast in the teleological model that is implicit in Plato's and Aristotle's conceptions of the polity. Let me single out as an example *The Civic Culture*, not because it is unique but because it is undoubtedly the most majestic work of this genre of research.[3] Almond and Verba discover nine relationships between level of education as the independent variable and a variety of political perceptions, attitudes and behavioral manifestations as the dependent variables. They conclude that "educational attainment appears to have the most important demographic effect on political attitudes."[4] I have no doubt that these relationships exist. But I believe that one or another mix of all the variables subsumed under what is called political culture—whether parochial, participant, subject or civic—is nothing but one huge tautology that, like Plato's *Republic*, so completely absorbs politics into education and education into politics that explanation of the relationship between politics and education is foreclosed. What is involved is, of course, more than formal education which, Almond and Verba point out, "may not adequately substitute for time in the creation of these other components of the civic culture."[5] But in their subsequent discussion the Platonic-Aristotelian model (which is basically a teleological and practically an engineering approach) implicit in their premises and inferences is made quite explicit: "The problem, then, is to develop, along with the participation skills that schools and other socializing agencies can foster, affective commitment to the political system and a sense of political community."[6] Now, these are not the words of Plato and Aristotle but their spirit is there. The good society will emerge if, through proper socializing and educational procedures, in whatever channels and by whatever agents, the right components of the political culture are harnessed in the right direction.[7]

The belief in the omnipotence of education in shaping the political order is reflected in much of the literature on political development. "The educational preparation of at least sizeable segments of a population," writes Robert E. Ward, "is a basic factor in the modernization of political cultures."[8] I find all of these writings troublesome because the formulation of the problem strikes me as eminently circular. For, it seems to me, the introduction of a sophisticated educational system is an *act* of modernization and can, therefore, not be its cause. In many underdeveloped nations which mobilize educationally there are, indeed, effects on the political order, but not necessarily effects that are conducive to a viable politics. The overproduction of high school and college graduates who cannot find meaningful employment often makes for disorder rather than order, but the resultant revolutionary regimes cannot solve the problems that brought them into being. Although an educated elite is a necessary condition of political viability, it is not sufficient. If the educated elite reinforce traditional status values or special privileges and, at the same time, betray a sense of insecurity as a result of the new education, the political process suffers. "Hence the paradox," writes Lucian Pye of Burma,

that is the common tragedy for so many underdeveloped countries: those who have been exposed to modern forms of knowledge are often precisely the ones who are most anxious to obstruct the continued diffusion of the effects of that knowledge; they desperately need to hold on to what they have and avoid all risks. The lasting consequence of their formal education has thus been an inflexible and conservative cast of mind. Modernization has bred opposition to change.[9]

Not all students of development follow the Aristotelian lead. Holt and Turner, for instance, posit the primacy of government. Referring to the government's participation in modernization, they point out that "during the take-off stage, however, the government became much more involved in the enculturation process through its contribution to and regulation of education, especially at the elementary level."[10] Political development in England, for instance, took place prior to educational development.

My point in all this is merely to suggest that a model that postulates the primacy of politics in the relationship with education may be more appropriate than the classical approach, and the underdeveloped nations certainly offer a rich field for testing relevant hypotheses.

Fortunately, modern political philosophy gives us an alternate to the classical model. But this brings us quickly into the nineteenth century. Hobbes, as far as I can make out, is silent on education, and Locke, though concerned with it, significantly did not see it as a function of education to develop in citizens a sense of civic duty—quite logically, I think, because in his view ideas solely stem from one's own perceptions and can therefore not be subjected to an authority other than that of the person himself. I do not want to dwell on Kant who, insisting on man being treated as an end rather than as means, is probably Plato's most distinguished antagonist; but the American tradition was barely influenced by him. I shall turn, therefore, to John Stuart Mill's *On Liberty*.

Mill's conception of education flows from the premise that, given the great variety of opinions on questions of value, moral training must leave room for error. Although one opinion may be dominant, the expression of contrary opinions is necessary and desirable because the dominant opinion may turn out to be partial, false or even dangerous. *On Liberty* was written before universal education, which Mill favored, had been introduced. "If the government would make up its mind to require for every child a good education," he wrote, "it might save itself the trouble of providing one." Implicit in this statement is an interesting distinction between "State education" and the "enforcement of education by the State." Arguments against the former, he believed do not apply to the latter "but to the State's taking upon itself to direct that education; which is a totally different thing." And why did Mill reject "State education?" Let me quote him, for this view is so very different from the Platonic-Aristotelian conception:

All that has been said of the importance of individuality of character, and diversity in opinions and modes of conduct, involves, as of the same unspeakable importance, diversity of education. A general State education is a mere contrivance for moulding people to be exactly like one another: and as the mould in which it casts them is that which pleases the predominant power in the government, whether this be a monarch, a priesthood, an aristocracy, or the majority of the existing generation; in proportion as it is efficient and successful, it establishes a despotism over the mind, leading by natural tendency to one over the body.[11]

I need not linger over the fact that the times have passed Mill by. Rather, I find his position remarkable for two reasons. First, if I do have to smell the scent of Utopia, I find Mill's version much more attractive and congenial than Plato's, for reasons that should be self-evident. But, second, just as the Platonic-Aristotelian conception provides the latent premises for the model of empirical research that takes education as the independent variable, so Mill provides the premises, I think, for any model that takes it as the dependent variable. Almost a hundred years after *On Liberty* was published, another eminent English political theorist and scholar, Ernest Barker, echoed Mill to the effect that "the field of education ... is not, and never can be, a monopoly of the State." And he gives a reason: "Educational associations—of parents, of teachers, of workers, and of members of religious confessions—are all concerned in the development of educational experiments, and in offering that liberty of choice among types of school and forms of instruction which is essential to the growth of personal and individual capacity."[12]

What I want to bring out, simply, is what we all know but rarely articulate as specifically as we might; namely, that our value bias is an important criterion in the specification of what we study and how we study it. Our research designs are not neutral by nature, but by articulating and guarding against our value biases, we can at least hope to neutralize them as long as we do our research. It seems to me that there is a profound difference between a research design that takes education (or related processes, such as socialization, indoctrination, propaganda, conditioning, and so on) as the independent variable and a design which takes it as the dependent variable. For if we start from the other end, I think we have a much richer area of investigation opening up before us. And this, I think, is what we mean when we speak of "politics of education" as a field of inquiry.

I do not know why the field has been neglected for so many years; why, in fact, there has never been a consistent effort to continue the research on "civic training" that Charles E. Merriam organized and directed in the late twenties. There were eight country studies and Merriam's own *The Making of Citizens*. Each study, Merriam reported, was given wide latitude, but each collaborator was enjoined "(1) that as a minimum there would be included in each volume an examination of the social bases of political cohesion and (2) that the various mechanisms of civic education would be adequately discussed."[13] Among these mechanisms, Merriam continued,

are those of the schools, the role of governmental services and officials, the place of political parties, and the function of special patriotic organizations; or, from another point of view, the use of traditions in building up civic cohesion, the place of political symbolism, the relation of language, literature, and the press, to civic education, the position occupied by locality in the construction of a political loyalty; and, finally, it is hoped that an effective analysis may be made of competing group loyalties rivaling the state either within or without.[14]

In his later *Systematic Politics*, Merriam emphasized that "the struggle for the schools is almost as significant as that for the control of the army, perhaps more important in the long run.... We may merely note that some of the most vital of the power problems center in processes often only remotely associated with the grimmer realities of conventionalized authority.[15]

There is certainly something of the prophetic in Merriam's appraisal. We surely witness today a struggle over our educational institutions unmatched in history. Unfortunately, empirical political science has little to contribute to either an understanding of the conflict over the control of education or to possible solutions (though I suspect we may have to learn to live with unsolved problems for a long time to come). I must plead a good deal of ignorance in the matter, but as I search through my library I find only a few items that, in one way or another, meet Merriam's challenge to investigation. If one leaves out the burgeoning literature on political socialization and related topics which, I argued, is really inspired by the education-as-independent-variable model, I can think only of such works as *State Politics and the Public School*, by Masters, Salisbury, and Eliot;[16] of *The Political Life of American Teachers*, by Harmon Zeigler;[17] and of the stimulating, if "soft," *The Public Vocational University: Captive Knowledge and Public Power*, by Edgar Litt.[18] And I don't think the situation in political sociology is much better. There are, undoubtedly, case studies of local situations (as in Dahl's *Who Governs?*), but a systematic, empirical body of knowledge on the politics of education does not exist.

I hope very much that this workshop will generate enough research ideas to remedy the situation. Just to be constructive, let me put in some input.

1. Instead of doing so much work on political socialization, we might ask how the rapid circulation of political elites in America influences the educational system. How is the educational system affected by the conditions of political recruitment and turnover in personnel among those who control it? Are some of the troubles besetting the schools due to the volatility of recruitment processes?
2. How is the educational system affected by the existence of individual differences in intellectual interest and capacity, on the one hand, and government policies to provide equal opportunities for education, on the other hand? How can the educational system be "calibrated" to meet the variety of societal needs for different jobs—from janitors and unskilled workmen to Supreme Court Justices? What are the political implications of "manpower manipulation" through education?
3. Why is it that the "educational lobby" is relatively weak? Who are the "natural" allies of education in the determination of national, state or local educational policies? Would education be better off, or would it be worse off, if it were "taken out" of politics or politics were taken out of education? Why do most interest groups other than those directly involved in education not see the stakes they have in education?
4. What are the consequences of centralization and decentralization of control structures for education? Although this has been much debated, I don't think there is much reliable evidence. Cross-national comparisons are indicated.
5. What are the effects on education of the continuing efforts on the part of those who would use educational institutions to achieve their own political ends? How can education resist the encroachment of outside interests, be they rightist-oriented legislative inquiries or leftist-inspired movements? How can the school be a "laboratory of democracy" and yet remain sufficiently autonomous not to become, as in the Soviet Union, an instrument of the garrison state?
6. In treating the school itself as a "political system," we must surely ask questions about the balance between authority and liberty that is conducive to education; in short, reconceptualizing the school as a political system cannot avoid the old controversy over "discipline." How true is the progressive notion that too much (what is "too much?") discipline makes for aggression which is the enemy of tolerance and corresponding guilt which is the enemy of political responsibility? (To judge from the current generation, presumably brought up in a relaxed manner, there is even more aggression and guilt.)

Let me leave it at that. Let me also reemphasize that my premise, throughout, has been the Millian view of the individual as the goal of all educational effort.

This is, of course, both a normative and an utopian premise. As I see the excesses now being perpetrated on our high school and college campuses in the name of freedom I am by no means sure that this premise is viable. But, I think, it is a premise worth defending. Perhaps it is up to government to protect the schools against their own excesses; which is, I posit, a nice twist on John Stuart Mill. But such must be the view of a latter-day liberal who, unlike conservative and radical, does not see in government the source of all evil.[19]

## Notes

1. Heinz Eulau, "Political Science: I," in Bert F. Hoselitz, ed., *A Reader's Guide to the Social Sciences* (New York: The Free Press, rev. ed., 1970), p. 132. I should say that this was written in 1956 and first published in 1959.

2. Ibid., p. 131.

3. I could cite here just as well the late V.O. Key's chapter on "The Educational System" in *Public Opinion and American Democracy* (New York: Alfred A. Knopf, 1961), pp. 315-343. Key orders his variables in the same way as Almond and Verba do. But I think both his premises and inferences are different—in fact inconsistent with his data presentation. Almond and Verba, on the other hand, are highly consistent and interpret their findings within the contours of the underlying model.

4. Gabriel A. Almond and Sidney Verba, *The Civic Culture: Political Attitudes and Democracy in Five Nations* (Princeton, N.J.: Princeton University Press, 1963), p. 379.

5. Ibid., p. 502.

6. Ibid., p. 503.

7. It is amusing, and I think ironic, that the author of a recent text in political theory entitles one of his chapters "The Aristotelian Bridge: Aristotle, Lipset, Almond." See William T. Bluhm, *Theories of the Political System* (Englewood Cliffs, N.J.: Prentice-Hall, 1965).

8. Robert E. Ward, "Japan: The Continuity of Modernization," in Lucian W. Pye and Sidney Verba, eds. *Political Culture and Political Development* (Princeton, N.J.: Princeton University Press, 1965), p. 29.

9. Lucian W. Pye, *Politics, Personality, and Nation Building: Burma's Search for Identity* (New Haven: Yale University Press, 1962), p. 220.

10. Robert T. Holt and John E. Turner, *The Political Basis of Economic Development* (Princeton, N.J.: D. Van Nostrand Company, 1966), p. 270.

11. John Stuart Mill, *On Liberty*, edited by R.B. McCallum (Oxford: Basil Blackwell, 1947), p. 95.

12. Ernest Barker, *Principles of Social and Political Theory* (Oxford: At the Clarendon Press, 1951), p. 277.

13. Charles E. Merriam, *The Making of Citizens: A Comparative Study of Methods of Civic Training* (Chicago: University of Chicago Press, 1931), p. x.

9

14. Ibid., pp. x-xi.

15. Charles E. Merriam, *Systematic Politics* (Chicago: University of Chicago Press, 1945), pp. 100-101.

16. Nicholas A. Masters, Robert H. Salisbury, and Thomas H. Eliot, *State Politics and the Public Schools: An Exploratory Analysis* (New York: Alfred A. Knopf, 1964).

17. Harmon Zeigler, *The Political Life of American Teachers* (Englewood Cliffs, N.J.: Prentice-Hall, 1967).

18. Edgar Litt, *The Public Vocational University: Captive Knowledge and Public Power* (New York: Holt, Rinehart and Winston, 1969).

19. Which explains, perhaps, why I find much of virtue in Emile Durkheim's *Moral Education*, edited by Everett K. Wilson (New York: The Free Press, 1961).

**Part 1: Normative Political Perspectives for Education**

# Introduction to Part 1

The papers in this section propose a new conceptualization of the normative assumptions underlying the goals of public schools, for instance, what should be taught and what is the difference between education and schooling. This concern with the "proper goals" also leads two of the authors to criticize the focus of existing social studies textbooks used in schools. They assert that these textbooks reflect an insufficient vision of the intersect between education and politics and do not adequately discuss the most important variables.

Specifically, Sheldon Wolin emphasizes "the task which confronts us requires a political theory that will illuminate both politics and education, but it must be a theory which starts from the assumption that the society is in deep trouble, proceeds by searching for a formulation which identifies those troubles, and concludes with some sketch of the possibilities, necessities, and dangers for a better politics and a better education." Underlying Wolin's education prescription is his contention that:

There can be no theory of technological society which is not also a theory of evil, and hence there can be no politics and no education worthy of their names which are not committed to countering many of the forces and promises of the new society and to preserving, rather than merely redefining, what is human.

Edward Greenberg agrees with Wolin that we are in the midst of a public crisis "which threatens to tear asunder the fragile network of sentiment and shared loyalties that constitute the social fabric of a people." Greenberg argues the current picture of American politics that students receive in the educational system (largely through civics and history courses) is inaccurate and breeds cynicism among the young. He outlines his view of the dominant paradigm of political science or social studies textbooks on American government. In view of recent events, he asserts this paradigm is filled with anamolies and the result is:

We are, I believe, in that disconcerting period of time when the old has lost its ability to make sense of the world, but a new formulation has not arrived to fill the gap. The young who have no strong attachment to older perspectives are conscious of the turmoil and are searching for new ways to deal with the world. We would do well to emulate some portion of their behavior by beginning to seriously re-examine the way we perceive the American polity.

Norton Long is interested in a different perception of the American polity by political researchers because:

Much of political science is concerned with activities in the palace and the capital, coup d'etats and elections. Similarly, studies in educational politics focus on the school board, the superintendent, and tax elections. While these activities are

13

highly consequential for the participants and their allies; they frequently seem trivial in their observable consequences for the bulk of the ruled as measured by changes in any of the dimensions of our inventory of the human condition, educational achievement, infant mortality, adequate housing, etc. The round of meaningless changes of juntas and military cliques in South America is an opportunity foregone of the possible use of government to improve the human condition. Analyses of school board elections and superintendent turnover may have little relevance to changes at the classroom level in teacher behavior or pupil performance.

Professor Long proposes a particular kind of follow-up study to the Coleman report to explore the "differences that make a difference."*

Robert Salisbury is also concerned with charting goals for education but he emphasizes the required redirection of research to direct consideration of how major change can be effected to accomplish concrete goals. In three midwestern states he proposes to ask education-elites their perceptions of "the problem" in public education and to outline a political strategy for major innovation, e.g., how they would bring about the changes necessary to correct whatever they thought was wrong. The second study phase would focus on two policy objectives: (1) the separation of financial support from policy making and administrative control, and (2) making the administrative structure more responsive (e.g., decentralization and community control). Salisbury's stress on the usefulness of elite viewpoints clashes with the position of Wolin and Greenberg.

---

*The Coleman report is a popular term for James S. Coleman et al., *Equality of Educational Opportunity* (Washington, D.C.: U.S. Office of Education, 1966).

# 1

## Politics, Education, and Theory

SHELDON S. WOLIN

The subject of this conference comprises two of the oldest, most pondered matters in the recorded history of Western civilization, education and politics. Shortly after the ancient Greeks discovered philosophy as a self-conscious activity focused upon a complex of "problems," of which politics was one of the most important, they made the same discovery about education: the latter, too, presented problems of which politics was one of the most important.[1] The union of politics and education within a common frame of philosophy was uniquely symbolized by the figure of Socrates. Socrates, who in the fine characterization of Cicero, "was the first to call philosophy down from the heavens and established her in the cities of men,"[2] was also the first to designate politics and education as distinct and, above all, interrelated subjects of systematic inquiry. The intimacy of the union was deliberately reenforced by the institution of the Academy founded by Socrates' greatest pupil and, somewhat less so, by the institution of the Lyceum founded, in turn, by Plato's greatest pupil.[3] The union was maintained despite, or perhaps because of, the continuous criticism directed at the Socratic conception by rival schools of philosophy as well as by rhetoricians, poets, and politicians. But the disputes were mainly over the proper admixture of the two elements, politics and education, not over whether education ought to be political or politics educational.

As I understand it, this conference is not about the problems arising out of the historical association of politics and education, but about how best to study the behavior of those who make, or who influence the making of, decisions about education. Or, alternatively, how best to study education as a political process. Judging by the papers which were sent as illustrations and examples to the participants, a strong predisposition exists among political scientists to recommend the use of "systems theory" as the preferred method of investigating the new subject-matter.[4] If we grant that a "field" is defined by the way we propose to study it and that the methods and/or theories brought to bear embody certain assumptions and discriminations, then we are justified in scrutinizing the proposed mode of inquiry, particularly if the field is thought to be relatively undisfigured by prior theories or if one has grave doubts about the utility of the theory being proposed. Mindful that the participants in this conference have been invited to submit their views on how best to study the politics of education rather than to criticize alternative approaches, my comments on

15

"systems theory" will be brief. They will mainly be directed at showing that the assumptions of the theory are symptomatic of a broader range of problems which constitute the proper starting point for thought and reflection on the subject of this conference.

Since every theory is an abbreviation of reality, it is, in varying degree, a distortion of reality. In social and political matters, it is not enough for proponents of a theory to acknowledge this. Distortions and omissions cannot simply be justified on grounds of convenience or because a certain amount of arbitrariness is inevitable. There is too much at stake to permit such an easy way out. Any theory which attempts to depict a society in broad, political terms and which also claims to generate propositions that are testable by the actual operation of that society is engaged in very serious business. Political theories deal with structures which embody and exercise a concentration of the most awesome powers of which man is capable. On some occasions these powers are used violently and destructively; more often they are used to intimidate; and still more often they are used to reenforce a going system of distributive inequities. Much depends, therefore, on how meaningfully a theory deals with these basic features of any political society. The capabilities of a theory are determined by the nature and type of distortions it embodies. In the case of systems theory these distortions are crippling. It enables its exponents to talk about "outputs" but not about distributive justice or fairness; about "steering" but not about statecraft; about "messages" or "inputs" but not about the quality of the citizens or their lives.[5]

These embarrassments may be of little consequence when a theory is being applied to that abnormal and deceptive state of politics which is called normalcy, and is supposed to signify a state of prosperity, peace, stability, and equity. But when a theory, with all of its distortions, omissions, and assumptions is applied to a deeply troubled domain like education, and when that domain appears to mirror the larger troubles of a society in crisis, there is reason to question its utility. If one thing can be confidently stated about the Miltonic chaos of political science it is that a great and pervasive doubt now surrounds the main assumptions that have governed "mainstream" political science of the past three decades and have been incorporated into systems theory.

Among the insecure assumptions are the following:[6] (1) that the best possible politics is one whose basic "rhythm" is set by the competing pressures of organized interest groups; (2) that the best mode of political competition consists of interest groups striving for material advantages and that the worst or most dysfunctional mode of competition occurs when political parties present sharply defined alternative programs and "ideologies" to the electorate; (3) that from the interplay of group pressures the most equitable distribution of material goods will emerge as long as no one group or permanent combination of groups exerts dominant influence; (4) that the main tasks of government are to mediate between group demands, enforce the standard of fair competition embodied in the constitutional and other legal rules of "the game," and somehow seek to reconcile the public interest with the self-serving thrust of group pressures. These tasks are commonly held to be discharged by showing either that no single group has consistently dominated public policies or that at certain times there has been manifest governmental concern over the plight of disadvantaged (i.e., unorganized or powerless) groups. Given the constraints of group power and influence and the resulting limits which fence political action, it is not surprising to find that in the eyes of most political scientists the "political system" has exhibited a natural and healthy genius for slow, piecemeal, incremental advance.[7]

The comparatively unenthusiastic support which these assumptions now command are directly traceable to the startling emergence of specific problems, such as environmental pollution, depletion of natural resources, the disappearance of habitable space, intensified racial conflicts, urban decay, campus unrest, and military disaster. As we are coming to recognize, these problems only appear to have emerged suddenly. Most of them have been in the making for decades, which suggests why it is that political scientists seem so uncertain about the main assumptions of the political system: the problems were concealed or misrepresented by the normal operation of the system, so much so that in many quarters it is feared that the problems have either become insoluble within the current terms of the system or worsened. Nowhere are these doubts more evident than in the field of education where there is widespread lack of confidence about the capability of existing educational institutions, practices, and values; deep scepticism about whether society can be persuaded to face up to the heavy financial, political, and psychic demands which radical change requires; and despair over whether the traditional methods of policy-making, supervision, accountability, and community involvement can cope with the dimensions of the crisis. Meanwhile, our schools, like our cities, are streaked with lawlessness, violence, alienation, and incivility.

The general situation which obtains both in politics and education is marked by fundamental disorder or derangement such that the ills reenforce the causes which have produced them. The political troubles arising from racial conflicts, poverty, urban decay, and campus rebellion have contributed to an educational crisis whose political effects will continue to be registered for several more years. Civic man is, in large measure, the product of our schools; and the future vitality of our civic life and its values is being determined in the present. If, in the midst of a profound political crisis affecting education, it is proposed that we study the latter by means of a theory which assumes that the former is functioning normally, the results are bound to be misleading. The task which confronts us requires a political theory that will illuminate both politics and education, but it must be a theory which starts from the assumption that the society is in deep trouble, proceeds by searching for a formulation which identifies those troubles, and concludes with some sketch of the possibilities, necessities, and dangers for a better politics and a better education.

No one, of course, is foolish enough to pretend that he has *the* theory which will solve all of our political and educational problems. However, it is possible to get some of the questions a bit straighter. Toward that end I shall contend that our present political condition is being shaped by many novel and unprecedented factors and that, consequently, the main theoretical task must begin with the search for new categories and concepts. Before turning to these novel factors, I would briefly mention two questions, first raised by the Greeks and then retained by later writers, that are central to any discussion of education and politics: What kinds of persons should education seek to encourage and, inseparably bound to that question, what is the proper image of the citizen which is to be followed in preparing the young for membership in the most general and inclusive association, political society?

These two elements, the quality of the individual person and his quality as a political or civic being, are complicated by a third consideration which forms one of the paradoxes of education: in a democratic society education is said to be justified by the extent to which it promotes the development of the individual—how far it develops his mind, cultivates his sensibilities, and equips him with a command over certain bodies of knowledge and skills which will enable him to move about in the world with some measure of confidence. From the standpoint of society, however, education rests on a different and sometimes contradictory justification. Society requires and demands certain skills of its members so that economic, administrative, scientific, military, and other socially necessary tasks will be performed efficiently. During the nineteenth century much of the momentum for popular education stemmed from the recognition of the growing needs of manufacturers for literate workers. In the 1950s the Sputnik crisis led to widespread demands for increased education in science and engineering.

Thus one justification is individual and qualitative, while the other tends mainly to be functional and quantitative, i.e., how many literate workers, how many and what types of engineers? But, as Plato discovered long ago in the *Republic*, the difficulty is to reconcile the two justifications and satisfy the legitimate claims of each. That difficulty is mainly what the politics of education is about, deciding what kinds of individuals should be cherished and encouraged by education and what kinds of social tasks properly require educational support. To clarify this conception of the politics of education it is necessary at the outset to identify those forces which are shaping our society and are at the heart of its crisis in politics and education. What are the most insistent imperatives which are shaping the contours of society, the forms of work and socially necessary skills, the relationships between classes and groups, the assignment of rewards and status, and the rating system by which some forms of knowledge are preferred? What are the imperatives which are causing many of our personal and collective tensions, providing much of the "stuff" of our major political decisions and policies, and dictating increasingly the style and means of political action?

Imperatives of this range and magnitude form the primary substance of a potentially significant political theory. In a preliminary way, they can be conveniently grouped under the concept of "technological society" or, more broadly, "technological culture." Today there is scarcely a sphere of society or a major aspect of human activity which is not infected or affected by a technological component. There is daily confirmation that contemporary politics is mostly about the future imperatives and past consequences of technology; that education is increasingly being affected by it; that popular culture has become inseparable from it; that, in short, our society can be most accurately described as technological. Neither politics nor education, nor any combination of the two, can be properly understood apart from technological society.

What, then would the beginnings of such a theory look like? It would start with an attempt at some general overview of the distinctive nature of technological society, some perspective which would help us to understand its nature and distinguishing features. Such an overview would form a network of concepts that would aid us in describing, explaining, and signifying the relevant phenomena. It would start from the common knowledge that technological society is distinguished by a special form of collaboration between modern science and modern industry and by particular institutional and organizational forms which have been evolved to promote and exploit that collaboration. The distinctive feature of technological society is that it is an order based upon the union of science and industry, and that that union has ushered in unprecedented forms of power which have created a constantly changing environment, natural and social, and give every indication of being able to change the human species as well.

In its several component parts, this ordered totality of activities does not appear novel. Other and earlier civilizations have cultivated science, technological innovation, social organization, and environmental change. What is unique is the union of these factors and the systematic and premeditated cultivation of that union. In this context, intense cultivation signifies more than the encouragement of techniques or methods, be they scientific or industrial; it points to a special ethos which has become generally diffused throughout society and definitive of the dominant values and socialized consciousness of the members. Thus society, environment, and man are being altered simultaneously. The future which looms already in the present is of an artificial nature surrounding a mechanized society inhabited by a species which has been christened a "bio-mechanical symbiote."[8]

There is little need to remind most of us that the main issues pressing upon our society have their origins in, or are powerfully affected by, the operation of technological society. A theory of technological society should be a response to the evident urgencies of our condition, not simply a search for explanation, much less a cause for self-congratulation. Toward that end, the concepts employed in that theory must not begin with an isolate, not even with "technological society," much less one composed from the vocabulary of technological society itself, e.g., "cybernetic society" or the "technotronic society." It is not merely that technological culture has a history, i.e., it came from somewhere, but rather that its novelty and significance depend upon the kind of contrasts which history alone can provide. To mention one obvious example: one cannot appreciate the significant changes in the nature of "work" unless one has a fair idea of what work has meant in other ages. But while some older concepts still retain vitality or can be modified by a new emphasis (e.g., "information" is an old notion but it has acquired a significant and new emphasis). there are others which may cease to be relevant. For example, it is no secret that in many sectors of advanced societies the absence of "authority" explains more than its presence. It may be the case that technological society will be governed by "processes" rather than authorities.

What, then, are some of the possible concepts which could form a theory of technological society and thereby help us to find our bearings, politically and educationally, in this "new world" which Saint-Simon prophesied more than a century and a half ago?

1. Like all previous societies, technological society constitutes an *order*, but of a distinctive kind. It is essentially an organizational society which integrates, coordinates, and subordinates activities in accordance with the requirements of science, technology, and industry. Much of modern science and most of modern industry are administered activities in the sense that their success and efficient operation depend upon a high degree of organization, the careful ordering of sequences, immense amounts of planning, and formalized methods of accountability and performance. It would be superfluous to add that the technological order thrives on impersonality—of effort, achievement, and service.

2. Although many previous societies have accorded high place to the pursuit of *knowledge* (and to the value of "useful" knowledge and have supported the institutions of knowledge, such as monasteries, academies, and universities), technological society is not only deeply dependent on knowledge, but peculiarly reliant upon knowledge which is systematic and interlocked. (Contrast, for example, the medieval preoccupation with distinguishing various bodies of knowledge, as in the Thomistic distinction between, among others, philosophy and theology, with the contemporary assumption about the interrelationships between "fields" and the constant search for new overlappings.) The contemporary emphasis upon the various sciences, mathematics, engineering, and, now, the managerial sciences is reflective of this dependence, as is the use of the phrase "knowledge-industry" to describe the modern universities. This dependency is further distinguished by a continual dynamic; particular forms of knowledge are not only specially cultivated but are cultivated in ways that are intended to make them continually expanding. Technological society is probably the first society in history that continually renders vast bodies of knowledge obsolescent and at the same time threatens

to engulf itself with ever-mounting heaps of new knowledge. It might also be noted in passing that the primacy of knowledge in technological society, as well as the rank-order in prestige among various fields of knowledge, will play a large role in assigning stations of power and powerlessness throughout society.

3. As the above suggests, technological society is not classless. Scientists, engineers, experts in management, "information" specialists, as well as hybrid types, such as the scientist-entrepreneur or the scientist-administrator, exert great power and influence throughout society. Within these categories, however, the growth of knowledge is so rapid that skills are constantly being rendered obsolete: today the engineer who specializes in space engineering enjoys greater rewards than the engineer who specializes in road construction. Perhaps more important technological progress has jeopardized most of the forms of work which were the lot of the vast majority of the working population less than a half-century ago. The destruction of work and the ever-changing demands of technology threaten the lower classes with permanent subjugation. The new structure of inequalities has a most important bearing upon education, not only for the obvious reason that education is looked upon as the means of outfitting new generations with new skills, but because education is being asked to prepare classes and groups which hitherto have lacked even rudimentary skills and which, at the same time, are becoming politicized before they have been "technicized." And all of this is in addition to the problem of whether technological society can continue to absorb vast numbers of college-educated persons and offer them meaningful work.

4. Technological society accentuates *concentrations of power and influence*. The clusters of skills which it demands and organizes, the goods and services which it produces, and the equipment which it employs are all extraordinarily expensive and beyond the reach of most small-scale enterprises. Heavy governmental support is needed, not only in the form of funds but in the form of future assurances. A web of mutual dependency grows between governmental bureaucracies and corporate bureaucracies, and its symbol is the governmental contract.[9] Any viable distinction between public and private enterprise disappears.

5. At the same time that technological society encourages the concentration of power and facilitates its exercise by means of rapid communication and ingenious forms of surveillance, it becomes increasingly difficult to alter or significantly modify the society by means of political action. The novelty of technological society is that incessant innovation flourishes amidst rigidity. As the present problems of the cities and of the natural environment have taught us, it is very difficult, perhaps even impossible, to separate the social costs of technology from its benefits, impossible to have the one without the other, and impossible to remedy the former by larger applications of the latter. Without the possibility of significant change, political action dwindles in

importance. Perhaps it is no accident that virtually all of the major prophets of technological society, such as Saint-Simon, Marx, Lenin, Bellamy, and H.G. Wells, have all reduced the role of politics to administration, as if to emphasize that in the society of the future efficient and stable routines are what matter and that creative politics is atavistic.

This list of concept could be prolonged. If space permitted I would want to examine such notions as "consumerism" and explore the new "rhythms" embodied in technological society. But a more important closing note would emphasize that whatever its benefits, technological society forms no exception to Freud's gloomy wisdom that all culture is purchased at a human price. There can be no true theory of technological society which is not also a theory of evil, and hence there can be no politics and no education worthy of their names which are not committed to countering many of the forces and promises of the new society and to preserving, rather than merely redefining, what is human.

## Notes

1. This is one of the major themes in the classic work by Werner Jaeger, *Paideia, The Ideals of Greek Culture*, tr. G. Highet (New York, 1945). See also E. Havelock, *Preface to Plato* (Cambridge, Mass., 1963).
2. *Tusculanae Disputations*, V. 4. 10.
3. See G.C. Field, *Plato and His Contemporaries*, 2nd ed. (London, 1948), Ch. III; W. Jaeger, *Aristotle*, tr. R. Robinson, 2nd ed. (London, 1948), Pts. I, III.
4. Michael W. Kirst and Edith K. Mosher, "Politics of Education," *Review of Educational Research*, Vol. 39, No. 5, pp. 623-40; Frederick M. Wirt, "American Schools as a Political System," Part 5 of this volume.
5. See the tortured attempts to include concepts of "sin," "guilt," and "grace" within a cybernetic system of politics in K. Deutsch, *The Nerves of Government* (New York, 1963), pp. 228-40.
6. For a convenient statement of these assumptions, see R.A. Dahl and C.E. Lindblom, *Politics, Economics, and Welfare* (New York, 1953), p. 324ff.
7. This is systematically developed by C.E. Lindblom, *The Intelligence of Democracy* (New York, 1965), pp. 3-17, 117ff, 274ff.
8. P.H.A. Snaith, *Planets and Life* (London, 1970).
9. H.L. Nieburg, *In the Name of Science*, rev. ed. (Chicago, 1970), p. 184ff.

# 2

## Inventorying the Human Condition and the Study of Local Educational Politics

NORTON E. LONG

Some years ago, Herson reproached the study of local politics in the United States with being a "Lost World." He found it largely lacking in theoretical concern and disconnected from the main body of the discipline. Its interests involved a narrow preoccupation with economy and efficiency, honesty and corruption, and formal structure. The same comments could have applied to political analysis of local school systems.

Since then, attention has shifted to the question of community power structure, a literature typified by Hunter's *Community Power Structure* and Dahl's *Who Governs?* Debate has centered on whether and to what degree American local governments are characterized by a monolithic, omnicompetent power elite or a pluralism of competing elites. This debate has obvious implications for local education politics. If Hunter is correct, an elite of economic dominants not holding official positions largely determines important educational policy as well as other types of local government policy.

The debate, however, has been largely focused on confirming or disconfirming the Hunter thesis. While seeming to have greater realism than the literature Herson deplored, in fact, the debate over *Who Governs?* has been well-nigh as disappointing as the controversy over power. The latter, at least, produced James March's *Power of Power*; as yet *Who Governs?* lacks a similar assessment. What the "who governs?" literature has done is to add a local chapter to the De Regimine Principum genre with Mayor Lee of New Haven as an American minor league analog to Machiavelli's Cesare Borgia. Like the Prince, this literature is suggestive for politicians and rulers but like the Prince it has little to say as to the consequences of "who governs?" for the governed. In education politics, the analyses of local school board-superintendent interaction or elections have been unconcerned with the impact on the educational attainment of youth.

The mode of governing and the structure of formal government have been major objects of inquiry. But like the literature on "who governs?," the literature on the modes of governing yields tantalizing glimpses and little more as to the consequences of the modes of governing for the governed. Anne Marie Hauck Walsh, in her book summarizing the results of some thirteen cities studied in a wide variety of countries and cultures, seems to conclude that while these studies of formal structures and their attendant party and group settings provide valuable insights, they by and large tell us all too little about system outputs.

23

The question who benefits from who governs, and the mode of the who's governing, remains largely unasked and well-nigh unanswered. A study of politics that neglects to inquire into who a politics benefits is likely to remain bemused in what Marx called bourgeois democracy or to concern itself with an elitist preoccupation with the doings of the palace and the ruling circles to the neglect of the consequences of these doings for the ruled. A bourgeois socialism might be equally oblivious of the consequences of the actual performance of the regime in terms of measurable dimensions of changes in the human condition.

A sociology of the knowledge of politics would emphasize the ready availability of decrees and government manuals to say nothing of a pervasive public law tradition as an explanation of the concentration on form and formal process to the neglect of output. In addition, a concern with rulers and ruling rather than with the measurable outcomes of ruling follows from the posture of political scientists as court chroniclers and princely advisers. Political science like the business schools is more concerned with the fortunes of rulers (school boards, legislatures, superintendents) than the consequences of ruling for the ruled (children). The subject needs a posture such as that of economics where concern with system performance takes precedence over concern with individual or corporate performers.

Such a concern might be generated by beginning with an inventory of the human condition along a number of major gross observable dimensions and seeking to account for changes in system performance as measured by changes in the dimensions. Thus ratios of doctors to inhabitants, hospital beds, infant mortality, tuberculosis rates, and the like could measure system performance along the health dimension. In education, we need to research the connections between political decision-making patterns and such pupil outcomes as achievement, attitude, absenteeism. Too much research stops at the level of the superintendent and never reaches classroom implications. Comparative figures not only for nations but for individual cities and the groups, classes, and races that compose them would be more enlightening than structural comparisons standing alone. Even ideological contrasts would take on added meaning if measures were possible to show what if any significant differences in health, education, housing, and the like are associated with ideological differences.

The impact of a vulgar logical positivism on political science has been unfortunate. Value-neutral science seemed to offer an escape from the perplexities of defending the grounds of choice and purpose. The reading of Hume popularized in American political science by Sabine seemed to deny that reasoning and reasons had a meaningful office in the enterprise of evaluation. The inconclusive debate between Simon and Waldo well illustrated an impasse that has dogged political science. Only recently has the spell of logical positivism begun to be lifted. Philosophers of science such as Carl Hempel are increasingly critical of the older formulations. They recognize both the importance of purpose and usefulness as definers of relevance and tests of truth.

Indeed, the paradigm *all swans are white, this is a swan, therefore, it is white* that has hung political science with a quixotic quest for universal nondiscoverable laws is recognized as an unattainable ideal. More, it is recognized that an unattainable ideal may well be a false god whose worship, however prestigious, condemns its votaries to scientific sterility. Eugene Meehan, among others, has recognized, following Toulmin, that the actual practice of science has not been to seek to acquire a statistical *n* of instances that can be illegitimately transformed into a universal from which logical deductions may be made. Meehan's view is that the logical entailment is in the patterned relations of the variables that comprise the explanatory theory. Whether the theory holds and where it holds are determined by isomorphism with the phenomena to be explained. The force of the logic depends not in the power of any *n* of instances but on the consistency of the pattern. The utility of the pattern depends on the nature and range of the phenomena it explains and the fruitfulness of the intervention strategies it suggests.

While the fashionable view of the current philosophy of science is seen by some as having misdirected political science toward a bootless and unending attempt to make statistics substitute for theory, its unfortunate impact is quite likely greater in denying the importance or possibility of reasoned valuation. Without such valuation, inquiry remains purposeless, pointless, and incorrigible. Aimless institutional description has been the bane of political science. This orientation has been the predominant research focus of local education politics either by political scientists or education administration scholars.

The subject remains in the natural history stage of science in which collecting the commonsensically indicated important or even existent flora and fauna of a territory is accepted as a self-evidently valid enterprise. To denigrate natural history would be to deny that it has on occasion provided useful nuggets of fact to edit theory. However, it exemplifies a theoretically undirected search procedure that well illustrates the problems of a common sense procedure that fails to take its common sense assumptions critically and seriously. The divorce between questions of value and questions of fact that has been blamed on Hume has obscured the basic fact that both explanatory (scientific) and evaluatory (ethical) theory alike have logics that cannot be excogitated from empirical data. They are alike in their logic being confined to their theoretical structures and their power being dependent on their usefulness as tools with which to organize and alter the phenomena of experience. As Terry Clark and Nelson Polsby have remarked, the propositions and issues of even our most empirically oriented community power studies have little to say of significant outcomes and issues. Given the lack of a critically conscious search procedure, it would have been pure good fortune had it been otherwise.

Health, security, income, jobs, education, housing, and recreation all have dimensions worthy of inclusion in an inventory of the human condition. Following Aristotle one can accept life as a fundamental value, the prerequisite for the attainment of any others. It gives a rough ordering of priorities among the dimensions. However, it leaves vexing questions as to the comparative value of lives present over future, old over young, unborn and born, as decision-makers in the undeveloped countries well know, as do even the legislators in developed nations, who ponder the perplexities of abortion laws. It would be idle to pretend that the above list of dimensions presents no problems of qualitative and quantitative definition. Detailing what is meant and arriving at meaningful standards of measurement is the business of any discipline with scientific pretentions. Methodological problems apart, what is here contended is that when we speak of political differences that make a difference we need to be able to specify to whom the differences make a difference, and in terms of what variations in the listed dimensions they make a difference.

The value of such an inventory to political science lies in its pointing to differences that make a difference and are, therefore, worthy of efforts to explain them. In effect, changes in the dimensions are the phenomena that a science of politics would seek to explain. Descriptions of political institutions, if they have value, have their value because they help to explain these changes. Focus on the movement of these dimensions would raise questions that now remain unasked by the enterprise of aimless institutional description. Much of political science is concerned with activities in the palace and the capital, coup d'états and elections. While these activities are highly consequential for the participants and their allies, they frequently seem trivial in their observable consequences for the bulk of the ruled as measured by changes in any of the dimensions of our list. The fact, when it is a fact, that the governors and their governing are trivial in their consequences for the ruled is itself not trivial. If the status quo is not worsened, it is not improved and that is a fact of considerable significance. The round of meaningless changes of juntas and military cliques in South America is an opportunity foregone of the possible use of government to improve the human condition. Similarly, analyses of school board elections and superintendent turnover may have little potential for exploring changes at the classroom level in pupil performance.

In Mrs. Walsh's work, *The Urban Challenge to Government*, we are given tantalizing glimpses of differences in governmental structures, functioning and staffing that may explain significant differences in dimensions of the human condition for members of the governed. Her interpretation of the results of thirteen case studies of cities undertaken by the Institute of Public Administration points among other things to the generalization that major concern for taking action to alleviate the condition of the poor is most often associated with the action of professionalized bureaucrats. Decentralization and even local self-government are not characterized by such concern. The local elites, whose power is enhanced by decentralization and local self-government, are less willing and probably less able to undertake a politics of resource redistribution than centrally positioned professional bureaucrats. On the other hand, decentralized administration, and even more, local governments tend to be the protagonists in the national system of the service functions housing, health, education, transportation, and the like. National bureaucrats, whether in France or India, most commonly concentrate on national plans that neglect the side of consumption and the social services. Only recently has the philistinism of economics begun to be tempered by a realization of the importance of the investment in people for the economy as well as for the people it should serve.

Michael Harrington's *The Other America* is a forceful presentation of aspects of the human condition in the United States that ordinarily do not bulk large in the consciousness of the political scientists describing American political institutions. It is a useful exercise to consider whether the perusal of any American government or educational administration text would lead one to expect the phenomena depicted in Harrington's work. At first glance *The Other America* seems in blatant contradiction to the impressions received from the ordinary American government text. On further examination however, the reader discovers that the contradiction derives from affect and the gratuitous common sense attribution, not from any logical entailment. What emerges is that educational administration or government texts predict no outputs good or bad. Lacking any consciously expressed explanatory theory, they are not organized to logically entail anything and hence suggest no intervention strategies that might alter the working of the variables affecting the human condition. Since they entail no outputs, they have no theoretical structure capable of being corrected by observation. They are radically incorrigible. This is the chief vice of institutionalism. To be sure, it has a sociology which doubtless explains its nonscientific merits.

By returning to the phenomena, the differences that make a difference to people, political scientists will not so much reclaim lost territory from the clutches of economists and sociologists as they will add explanatory dimensions to phenomena now only partially and inadequately explained by the sister disciplines. Robert Dahl's *Who Governs?* needs to be expanded to ask why socioeconomic issues are not raised in the political life of his New Haven and what differences it would and might make if such issues were raised. The political scientist needs to treat the going economy as subject to political explanation both with respect to why it is presently treated as for the most part politically nonproblematic and under what circumstances this situation might alter with what likely results. For some time in the United States, education was treated as a realm apart from politics and the inquiry of political science.

It took the civil rights revolution of the blacks to shake America's political science loose from its traditional preoccupation with the formal institutions conventionally accepted as political. Indeed one might regard the status of education as outside of formal politics as most fundamentally political. As long as blacks could believe their fates were determined by forces of nature (the IQ tests) they might accept their educationally determined role assignment as legitimate. As the untouchables of India, they needed to recognize the educational system as profane, man made rather than sacred to make it politically problematic and susceptible of purposive human action.

Despite a tradition running from Plato to Bodin and Burke, the family has been a neglected institution in the concerns of political science. Only recently has political socialization and the voting studies given it a limited revival. More in the older tradition is Moynihan's rediscovery of the significance of the family in the normative structure and the maintenance of social organization. The uncritical, radical eighteenth century type individualism that has unconsciously characterized the dominant trend in American political science tended to view concern with, and appreciation of, the family as Burkean conservatism at best, fascist authoritarian reaction at worst.

A way of clarifying what the enterprise of comparative government might be up to is to consider the perspectives and purposes from which, and for which, one might be doing the comparing. A black, or anyone else for that matter, in the United States might be considering alternative cities as a place of residence and education for his family in addition to a place of work for himself. Realism and focus would be added to comparative local government studies if they addressed themselves to and were able to suggest what political variables might enter into a rational comparison. For whom does it make what differences that the mix of variables differ in what ways as between cities? The rational chooser has to make comparisons. The relevant elements of his comparisons depend on his explanatory theories that indicate the weight of differing variables in differing cities in entailing the position of likely outcomes on his preference scale. Only with some such device as a rational chooser, endowed with properties entailing a preference scale, can we develop a critically held perspective and purpose from which comparisons can be meaningfully made. Indeed, only with this clarified can we give an intelligent and intelligibly honest answer to the question "why compare?"

## Community, Neighborhood, and Educational Performance

James Coleman's massive investigations into educational achievement invite inquiry into the significant characteristics of educative environments. Political scientists, with their interest in Greek political theory and institutions other than sentimental or honorific, might have been expected to be among the first to recognize the city as the educational institution. Indeed, for Plato education was the main spring of politics. The late V.O. Key in the first edition of his party's text had chapters on violence and education. These chapters were prescient beyond their time and were removed in subsequent editions. Even earlier than Key's work, Merriam's *The Making of Citizens* series concerned itself with the newly rediscovered subject of political socialization—itself an educational field. Doubtless Merriam's work was inspired by the problems of post-World War I nationalism as similar current interests have been by the new nations of World War II. The interests of V.O. Key and Merriam are a far cry from the extension of conventional political institutional interests that are exhibited in political science concern with educational referenda on school bonds and taxes and apportionment of funds by legislatures.

The superficiality of this latter concern is partially due to the self-serving and simplicist identification of quality of educational output with quantity of dollars input. Coleman's studies and those of others have cast doubt on what had been a pleasing and labor-saving assumption. With its own preoccupation with aimless institutional description to the neglect of the selection, explanation, and evaluation of important outcomes, political science is scarcely in a position to throw stones. It has never quite assumed that governments that raised or spent the most money had the best product. Perhaps if it had made such an explicit assumption it might have gone further along the road of explaining and evaluating outcomes than it has. The uncriticized common sense imputation of outcomes to the institutions laboriously described has served both to justify the effort to institutional description and to inhibit realization of the critical need for explanation and evaluation of the outcomes of the institutions described if political science were to go beyond mere institutionalism.

As so often, the acute problems raised by social change force a relevance on a discipline that has become remote from everyday life. Black concern with education and its crucial place in determining and legitimizing role assignment in a society putatively meritocratic and increasingly credentialist, has revived interest in the Platonic politics of the who and the how of the determining of the men of gold, silver, and brass. Ciccourel and Kitsuse's study of college counseling in the high school shows that not only blacks need to be concerned with the Platonic politics of education. Chalmers Johnson, in his essay on revolution, maintains that a critical stage in the process is the erosion of the accepted legitimacy of the system of role assignment. While the IQ provided the analog of the Indian caste system in explaining a bad karma, the problem of role assignment was social and divine or natural rather than secular, human, and political. Even the supposition that education gave skills such as reading, which in their turn justified role assignment, has been called in question. Thus, Christopher Jenckes, reviewing the Coleman report a year after, expresses doubts that the schools ever taught great numbers to read and surmises that their real contribution to employability was docility. Ivar Berg, in his *Education and Jobs: The Great Training Robbery*, in similar fashion calls in question the reality of the manifest function of industry's educational job prerequisites.

A slaveholding society passed laws forbidding blacks to learn to read. It would be ironical indeed if schools succeeded where slave state laws failed. What the Coleman report suggests is the critical importance of the environment outside the four walls of the school for what goes on or fails to go on inside them. We have known from our experience with the Peace Corps that it is difficult, if not impossible, to teach the children of a village if the teachers are unwilling or unable to live in the village. If there is one thing our expensive experience should have taught us in Vietnam it is that if the village chief cannot or will not stay the night in the village you do not own the village. While Bowles and Levin have raised fundamental questions about the methodology of the Coleman report, if Coleman is right there is a politics and a sociology of a school's environment that disposes children favorably or unfavorably for educational achievement. Lyford has portrayed achieving schools in a most untoward environment and Havighurst asserts that exceptional principals in Chicago have achieved superior results. However this may be, the cases are likely exceptional and dependent on unique factors with the Coleman findings representing the norm.

The paradigm case for an untoward environment such as depicted by Lyford in *The Airtight Cage* and by Greene and Ryan in *The School Children* might well be the Muslim Church as described in an autobiography of Malcolm X. Malcolm describes an institution with the power to grip much of the humanity whose condition is so desparingly described. The logic of such an institution, if it is susceptible of practical realization, would entail children with the quality Coleman finds preeminently important, a sense of capacity to meaningfully determine their own fate. Such children could be expected to learn to read and the schools of such a church, like that of Calvin, could be expected successfully to teach. Clearly the Muslim model has drawbacks, not least of which is that the severity of its demands may severely limit the range of its application. Its value is that it does suggest a social organization of a neighborhood that might motivate children to learn. The model of this organization may reveal one of the logics by which desired educational results might be achieved. It suggests a politics by which such a model might be brought into play.

The politics it suggests may be most relevant to those for whom large money expenditures to purchase educational results are out of the question. The politics of the model are of course repugnant to the ideals of privacy, individualism, and limited community involvement. Like the Calvinist Church, they make unpleasantly personal and onerous demands. The demands, nonetheless, are highly rewarding to many despite their invasions of privacy and their incompatibility with a merely dues paying membership. A revival of the closed or partially closed highly interactive neighborhood community that has been eroded by the national market, a free-floating national and state citizenship, and a monetized set of social relationships, is an alternative for those who have not the means to purchase their amenities but must resort to collaborative social self-help if they are to enjoy them.

If Coleman is right that the attitude of the child, his sense of efficacy, is critical, and if this attitude is the result not only of family but of neighborhood functioning, we badly need to know what are the characteristics and the dynamics of the educationally achieving neighborhood. This suggests the desirability of doing some intensive neighborhood ethnography in areas whose educational performance indicates that their intensive study might yield insight into the variables whose interaction may account for differential neighborhood educational performance. Appreciation of the critical variables and the manner of their interaction that accounts for significant variations in educational performance is a first step toward the development of explanatory theory and might shed some light on the methodological criticisms of Coleman's study. This, in turn, is a necessary prerequisite to informed intervention strategies which can serve to alter existing logics in desired ways and whose results can serve to edit and improve theories. The Muslim Church is a useful example of a bundle of interacting variables whose examination may yield an underlying logic of wider and potentially useful applicability.

With some notion of the kind of neighborhood variables whose interaction might produce attitudes among children favorable to educational achievement, it may be possible to locate sites of natural state experimentation whose examination would help both to build and edit theory. In the country at large the play of events must be producing wide variations in the mix of critically relevant educational variables. If we could spot the interesting natural state experiments, their study *in situ*, like natural state medical experiments, could be highly rewarding. The problem is to locate the sites of these experiments to make possible their intensive ethnographic study. What one might be looking for is a critical educational dimension such as literacy.

Performance on the literacy dimension that would widely diverge from what census characteristics of neighborhood population would lead one to expect would indicate a territory that might be promising for study. Substantial change in favorable or unfavorable direction of the literacy performance would also indicate interesting sites. The value of these sites is the likelihood that they would highlight the action of variables that are critically important for an explanation of system performance.

A major reason for the failure to measure and explain outcomes of the political and, more to the point, the educational system has been the lack of available comparative performance indicators. In part, this has been due to schoolmen's concern with the insidious and politically uncomfortable nature of other than dollar comparisons. In part, it has been due to a metaphysical quest for an educational standard. This last is an outgrowth of an inappropriate conception of the task of evaluation and the function of standards as tools whose justification is in use rather than in essence. In a discipline heavily indebted to John Dewey, it is surprising that other than politically pragmatic tests should have failed to develop, gain acceptance, and improve with use. Be this as it may, the attainment of literacy seems a good first approximation standard of at least an important dimension of educational performance. Hopefully, it will prove to covary in interesting ways with other significant educational and societal dimensions. This approach would be enhanced if a useful available indicator of comparative literacy performance should prove forthcoming from the congressional interest in designing social indicators.

The selective service tests contain a literacy predictor which should be susceptible of disaggregation to area levels that might approximate neighborhoods. A major problem consists in the territorial definition of likely local social systems whose characteristics may account in important degree for educational successes and failures. Existing concern with community control of local schools to the extent that it has a rational base depends upon a reasoned belief that a local community relevant to school performance exists or could be brought into being. Indeed, much of the Ford Foundation advocacy of decentralization, and the hopes for experiments, and disasters such as Ocean Hill-Brownsville seem to be based on the assumption that power over a school could activate latent neighborhood potentialities and in doing so prove therapeutic for neighborhood and school alike. Much of these hopes may be as well- and as ill-grounded as many of those of colonial nationalism. Neither community nor self-governing capacity are free gifts of nature.

What might be attempted is to take some of the existing territorially defined areas, school districts, and perhaps other minor civil jurisdictions and see if in the general performance of the draft literacy predictor an areal performance that approximates neighborhood size shows up. Hopefully, the social interaction patterns of limited definable territories will prove significantly related to the behavior of the literacy predictor of the draft test. If this proves the case, it should be possible to spot areas in which, despite highly adverse or highly favorable census characteristics, the literacy predictor behaves in unexpected ways. Dramatic changes in the behavior of the literacy predictor over time might turn out to be connected with observable movements of other variables suggesting causal connections. The literacy predictor of the draft test then, if it can be meaningfully disaggregated to interesting local areas, might enable research to zero in on the active sites of natural state experiments. These natural state experiments quite possibly will prove theoretically heuristic by exemplifying the action and interaction of critical variables in a more readily observable way. Observation of this interaction should prove helpful both in the building and the editing of explanatory theory concerning the societal variables associated with variations of the localized educational performance along the dimension of literacy.

Explanatory theory that embraces the social variables significantly accounting for the localized literacy performance should suggest intervention strategies that would in principle alter the existing logics in desired ways. Thus, a successful mapping of patterns of localized interaction accounting for literacy performance might yield an understanding of the relevant structure and process and the means to its desired modification through political action. It might be that a local neighborhood that is achieving a significant aptitude for literacy on the part of its young is producing an effective normative structure that would significantly affect rates of crime, deviancy, dropouts, work attitudes, and other important dimensions. If there proves to be a societal interaction, a sociopolitical process whose variations account significantly for differences in the behavior of the literacy predictor, we may advance our understanding both of the way in which neighborhood forces as well as family generate the youth attitudes Coleman finds critical. In doing so, we may learn what constructive intervention strategies are possible. If nothing more, we can explore the behavior of a seemingly significant social indicator that the social accounting routinely produces. This indicator is all the more valuable since we so sorely lack available means of standardized comparison over places and times.

## References

Berg, I. *Education and Jobs: The Great Training Robbery*. New York: Frederick A. Praeger, 1970.

Bowles, S. "Towards Equality of Educational Opportunity?" *Harvard Educational Review* (Winter, 1968), Vol. 38, No. 1.

Cicourel, A.V., and Kitsuse, J.I. *The Educational Decision Makers*. Indianapolis: Bobbs-Merrill, 1963.

Clark, T.N., ed. *Community Structure and Decision-Making: Comparative Analyses*. San Francisco: Chandler, 1968.

Coleman, J.S., et al. *Equality of Educational Opportunity*. U.S. Department of Health, Education and Welfare, Washington, D.C.: U.S. Government Printing Office, 1966.

Dahl, R.A. *Who Governs? Democracy and Power in an American City*. New Haven: Yale University Press, 1961.

Greene, M.F., and Ryan, O. *The School Children: Growing Up in the Slums*. New York: Pantheon Books, 1965.

Harrington, M. *The Other America—Poverty in the United States*. New York: MacMillan, 1962.

Havighurst, R.J. *Education in Metropolitan Areas*. Boston: Allyn and Bacon, 1966.

Hempel, C.G. *Aspects of Scientific Explanation and Other Essays in the Philosophy of Science*. Glencoe: Free Press, 1965.

Herson, L.J. "The Lost World of Municipal Government." *American Political Science Review*, No. 51 (June, 1957).

Hunter, F. *Community Power Structure: A Study of Decision Makers*. Chapel Hill: University of North Carolina Press, 1953.

Jencks, C. "A Reappraisal of the Most Controversial Educational Document of Our Time." *The New York Times Magazine* (August 10, 1969) Part 1, p. 12.

Johnson, C.A. *Revolutionary Change*. Boston: Little Brown, 1966.

Key, V.O., Jr. *Political Parties and Pressure Groups*. New York: Thomas Y. Crowell Co., 1942.

Kirst, Michael W., ed. *The Politics of Education at the Federal, State, and Local Level*. Berkeley: McCutchan, 1970.

Levin, H.M. *Community Control of Schools*. Washington, D.C.: Brookings Institution, 1969.

Levin, H.M., and Bowles S. *The Determinants of Scholastic Achievement: An Appraisal of Some Recent Evidence*. Washington, D.C.: Brookings Institution, 1968.

Lyford, J.P. *The Airtight Cage: A Study of New York's West Side*. New York: Harper & Row, 1966.

Malcolm X *The Autobiography of Malcolm X*. New York: Grove Press, 1966.

March, J.G. "The Power of Power" in *Varieties of Political Theory*. David Easton (ed.) Englewood Cliffs: Prentice Hall, 1966.

Mayer, M. *The Teachers Strike—New York, 1968*. New York: Harper & Row, 1969.

Meehan, E.J. *The Foundations of Political Analysis—Empirical and Normative*. Homewood: Dorsey, 1971.

Merriam, C.E. *The Making of Citizens*. Chicago: University of Chicago Press, 1931.

Polsby, N.W. *Community Power and Political Theory*. New Haven: Yale University Press, 1963.

Rosenthal, Alan. *Governing Education*. New York: Doubleday, 1969.

Sabine, G.H. *A History of Political Thought*. Third Edition. New York: Holt, Rinehart, Winston, 1962.

Toulmin, S. *The Philosophy of Science: An Introduction*. London: Hutchinson University Library, 1953.

U.S. Department of Health, Education and Welfare. *Toward A Social Report*. Washington, D.C.: GPO, 1969.

United States Senate, Committee On Government Operations, *Hearings on Full Opportunity and Social Accounting Act*, S843, Ninetieth Cong., 1st Sess., June 1967.

Walsh, A.H. *The Urban Challenge to Government: An International Comparison of Thirteen Cities*. New York: Frederick A. Praeger, 1969.

# 3 Political Strategies for Educational Innovation

ROBERT H. SALISBURY

I begin from the following baseline assumption: Social science research has been inadequately linked to the future. At its best, social science has provided sensitive analysis of past performance. Its theoretical imagination and empirical richness have been almost entirely confined to looking at the way things are and have been hardly at all addressed to the way things might become.

This existential bias of social science research has a very important result. It limits our conception of the future to whatever paltry vision can be developed through extrapolation. We are trapped by our conviction that the past is prologue to the future and that the only possible worlds must emerge incrementally out of those we already know. Small wonder that brave new policies so often consist of spending more money on the same old programs. And small wonder that the radical young, unwilling to accept a future so bound by the present but every bit as trapped by extrapolation as the rest of us, simply refuse to talk much about new social designs and strategies for achieving them.

It follows from this argument that social science research should be redirected so as to encourage more direct consideration of how major social change can be effected. I regard this position as valid for nearly all of social science, but with particular respect to politics and education it seems to me especially crucial. It is beyond dispute that the mighty edifice of American elementary and secondary education falls woefully short of accomplishing or permitting the accomplishment of the educational and social responsibilities placed upon it. Moreover, it is apparent that extrapolation of programs and policies from the past will leave us even farther behind. We must find out what quantum shifts are possible and, unless we intend to rely as before on traditional lore and dumb luck, social science had better help chart the territory.

How can social science, *qua* science, bridge with imagination the gap between description and prescription? First, description can address strategies and goals of social change far more directly than it customarily has done. Second, empirical investigation can uncover previously inarticulate visions and unformed utopias by asking normative, future-oriented questions of people. Third, serious theoretical and conceptual inquiry into public policy alternatives, especially at more abstract levels than have usually been attempted, can enrich our understanding of what can usefully be done and of which routes have less promise of taking us anywhere. The first two points can be addressed through the empirical

35

investigation proposed below. The third point calls for imaginative theorizing which, I believe, would be much enhanced by the empirical work outlined.

**Proposed Research Topic**

The institutional structures and rules governing public education are specific to each state, and although there are regional and national commonalities of importance it remains true that programs of institutional change will differ from state to state. Accordingly, I propose to study three states only, seeking intensity of coverage rather than a nationwide perspective. Because of previous research experience on their politics of education I would choose Missouri, Illinois, and Michigan. The study would consist of extended interviews with education-related elites. Initially, four categories of relevant elites can be identified. State legislators and executive officials including the governor, the chief state school officer, and perhaps additional administrative staff personnel would comprise one set. School administrators, classroom teachers, and other "schoolmen" would constitute the second group. The third category would be school board members. The fourth would be drawn from community elites, official and non-official.

Legislators and community elites would be sampled so as to include those most directly concerned or actively involved with school matters as well as some in each group who were not so engaged. Samples of "schoolmen," board members and community elites would be drawn first on the basis of community type. Core cities of Standard Metropolitan Statistical Areas (SMSA's) would all be included and it might be desirable to oversample suburban districts also. There would be no special effort to match schoolmen, board members, and community leaders from the same communities. Such an effort might entail problems of confidentiality and access and in any case would not be particularly germane to the main theoretical interests of the inquiry.

The size of the samples would depend partly on the available resources, of course. Face-to-face interviews would be required, and it might not be feasible to get more than fifty state officials and one hundred from each of the other three groups. If a clear choice were required, it would seem preferable to interview larger numbers in two states rather than have fewer respondents in three states.

*The Interviews*

The focus of the interviews would be two-fold. One would be to probe the respondent's perceptions of "the problem" in public education and how he would proceed to make the necessary changes to correct whatever he thought was wrong. The respondent would be pushed and prodded to offer his diagnosis and policy remedy and also to outline the political strategy by which the remedy might be effected. As far as possible respondents would be discouraged from expressing a preference for the status quo as long as there was any glimmering of even a half-formed idea concerning change. Respondents would be encouraged to contemplate *major* innovations, particularly those which they felt might get at the roots of what they regarded as central problems. They would also be encouraged to think in terms of how to formulate appropriate policies that would, in fact, achieve the educational ends they desired. In asking about political strategies, specific probes would explore the principal sources of support and opposition, anticipated methods by which to alter the balance of friends and opponents, whether to pursue an "inside" strategy working within the institutionalized areas or an "outside" strategy of public pressure, and so on.

The second phase of questioning would focus on two rather specific policy objectives. Respondents would not be asked whether they favored or opposed them, but only what formulation of policy and what strategies they would recommend in order to accomplish the objectives. One objective would be the greater separation of school financial support, on the one hand, from policy-making and administrative control, on the other. In other words, what would the respondent recommend to overcome the tradition that those who pay the piper should call the tune? The second question is somewhat more general but it also involves the institutional structures in which schools are embedded. The question is how to make the administrative and control structure of the schools more responsive. Respondents would need to indicate something of how they interpreted the notion of responsiveness and to whom responsiveness was mainly owed, as well as suggesting policies and strategies for increasing it.

It would be useful to establish not only the respondents' vision of desirable change, but also their sense of its urgency and the likelihood of making significant progress. One would expect, a priori, that state officials and perhaps general community elites would have less sense of urgency and more optimism than the schoolmen or board members. Length of residence, time in position, and other mobility items might also be expected to relate to both the style and the substance of respondents' views about policy change. Cosmopolitans would presumably have a different orientation toward the strategy options than locals. "Localism" may not be adequately identified by simple indicators like age, position, or geographical mobility, however, and an important by-product of this research would be to identify the variables leading to local and cosmopolitan perspectives.

This kind of study would provide systematic data regarding the range and distribution of views on interesting questions among these elites, and these data alone would be most intriguing. How much clustering is there, and among whom, on the questions of what is wrong with public education, and what it would take to change it? Do views regarding workable strategies of action cluster according to position, community type, age, or indeed is there much range at all? Hopefully, too, some usable visions of the future might be generated as respondents are encouraged to talk explicitly about matters that previously had remained below the line of self-conscious articulation.

## Improving the Theoretical Understanding of Structural Reform

We cannot be overly confident that elites will, when asked, think of stimulating policy ideas to solve complicated social problems. I cannot read the voluminous literature on educational reform without being impressed by how seldom there are public policies, even implicitly, to accompany the diagnosis. I believe this is due in part to a pervasive confusion in the minds of many between policy and outcome. Educational reformers generally focus on outcomes. They want Johnny to read better, to love learning, to love other children, or at least not hate them or beat them up, and so on. Reformers may realize that the choices public officials make are not whether or not Johnny shall read well but how much money will be spent, where to build the new school, how to draw district boundaries, whom to hire, etc. These are not, for the most part, educational outcomes, but they are *the only questions amenable to authoritative public action*. We need to address far more attention than we have done to the forms public action can take, to the conceptual and theoretical analysis of public policy so that we can gain a better perspective on how public policy can be expected to affect outcomes.

Apart from the perennial cry that additional money is required for the schools, an almost equally perennial request is for reorganization. Consolidation and decentralization are two of the themes in the long contrapuntal flow, and there are others. In other work I have explored the difference, which I think is fundamental, between what I call allocation policies and structural policies. Reorganization is a structural decision, and further theoretical consideration of this kind of policy seems to me to be very much needed. For example, if blacks are to urge decentralization of control, do they mean that to apply to white suburbs as well? Or do they want a policy which gives self-determination to black ghettoes but requires middle class whites to accept greater socioeconomic diversity? And is it the symbols of power that are at stake, or is it substance? What kinds of substance are affected by particular types of decentralization? A very large part of the *possible* public policy decisions in education involve changing the institutional structures, and it would behoove us to contemplate these questions at length and at every level of abstraction.

One approach to the particular organizational problems of public education would be to establish multiple organizations for the several distinct activities schools engage in. Thus there seems no good reason to have a "city-wide" system for all the school purposes of Chicago or St. Louis, and indeed there is, de facto, all sorts of administrative decentralization and diversity on the organizational chart. But there is only one authoritative control source—one board and one superintendent—and as we now see this presents some serious difficulties. What would it be like if "the" schools were converted into a dozen or more autonomous systems, whose boundaries might sometimes be functional, sometimes geographic, sometimes defined by clientele? What theoretical criteria do we have for contemplating such "messy" schemes? Our capacity to think about these questions is underdeveloped and needs attention.

It is to be hoped that the responses provided by interviewees in the empirical phase of this project would enlarge the possible alternatives that theoretical inquiry into structural reform could take into account. In any case, however, we must expand the list of values which are linked explicitly to organizational structures so that we can evaluate the available choices on grounds other than efficiency. We have come lately to recognize that both symbol and substance of significance to blacks are involved in the organizational pattern of the schools and that, indeed, any complex institution has a myriad of social values tied up in it. We need more carefully to sort out these normative implications of our structural arrangements and this is, in large measure, a task for theorists.

## Summary

I propose, then, two complementary undertakings. One is an empirical investigation of the images and conceptions of policy changes and strategies for accomplishing them that are held by four elite cohorts of critical importance to the making of educational policy. The second task would concentrate on improving the theoretical understanding of the forms public policy can take regarding educational affairs and especially of the alternative patterns of organization that might be contemplated.

# 4 The Civic Miseducation of American Youth: Political Science and Paradigm Change

EDWARD S. GREENBERG

We are in the midst of a public crisis. The continuing debate over the questions of American foreign policy, racism, and economic justice threatens to tear asunder the fragile network of sentiment and shared loyalties that constitutes the social fabric of a people. Few Americans are any longer shocked by riot, arson, bombing, police repression or the taking of political prisoners. Mass habituation to such horrors is perhaps the truest operational indicator of the depth of the crisis.

The crisis is and will continue to be nourished by the growing alienation of American youth, whether they be black youth from America's wretched ghettos or privileged white youth at elite universities.[1] The most pervasive orientation I have personally encountered among the young in teaching and research is a deep cynicism about the American political process. Students claim that what they hear and read in the classroom fails to correspond to the world as they experience it.

It is the argument of this chapter that the sanitized, perfumed, and inflated picture of American politics that students receive at all levels of the educational system is grossly inaccurate, and feeds the cynicism of the young. It is further argued that we, as professional political scientists, have contributed to this problem by the way we interpret the world and convey it in our work. And, finally, it is argued that we may have something to learn from the often incoherent ramblings of the young; that many of their admittedly unsophisticated critiques still manage to strike at the very heart of the prevailing paradigm of political science.

We have been charged by this conference to raise for examination the question or questions we feel are of greatest import for education and politics. I can think of no more pressing public issue or intellectual problem than the growing alienation of youth. The roots of growing alienation are no doubt multifaceted and I do not for a moment believe that changes in civic education will necessarily change the drift toward alienation. Yet the educational process is a promising place to begin, not only because educational institutions touch upon the lives of all young people, but also because these institutions are one of the few upon which change can be wrought. We, as political scientists, have more impact than we perhaps imagine. Our work finds its way into elementary and secondary

41

school texts, curriculum materials, and the college education of school teachers. We have, I am afraid, contributed to the miseducation of American children by offering them a picture of a society and a polity that cannot but lead to disappointment and disillusion. I believe that we have been a part of the problem and that it is time to become part of the solution. Such a process first requires some serious self-examination.

## The Paradigm of Political Science

A past president of the American Political Science Association recently announced the arrival of a paradigm of political science.[2] My own claim is somewhat narrower. While it is still questionable whether a paradigm of political science exists, I believe that one exists among those whose specialty is American politics. There exists among such scholars a certain commonality of perspective, a commonality of perspective that incorporates both empirical and normative elements. In short, these scholars tend to share, in Kuhn's terminology, a paradigm.

A paradigm is a very powerful tool indeed, for it represents a "strong network of commitments—conceptual, theoretical, instrumental and methodological . . . it provides rules that tell the practitioner of a mature specialty what both the world and science are like . . . "[3] Such a phenomenon is not to be sneered at. A paradigm simplifies and defines the world in such a way that it allows for the advancement of what Kuhn calls "normal science." This concentration of perspective has its price, however, and that is the failure to perceive, incorporate or take account of phenomena outside the boundaries of the paradigm. Political science has made very impressive strides in its normal science, but it pays a price in its failure to deal with matters inconsistent with the paradigm.

Following a suggestion implicit in Kuhn's analysis, I turned to an examination of leading and representative political science textbooks of American government in order to elucidate the main components of the paradigm. While textbooks do not seem to play as important a role in the social sciences as in the natural sciences, it still remains the case that it is in textbooks that the orthodoxy of a discipline may best be found. This is probably true for two reasons. Almost by definition, a textbook is based upon the cumulative work of a field of study; it is the distillate of the hundreds of research monographs that make up the literature of a field. Moreover, simple economics enters the equation. In order to enjoy wide sales, the authors of a textbook must convince other political scientists of the reasonableness and propriety of their treatment, and as a consequence rarely venture beyond the bounds of acceptability.

I turned, therefore, to three of the most generally respected and best selling textbooks in the field of American politics: Burns and Peltason, *Government by the People*; Dahl, *Pluralist Democracy in the United States*; and Irish and

Prothro, *The Politics of American Democracy.*[4] While each differs in style, in favored methodological approaches, and in several other nuances, the shared perspective that undergirds them is rather striking. The three elements which follow are, I believe, the building blocks of the paradigm.

### 1. *American politics is best described as a pluralist democracy.*

Group theory or the pluralist model is probably the dominant point of view among political scientists today. In group theory, mutual noninterference is replaced by conflict among groups with "shared attitudes." Majority coalitions must be created on each issue, and many individuals and groups fail to apply their potential resources in the coalition-building effort. As a result, the system contains considerable "slack" . . . power is highly decentralized, fluid and situational. There is no single elite, but a "multicentered" system in which the centers exist in conflict-and-bargaining relation to each other.[5]

The authors take their stand with pluralist democracy. With all its failings, this kind of democracy nourishes a tolerance for differing ideas, a respect for minority rights, and a concern for the individual that we consider essential in a decent and ordered society. But our intention in this book is not to defend pluralist democracy; our intention is to show, as objectively as we can, how it works in the United States.[6]

Because one center of power is set against another, power itself will be tamed, civilized, controlled and limited to decent human purposes, while coercion, the most evil form of power, will be reduced to a minimum.

Because even minorities are provided with opportunities to veto solutions they strongly object to, the consent of all will be won in the long run.[7]

How is it that the system which exalts freedom over order actually enjoys greater order with its greater freedom?[8]

Decisions are made, even in a pluralist democracy, by a relatively small group of decision-makers, with most of the public on most issues being unconcerned and uninvolved. Yet there is a rough correspondence between what public officials do and the interests of most of the people because of competition among political decision-makers.[9]

### 2. *American history is best characterized as a history of progressive change; a history of the steady improvement of the life chances of the average man.*

. . . The Civil War has been the only major breakdown in our political institutions during two centuries of continuous development in the arts of operating, on a national scale, a democratic republic in which unity yields to diversity, and diversity to unity: not without strain and conflict, to be sure, but without extensive civil strife or the introduction of those poisonous hatreds and resentment that seep through a system until it collapses in paralysis or in violent paroxysm.[10]

The United States . . . has undergone changes that half a century ago no one foresaw: the expansion of welfare measures and government intervention in the

44

economy; the almost overnight assumption by the United States of its role as a major, the major, world power; and since the early 1950s huge steps toward the ultimate political, economic and social liberation of Negroes.[11]

... of increasing political significance is the differential in incomes between white and nonwhite families. In 1966, the average nonwhite family income was only about 60% of the average white family income. But that was an improvement over the 51% of 20 years ago. Moreover, the improvement is likely to continue if nonwhites are able to take advantage of better educational opportunities.[12]

3. *Elites are the repository of democratic convictions and the guarantors of the viability of the democratic system. The masses, on the other hand, are to be feared because of their anti-democratic intolerance and proclivity for mass action.*

... democratic values and habits are more prevalent among the politically active minority. However much they may disagree on issues, political activists seem to serve as the carriers of the democratic creed, learning through actual experience to recognize the problems of others, to compromise differences rather than insisting on total acceptance of their own particular principles, and to appreciate the relation of specific actions or issues to broader democratic principles. ... Discussions of democracy tend to overlook the functional nature of apathy for the system ... many people who express undemocratic principles in response to questioning are too apathetic to act on these principles in concrete situations. And in most cases, fortunately for the democratic system, those with the most democratic principles are also those who are least likely to act.[13]

The Framers tended to think of government as kings and ministers who were not politically accountable to the electorate and who were likely to suppress legislatures, arrest citizens for criticizing the authorities, search homes without warrants. Today, many of us think of the government as our own elected officials and responsive to us.[14]

Democracy is preserved not only by the convictions of the mass but also by agreement among leaders on the basic rules of the game. Competition among leaders is indispensable to democratic government.[15]

[Democratic government is the outcome of] a series of responses to problems of diversity and conflict, by leaders who have sought to build and maintain a nation, to gain the loyalty and obedience of citizens, to win general and continuing approval of political institutions and at the same time to conform to aspirations for democracy.[16]

While I am sure that there may be additional elements of a world view to which many political scientists would adhere, I believe that these three are shared by almost all working political scientists and thus comprise a paradigm, no matter how crude. Like all paradigms, this paradigm structures the world in such a way that some phenomena are incorporated, whereas other phenomena make no impact. Thus, the above textbooks are as interesting for what they fail to say as for what they say. All of the texts attempt to be contemporaneous by including materials on black power, Vietnam, and the urban crisis, but none of the authors are led by this material to ask very hard and searching questions about their paradigm. Irish and Prothro, for instance, honestly deal with the use of a military-industrial complex, the failure of the civil rights movement and the increasing bureaucratization of decision-making, but never allow such matters to shake the faith in their view of America as democratic, pluralistic, progressive, and ruled by benevolent elites.

### Anomalies

Kuhn has suggested that revolutions in scientific paradigms are processes whereby cumulative anomalies arise which cannot be explained or fit into the dominant paradigm. A series of phenomena are discovered which violate the expectations formed by the dominant world view. There comes a point when so many anomalies have arisen that the old paradigm no longer makes sense of the world. It is then time for the formulation of alternative modes of explanation.

I believe that we are at such a juncture in political science. The sound and tumult raised by the young in the past decade and a half over the issues of American foreign policy and domestic racism raise some very serious questions about how the majority of political scientists look at America. I realize that some will argue that as scholars we should shun the type of phenomena usually referred to as "current events" and focus our efforts instead upon questions that have scientific payoff. I would suggest, however, that a focus on "current events" can lead to the raising of issues that are the equivalent of Kuhn's anomalies and thus scientifically important.

Take, for instance, political science's glorification of elites and fear of the masses. Such a perspective arises out of the rather impressive voting and opinion studies of the past three decades. The evidence gathered in these studies documenting the greater knowledge, sophistication, and expressed compliance with democratic norms by elites is certainly incontrovertible.

And yet it must also be acknowledged that the voting and public opinion studies represent a rather narrow peninsula of evidence, and interpretations of American politics based on them alone ignores a great deal about American political life that is neither open to the opinion survey nor relevant to elections.

The Vietnam War and American foreign policy in general should suggest to us that if elites are the repository of democratic values, they don't allow it to show in the area of foreign policy. Very few people can agree on very much about Vietnam, yet I believe a generalization that can be accepted by all is that that abomination was and is an elite adventure. The masses certainly did not force elite national decision-makers to intervene first with advisers and then with mas-

46

sive air and ground power. I doubt that the masses really fear for something called American "credibility." It was not the masses that forced cruel and inhuman tactics such as search and destroy, strategic hamlets, saturation bombing, and the forced urbanization of the peasantry.

If Vietnam were an isolated mistake in a sea of American benevolence, one could excuse political scientists for constantly praising elites. That national tragedy has, however, helped stimulate a second look at the history of American foreign policy, particularly the post-World War II period. The research results of the "revisionist" school of historical scholarship sheds a very different light on the cold war years than most Americans encounter in the media and in their schools.

One might argue that generalizations made by political scientists about elites are only meant to apply to the domestic scene; that the foreign policy arena represents an entirely different set of ground rules and considerations. And yet the issue of racial justice raised by the tumult of the past few years must serve to seriously call into question the vision of elites as the repository of the democratic ethic.

It has only been very recently that we have begun to look to the heart of interracial relations in the United States. For years social scientists have focused primarily upon individual prejudice. The research in this area has been most impressive to be sure, and the evidence demonstrating the greater tolerance of the upper reaches of the education-income-occupation hierarchies is uncontestable. And yet, that research is terribly limited in that it failed to examine and seriously consider the institutional nature of racial oppression in the United States.

In almost every institutional sector of American life, governmental and nongovernmental elites have had a hand in national policies that have been to the detriment of black citizens. It is a harsh fact indeed, but true, that almost without exception the institutions of American life are racist. Whether we look at business, education, the administration of justice, health care, housing or politics, major institutions have worked against the liberation of black citizens.

Housing is a particularly apt example. Government policy until quite recently has served to, in effect, concentrate black people in the inner city and provide cheap housing in the suburbs for fleeing whites. FHA loans were confined primarily to suburban housing beyond the financial reach of most black citizens. Until the courts intervened, the FHA actively encouraged the use of restrictive covenants in order to protect the financial position of investors. Public housing and urban renewal served to exasperate problems by destroying more low-income housing than it provided in return and leaving no decent place for the poor to live. Financial leaders, builders, and real estate men were of course quite enthusiastic about these policies and, not surprisingly, profited enormously. In short, many groups that would probably score high on any test of tolerance toward minorities increased their life chances by diminishing those of blacks.

The story could easily be repeated for almost every other sector of American life. In education, elite decisions have been an important element in the miseducation of black children. They helped write the texts which perpetuated myths of white superiority and black inferiority, formulated culturally biased IQ tests and established tracking systems that doomed many black children to menial futures. In business, elites denied black people adequate credit or insurance and helped insure white domination of ghetto businesses. The legal system oppresses black people through racially biased and often brutal police, white dominance of the legal profession, bond and sentencing practices, and lack of adequate counsel. The list could go on. Let is suffice to say at this point that while individual prejudice has always been a problem in American life, black advancement is hindered more by the major institutions of our society, all of which are run, by definition, by elites.[17]

In view of all of this, is it any wonder that a goodly number of our best students sneer at the picture of American society painted by political scientists. There is a basic incongruency between the harsh realities of American life and our dominant paradigm. Discomforting anomalies arise all around us whether they be raised by intemperate students, desperate ghetto residents or respected scholars like Lowi, Edelman, Rogin, Gamson or Mills, among others.

I believe that we are in the midst of that process whereby scientific revolutions come about. We are only at the very earliest stages of what may prove to be a long process. We are at the point where anomalies are beginning to appear and to accumulate. We are at the point where younger scholars are beginning to struggle with the inappropriateness of our current model for the understanding of American life.

We are not at the point, however, where a new paradigm has been formulated to take its place, and that fact contributes to our problem. Kuhn has demonstrated that old paradigms are not discarded until a new one is at hand that explains both phenomena incorporated in the old paradigm and the accumulated anomalies.

We are, I believe, in that disconcerting period of turmoil when the old has lost its ability to make sense of the world, but a new formulation has not yet arrived to fill the gap. Because they have no strong attachment to older perspectives, the young are especially conscious of the turmoil and are searching for new ways to deal with the world, whether it be in new political perspectives, cultural stances or family arrangements. We would do well to emulate some portion of their behavior by beginning a serious reexamination of the way we perceive the American polity. To cling to the outmoded paradigm not only feeds the disenchantment and cynicism of the young, but, I might add, distorts our analysis of American political life as well.[18]

**Notes**

1. To say that significant segments of white and black youth are politically alienated does not imply that their alienation derives from similar problems or demands similar solutions. Research on these matters is sorely lacking and much needs to be done. In addition to the sense data we receive from our not so tranquil sojourns on college campuses, there are some longitudinal survey data which support the generalization of increasing political alienation among the young. See Roberta S. Sigel, "Political Orientations and Social Class: A Study of Working Class School Children," paper prepared for the VIIIth World Congress of the International Political Science Association, Munich, 1970. A recent Harris poll in *Newsweek* ("The Black Mood—Summer, 1970," June 8, 1970) reports a fantastic increase in the percentage of blacks under twenty-five now willing to use violence in their struggle. A recent report in *The San Francisco Chronicle* offers convincing evidence that a majority of black soldiers (as opposed to just two years ago) now think that it might be necessary to apply the weapons and skills acquired in the military to the domestic needs of the black population.

2. Gabriel A. Almond, "Political Theory and Political Science," *The American Political Science Review*, LX (Dec. 1966), 869-879.

3. Thomas S. Kuhn, *The Structure of Scientific Revolution* (Chicago: University of Chicago Press, Phoenix Books, 1965), p. 42.

4. James MacGregor Burns and Jack Walter Peltason, *Government by the People* (Englewood Cliffs: Prentice-Hall, 1969); Robert A. Dahl, *Pluralist Democracy in the United States* (Chicago: Rand-McNally, 1967); and Marian D. Irish and James W. Prothro, *The Politics of American Democracy* (Englewood Cliffs: Prentice-Hall, Fourth Edition, 1968).

5. Irish and Prothro, p. 255.

6. Burns and Peltason, p. 7.

7. Dahl, p. 24.

8. Irish and Prothro, p. 88.

9. Burns and Peltason, p. 480.

10. Dahl, p. 4.

11. Dahl, p. 262.

12. Irish and Prothro, p. 56.

13. Irish and Prothro, pp. 77-78.

14. Burns and Peltason, p. 472.

15. Burns and Peltason, p. 480.

16. Dahl, pp. 22-23.

17. Because of time and space limitations, I have chosen not to deal directly with the other two elements of the paradigm. Sufficient research and interpretation critical of these elements is at hand and there is no need to be repetitious. The literature critical of the pluralist interpretation of American politics, for instance, is every bit as persuasive as those supportive of that interpretation, and I

suggest that the reader turn to the standard sources. Worthy of special attention, however, are the following: Ted Lowi, *The End of Liberalism* (New York: Norton, 1969); Murray Edelman, *The Symbolic Uses of Politics* (Urbana: University of Illinois Press, 1964); William Connolly, *The Bias of Pluralism* (New York: Atherton, 1969); William Gamson, "Stable Unrepresentation in American Life," *American Behavioral Scientist*, vol. 12 (Nov/Dec. 1968); and Seymour Melman, *Pentagon Capitalism: The Political Economy of War* (New York: McGraw-Hill, 1970).

It should be noted that Robert Dahl reports that one of his students measured the degree of poliarchy and pluralism in ten countries and found that the United States did not rank particularly well, namely, eighth. See Robert Dahl, "The Evaluation of Political Systems," in Ithiel de Sola Pool, *Contemporary Political Science: Toward Empirical Theory* (New York: McGraw-Hill, 1967).

18. If prediction is the companion of explanation in the scientific enterprise, then recent events attest to the failure of political science. A reading of recent political science literature fails to prepare us for the public crisis in which we are now embroiled. There is no hint in that literature of the alienation, passion and energy loosed in the ghettos and on the campus.

# Part 2: The Political Education of Youth

# Introduction to Part 2

A common theme of the writers in Part 2 is to challenge the traditional strategies, assumptions, and predominant values of prior research on the political education of youth. Hans Weiler argues "the maintenance of the political system" featured by most studies constitutes only one of the possible frameworks for the concept of political socialization. This maintenance focus should be supplemented by the inherent conflictual properties of political systems in general, and pluralist systems in particular. He advocates a reexamination of the dominant research assumption concerning the need for a substantial congruence between the outcome of the ongoing political socialization process and the belief systems already prevalent in the political system. He develops a concept of "conflict socialization" primarily in terms of the capacity for a nation's capacity for dissent toleration, or—in terms of group psychology—of the "latitude" of accepting deviant, dissenting, or nonconformist types of politically relevant behavior.

In a memo to the conference participants, Robert Hess (a Professor of Education at Stanford who studied the political attitude formation of 12,000 children in the early sixties) pursued some of the same lines of inquiry. He stressed that in 1961 he was explaining why American youth were so uninvolved in political controversy. He concluded it was because the socialization process was unusually effective and the system secure. Trust and confidence in the system were high, so why get worked up about politics. The contemporary scene is obviously quite different and it is difficult to explain it by applying traditional socialization modes to political behavior in young people. A few years ago he was stressing models of political learning (rather than socialization) that made allowance for acquiring political attitudes and behavior. His memo continues:

It seemed to me a couple of years ago that a model of political learning which made allowance for acquiring political attitudes and behavior from peers was more realistic than a model which conceptualized socialization as the transmission of belief systems and behavior patterns from the adults to the pre-adults. I found the notion of political learning more comfortable than political socialization in attempting to understand anti-establishment feelings and activities on the part of students and other minority groups. It was not completely satisfactory, but it helped me move out of a too-rigid way of thinking about the growth of citizen-type behavior.

The major concern I have at the moment about political socialization in this country is the extent to which political behavior in young people is learned or whether it is spontaneously derivative from a confluence of internal states and external pressures and appeals. From both an individual and group perspective, political behavior (as contrasted with political beliefs, attitudes and knowledge) is in part a matter of maintaining existing status and power relationships within a social structure and of attempts to change these relationships. Such maneuvers involve profound responses at the visceral level which may be accompanied by

53

verbalizations and more "cognitive" operations but are not necessarily controlled or initiated by them. In short, having observed my students and colleagues and been sensitive to some of my own responses during campus protests and near riots, I am very skeptical about the usefulness of concepts of political socialization to explain what happened to us as individuals or to the departments, schools and universities involved as social and "political" units. The responses of faculty members to students who demand in non-traditional ways a greater share in decision making may be understood by some behavioral dynamics other than the socialization of these faculty members when they were in elementary and high school. Not that the early belief systems are irrelevant; they are simply not adequate to explain political behavior when we get down to nonroutine cases. Similar arguments can be made with regard to ethnic nationalism and power, and probably to women's liberation movements.

Occasionally I wonder if the origins of political behavior in pre-adults cannot be better understood in terms of alignments and emotional sympathies rather than formal learning. The identification of the young with political structures, both formal and informal, may do more than slogans and concepts learned at school to influence their political behavior. If political behavior in the young is derivative rather than learned, what is the role of the kind of teaching that goes on in civics, government, U.S. history courses, etc. in the schools? Perhaps it is to provide verbalizations which enable the individual to articulate, in social discourse, underlying political alignments and to recognize in others the signs of one or another type of affiliation and alignment. Certain phrases or words in conversations, for example, will quickly signal to a listener how a speaker feels about black power, women's liberation, or the war in southeast Asia, and as such provide the listener with options as to what his own response might be and how it will be received.

In this formulation, the socialization of the young into patterns of political behavior could be more adequately studied as an indirect outcome of socialization in other areas, such as moral ideology, attachment and dependency, modelling, etc., than as a body of information, concepts and knowledge passed on by an older to a younger generation. Perhaps these comments naturally lead to a suggestion that a proper area for the study of political behavior among the young is political alignment, identification and affiliation with visible established politically oriented groups and structures. Such a perspective might allow us to bring to bear concepts about human behavior which are of a dynamic sort appropriate to an analysis of political action, energy and conviction in the young.

Edgar Litt pursues Hess' conception of political learning in a specific direction. He laments that too often research has tapped student responses within closed educational systems as if political learning was equated with cognitive learning within formal educational systems. In his view, experimental learning in which the young cope with the realities of politics in America becomes the only way of breaking the binds that have gripped researchers. He advances a specific design for experimental research in order to discover what values are capable of being changed by politics and which are simply incapable of being negotiated, modified, or changed in any fundamental way.

Kenneth Prewitt and John Meyer turned their attention to a different aspect of political socialization. Schooling is socially chartered to direct students toward adult social and political status positions. Schools help define these positions as well as legitimate the assignment of differentially educated people to them. In so doing schools are affected by and affect the political structure of society.

In short, school structures provide an important means of legitimating a whole system of inequalities, both in the eyes of students or graduates, and in the view of sectors of the adult population including government officials. Clearly when we view schools in this light we see a broader intersect between schools and the political order than if we concentrate on school board decision-making or the attitudes of children toward political parties. We also see the political stress inherent in our educational institutions that are responsible for teaching youth about the American ideal of equality and at the same time sorting people out to unequal social-economic positions.

# 5

# Political Socialization and The Political System: Consensual and Conflictual Linkage Concepts

HANS N. WEILER

For a while, it seemed as if the study of political socialization, after its surge to an unprecedented level of popularity among political scientists, had become fairly content with its new role as an established "sub-field" of the discipline, and had largely ceased to question some of the basic assumptions on which its initial emergence was predicated. To be sure, the discussion on where to go next in the study of political socialization continued,[1] and contributed to some noticeable improvement especially in the methodological quality of political socialization research.[2] By and large, however, the field of political socialization studies, and its cultivators, had grown accustomed to the existence of a distinct area of scholarly concerns within political science, and to its definition in terms of the "diffuse support" notion as developed in Easton's conceptual framework for the analysis of political systems.[3]

More recently, however, some instructive and potentially significant challenges to the prevailing notion of political socialization, and to the accepted parameters for research in this area, have been expressed. For one thing, the validity and usefulness of the distinction between political socialization and other areas of political science research is being questioned; a particularly persuasive case is made for reexamining the relationship between political socialization and political recruitment.[4] Furthermore, increasingly frequent excursions of political socialization researchers into studying political learning processes among post-juvenile populations[5] have tended to raise another kind of "boundary" issue, namely, that of the relationship between political socialization and the discipline's broader concerns with the study of political attitudes and behavior as represented in some of the studies of voting behavior and political belief systems.[6] Questions like these are bound to lead to a reexamination of the terms of reference of political socialization research, and of its relationship to other areas of political analysis.

An earlier version of this paper was prepared for a research workshop on "The Politics of Elementary and Secondary Education," sponsored by the Committee on Basic Research in Education, Division of Behavioral Sciences, National Academy of Sciences, at Stanford University, September 14-19, 1970.

The author acknowledges the suggestions and criticisms made by other participants in the workshop, especially Herbert Jacob, Edgar Litt, John W. Meyer, and Kenneth Prewitt, as well as his colleagues in the Department of Political Science and the School of Education at Stanford University.

This chapter proposes to pursue yet another challenge to the established conception of the field of political socialization. In an as yet rather preliminary form, several authors have recently questioned what, pending a more adequate description, could be characterized as the "consensual bias" in existing political socialization research.[7] This paper will attempt to (a) identify and describe the nature of such a bias; (b) argue its inherent limitations for an adequate study of the processes of political learning and attitude formation; and (c) develop a preliminary framework for a more balanced view of political socialization with regard to both the consensual and conflictual elements of political systems. It is expected that to revise the notion of political socialization in this way will also open up new perspectives on the role of formal schooling as both a source and a context for the learning of political beliefs, and the acquisition of political attitudes.

## Political Socialization and the
## Political System: Consensual Linkages

Our criticism of what we perceive as a somewhat unbalanced conceptual and theoretical notion of political socialization can probably be best expressed in terms of the various propositions which Dennis, among others, has grouped together under the aspect of the "system relevance" of political socialization. He refers to "the question about what effects political socialization has upon political life" and conceives these effects in terms of the alternative that "political socialization may either contribute or serve as an impediment to the persistence and stability of the political system and its component parts."[8] Dennis' basic reference in so defining the linkage between political scoialization and the political system is, of course, Easton's concept of political socialization as a source of "diffuse support" for the stability and cohesion of the political system—a kind of support which is generated by "the positive encouragement of sentiments of legitimacy and compliance, the acceptance of a notion of the existence of a common good transcending the particular good of any particular individual or groups, or the kindling of deep feelings of community."[9] Most research and writing on political socialization to date (to the extent that it has used a coherent conceptual framework on the linkage between political socialization and the political system at all) has been concerned with the elaboration and operationalization of this basic proposition. Furthermore, it has moved in the direction of interpreting it in essentially "conservative" terms, assuming "that in one way or another socializing processes assure the continuity of a political system in relatively unchanged form," and thus relegating change to the role of "a residual rather than a central or expected product of socialization."[10] One of the most unequivocal commitments to this concept of the role of political socialization in the political system is found in the lead article of one of the more respectable symposia on the subject:

Having once internalized the society's norms, it will presumably not be difficult for the individual to act in congruence with them. A politically organized society has the same maintenance needs and consequently has an additional function: the political socialization of the young. Political socialization is the gradual learning of the norms, attitudes, and behavior accepted and practiced by the ongoing political system . . . . . . The goal of political socialization is to so train or develop individuals that they become well-functioning members of the political society . . . . . . a well-functioning citizen is one who accepts (internalizes) society's political norms and who will then transmit them to future generations. For without a body politic so in harmony with the ongoing political values the political system would have trouble functioning smoothly and perpetuating itself safely.[11]

In one of the most recent and extensive reviews of the state of political socialization research, Dawson and Prewitt see fit to speak of the "generally conservative bias of political socialization,"[12] and conclude their book with a plea for mobilizing the concept of political socialization as a potentially important explanatory tool in an effort to understand "the mechanisms which transform one network of social relations, one pattern of cultural values, into another."[13]

In their own major contribution to political socialization research, Easton and Dennis deplore the narrowness and inadequacy of a "system-maintenance theory" of political socialization as tending to "bias research toward investigating those conditions favoring the perpetuation of stability of the status quo"[14] and call for "a more comprehensive conception of the theoretical relevance of socialization for the political system, one in which change is not interpreted as a failure of the system to reproduce itself but is viewed positively."[15] Whether their own attempt to overcome this problem by developing a "neutral" conception of political socialization has been entirely successful is, in our view, arguable, in spite of their theoretical allowance for political socialization being able, under certain conditions, to contribute not only to the maintenance or replication of a given system, but also to its transformation or even its total destruction.[16] This, however, is not the place to argue how close Easton and Dennis in their actual research come to the requirements of a "neutral" persistence model. What we are primarily concerned with is that the linkage between political socialization and the political system could and should be conceptualized in terms different from both the stability-oriented "system-maintenance" model *and* a more "open-ended," presumably less biased persistence model such as postulated by Easton and Dennis. Furthermore, we would argue that the theoretical decisions involved in designing an alternative model of the socialization-system linkage will bear significantly on the design of political socialization research in general, and on further inquiries into the role of education therein, in particular.

## Consensus and Political Socialization

Before we proceed, we need to make an important distinction between the two prevailing modes in which a "consensual" notion of political socialization expresses itself. While these are by no means strictly separable, each of them contributes in its own way to a rather unbalanced perspective on the process of political learning, and its relationship to the political system.

The first mode of a consensual perspective on political socialization implies the notion of what one may call a "vertical" consensus, i.e., an essential congruence between the norms and beliefs of the *existing* political system, and those of the projected or anticipated political system of the future. Such a model implies a process of political socialization which is oriented towards the existing belief system, on the assumption that it is that same belief system which will constitute the frame of reference within which today's socializees will operate as tomorrow's citizens; the modal case is that of the youngster acquiring the political norms of his elders, thus facilitating and assuring his smooth and frictionless transition into an essentially unchanged framework for his adult political life.[17] Major discontinuities in the socialization process, or inconsistencies between what the socialization process intends, and what it achieves, are incompatible with the model of continuity, and can at best achieve the status of deviant cases, or be excluded from what is conceived to be "political socialization." There is no room in this model for the possibility of conflict between the existing belief system and the results of the political learning process of the following generation; it would be extremely difficult, for example, to conceive in this context of something like a "counter culture" as an agent of socialization which is deliberately predicated on the notion of discontinuity.

While the basic presupposition of this mode of "vertical" consensus is the notion of *stability* over time, the second mode is based on the notion of intra-system *harmony* in a "horizontal" sense. In this perspective, the modal situation is characterized by the absence of major and persistent conflicts and cleavages in the political belief system, and implies a socialization process which, as a rule, is characterized by a high degree of internal consistency and conformity. The possibility of different socializing agents delivering inconsistent or even conflicting messages to a given group of socializees is again relegated to the realm of deviancy, and the research task is confined to studying the individual's progressive approximation of the prevailing value consensus.[18]

Both of these conceptions of the political socialization process, it is argued, tend to narrow the possible range of research questions in that they introduce, on a pre-empirical level, assertions about the "normalcy" of one type of socialization-system linkage over another, thereby reducing the openness of a balanced consensus-conflict continuum in the relationship between political socialization and the political system.

## Political Socialization and the
## Political System: Conflictual Linkages

Essentially, one could question the prevailing consensual model of the role of political socialization in the political system on two grounds. On the one hand, protest, dissent, and conflict have dramatically increased in both extent and intensity in contemporary American and Western European societies as well as in some non-Western systems. Consequently, one may come to realize that both intrasystem cleavages and discontinuities in the condition of political systems over time can no longer be relegated to the position of "marginal" or abnormal societal phenomena. The ubiquity of conflict as "the increasing imperfection of the consensus"[19]—while by no means new to any kind of social or political system at any point in time—has manifested itself with much greater drama and visibility than before, and it is from this observation that authors such as Hess derive the necessity for a new look at the linkage between socialization and political system.

While one could hardly argue with either the accuracy of the observation or the relevance of the propositions derived from it, there still is something of an "ad hoc" quality about this argument which leads us to search for a further and perhaps more generic basis on which to build a revised notion of the political socialization process and its relationship to the political system. Our search for such a modified conception of political socialization leads us, perhaps not surprisingly, to some of the work in the fields of political sociology and social psychology; while we could not claim to provide, in the framework of this brief chapter, a thorough and exhaustive review of the many relevant propositions that have been generated by these two burgeoning fields of inquiry and theory-building, we hope to show that some selected contributions in these areas lend considerable support to, and provide helpful explications of, our own preliminary notions about a "conflict model" of political socialization.

As we have indicated, our objection to much of the conceptual and theoretical basis of past research in political socialization results from the fact that this research is largely guided by one or the other mode of expressing an essentially consensual assumption about the role of political socialization in the political system, and that it tends to neglect the crucial importance or conflictual elements in the system's operation. It seems indeed odd that theoretical concerns in the field of political socialization have remained largely unaffected for so long by the challenge to consensus theory which has loomed large in the development of political sociology over the past decade. Some time has passed since Lipset stressed "the proper balance between conflict and consensus" as a crucial element in the nature of social and political systems,[20] and argued for acknowledging the interdependence of conflict and consensus in the sense that "consensus on the norms of tolerance which a society or organization accepts has often developed only as a result of basic conflict, and requires the continuation of conflict to sustain it."[21] Another early and important contribution to this debate was Dahrendorf's attack on consensus theory and his attempts to develop a theoretical framework for "the explanation of systematic social conflict in industrial societies" that would go beyond the Marxian theory of class and supersede it by a new and similarly comprehensive formulation[22]—an attempt which has led Dahrendorf to recognize that "class conflict is but a special case of an even more general phenomenon," and that "a new departure is needed in the sociological theory of political conflict and social change."[23] Such a new departure, while strongly influenced by Dahrendorf's further work, also stands to benefit from reexamining the work of such scholars as Schattschneider and the rich contributions to the theory of conflict provided by Lewis Coser.[24,25] The degree to which political science research has paid attention to this discussion has been notable in some instances,[26] but has, on the whole, fallen far short of a fully adequate utilization in the study of political systems.

It is characteristic of these and many other similar contributions to consider the ubiquity of conflict ("Societies do not differ in that some have conflicts and others not; societies and social units within them differ in the violence and intensity of conflicts"[27]), not just as an unavoidable deficiency of the human condition in its social manifestations, but rather as an essential requirement for the cohesion and integration of social systems in general, and political systems, in particular.[28] From this point of view, the argument that "the stability and 'success' of democratic societies depend on the sharing of general political and prepolitical values"[29] is subjected to severe criticism which, explicitly or implicitly, extends to a good deal of work in the field of political socialization.[30] Whether criticizing the biases of consensus theory must of necessity lead to the adoption of Marxist theories of "pragmatic role acceptance" and "manipulative socialization" would seem—Mann's interesting argument in that direction notwithstanding—open to further theoretical and empirical examination. What does seem indicated, however, as a result of the various challenges to the notion of the beneficial effects of consensus and intrasystem harmony on the stability of the system, is a reappraisal of the categories in which we have tended to view the process and outcome of political socialization.

How, then, would we begin to conceive of political socialization as a process which leads not only to certain levels of regime norm acceptance, political efficacy, trust, etc., but also to types of orientations which pertain much more directly to the individual's ability to cope with dissent and conflict, and hence to the system's ability to manage such conflict? We would argue that such an attempt will have to focus primarily on the choice and the conceptualization of the dependent variables of political socialization research; in a further step, we should try to formulate some tentative assumptions on the ways in which various factors associated with the individual's political learning experience can be expected to affect such variables.

*Factors That Enhance Dissent Toleration*

With regard to the choice of dependent variables, we would like to illustrate our point by elaborating on one type of attitudinal orientation which we perceive as being particularly relevant to a conflict-oriented notion of political socialization. If we follow V.O. Key's notion of political conflict as being represented by a more or less polarized bimodal (or, in some cases, multimodal) distribution of public opinion,[31] then the question of how individuals and groups identifying with one of the opinion clusters perceive of, and relate to, adherents of a different or even opposite opinion becomes of major concern to the student of the system's ability to manage conflict. Answering the question becomes all the more crucial the more one is interested not just in stating and describing the presence of conflict, but also in its future development, its persistence, its effects on the system's operation, and its possible regulation, resolution, or disappearance. On a preliminary level, for instance, one might argue that (in Rokeach's terms) the degree of "dogmatism" which prevails in the relationship between holders of diverse opinions would substantially affect the system's ability to "process" existing conflicts in such a way as to maintain the system's basic cohesion without at the same time taking recourse to repressive action against one or the other group. The complexity of the relationship pattern is, of course, bound to increase the more political reality differs from the pure and simple model of a bimodal distribution of opinion.

We would argue that the ways in which the holders of diverse and conflicting opinions regard each other could and should be systematically conceived as one of the possible outcomes of the political socialization process, and should thus be an explicit object of inquiry. Furthermore, our attention ought to be focused on the factors which can be shown to influence such outcomes under identifiable and specified conditions. It would seem that Rokeach's notion of a distinction between "open" and "closed" cognitive systems and his discussion of their respective properties and correlates[32] provide useful guidelines for the more elaborate and specific formulation of the kinds of dependent variables which we ought to be studying, although some other approaches to the problem could probably yield similarly useful conceptual and theoretical assistance.[33] If we succeeded in operationalizing intergroup attitudes in situations of conflict over political or politically relevant values, and then developed research designs which would test our assumptions about how different socialization agents contribute to the formation, maintenance, and change of such attitudes, political socialization research could significantly enhance its contribution to the understanding of not only the emergence of conflict in political systems, but also of the determinants of its intensity and the chances of its "successful" regulation or resolution.

Our discussion may be carried one step further by specifically looking at one aspect of the "open-closed" dichotomy: Rokeach assumes that, in the overall dogmatism syndrome, the degree of "closeness" of a cognitive system is highly related not only to authoritarianism, but also to intolerance.[34] If we pursued this further in the context of our thinking about conflict and political socialization, we should find it useful to concentrate on toleration, or the lack of it, as one important attitudinal dimension of both the antecedents and consequences of conflict. In doing this, we would follow Rokeach's plea for a more generic definition and use of "intolerance" than the narrower and particular concept of ethnic or radical intolerance of the "Authoritarian Personality" variety has provided.[35] At the same time, however, we would have to realize that "current concepts and measures of intolerance seem to be woefully inadequate in addressing themselves to non-ethnic forms of intolerance"[36]—a statement which would naturally hold as true for the obverse of intolerance, tolerance or toleration. It is here that the Sherifs' notion of "latitudes of acceptance and rejection"[37] of others' behavior would seem to provide a helpful construct in our attempt to formalize the inquiry into socialization processes which may lead to different levels of toleration in the political realm: "The latitude of acceptance and the latitude of rejection, relative to a given sphere of behavior, together constitute the reference scale on the basis of which evaluations or appraisals of specific behaviors are made."[38] This "reference scale" may vary from one setting to the next, both within and between societies, and would, if adequately and validly operationalized, become an appropriate measure of the kind of "dissent toleration" in which we are interested.

Thus, it should be possible to design measures which could serve as specific indicators of the acceptance and rejection latitudes with regard to various types of controversial political behavior,[39] and to begin to develop testable assumptions about the ways in which the variance in these latitudes across different subgroups of the political system can be accounted for by different socialization agents and processes. It will be important to bear the behavior-oriented nature of these "reference scales" in mind when one sets out to design appropriate measurements of "toleration." For instance, it will be insufficient to just solicit reactions of agreement or disagreement with statements representing more or less purely attitudinal orientations without referring rather explicitly to the type of behavior in which such attitudes would be most likely to manifest themselves. One direction which it has been found useful to explore further would be to measure latitudes of the acceptance or rejection of controversial political issues through a modified "social distance" scale: the level of acceptance of a dissenting position on a presumably controversial issue would be indicated by how "close" a role the respondent would allow the holder of such a position to assume—with the scale ranging from the "dissenter" holding such "distant" roles as speaking on TV or publishing a book, to his being acceptable as a personal friend.[40] It remains a matter of further inquiry whether attitudes of dissent toleration in the realm of politics constitute an integral part of a more encompassing psychological or personality disposition. As a first step, it will have to be ascertained whether toleration of dissent is contingent on the kind of issue over which dissent arises, or whether it is found to exist more or less regardless of the issues involved. Preliminary evidence suggests that, to a remarkable degree, the latter seems to be the case, and that the level of toleration of dissent in one area (e.g., politics) is an excellent predictor of the level at which dissent in other areas (e.g., sexual and marital norms) is considered acceptable.[41] The issue might be further explored with regard to the relationship between attitudes towards dissent and conflict and Berlyne's notion of "uncertainty tolerance."[42] What we are suggesting here is a substantial association between a "cognitive style" characterized by a high ability to tolerate, and live with, uncertainty, and an attitudinal orientation favorable to the continued existence of dissent and conflict in one's environment.

While the problem of measuring latitudes of accepting or rejecting positions on controversial and at least potentially conflict-generating issues will require further study and empirical validation, the major analytical problem arises with regard to the factors that affect the development and change of such attitudes. Some of the hypotheses developed and tested in connection with the Sherifs' work on the salience of accepted or rejected behaviors could lead to useful propositions for the more specific realm of political behaviors.[43] Thus, the finding that "the latitude of acceptable behavior, defined by the norms of the group, varies according to the importance of the activity to the members"[44] (which is subsequently differentiated by referring to the different standing of members in the group as a further factor) should provide an adequate starting point for the analysis of differences in dissent toleration between, say, different age groups or groups of different sociocultural background. While we find this particular set of propositions especially appealing and useful, there are other ways in which theories generated by research on small groups can be made directly relevant to the study of variation in the toleration of dissent and conflict as a result of political socialization processes.

Some important propositions for the further inquiry into the experiential correlates and sources of attitudes towards dissent and conflict could also be developed from the increasing literature on patterns of conflict resolution. A case in point is Steiner's work, which indicates a remarkable degree of association between certain types of interaction behavior and nonviolent patterns of conflict resolution.[45] For the kind of socialization research which would attempt to go beyond the description of conflict-related attitudes into a study of their formation and change, it would seem to be particularly important to test the effect of certain types of group interaction patterns on the emergence of attitudes towards conflict and dissent.[46]

## The Role of Education

It is possible to elaborate further on the kinds of research possibilities suggested in the preceding discussion by considering one of the various sources of political learning, namely, the instructional, experiential, and contextual influence of formal schooling. This is not the place to argue the relative significance of the school as a source of political learning, compared to such other sources as the family, peer group, media, etc.;[47] it should suffice here to assume, as available research entitles us to do, that formal schooling does play a role in the process of political learning, and to proceed to some specific propositions on how to identify the nature and strength of that contribution to the specific process of learning attitudes towards the acceptance or rejection of dissent.

Previous research shows that, at least in the case of political efficacy and related attitudes, the formation of political attitudes is strongly influenced by the "practice" of related kinds of behavior in other, nonpolitical social contexts. The findings reported by Almond and Verba, for instance, indicate a strong relationship between the degree of participation in family, school, and job decisions, and scores on their "subjective political competence" measure; furthermore, the data suggest that the effect of these various participatory experiences is cumulative.[48] Analogously, we might argue that the degree of involvement in situations which are characterized by a consistently high level of dissent and diversity of opinion, especially if the assumption about the cumulative effect of such experiences could be generalized, may well be an important factor in accounting for varying "latitudes" of accepting dissent in the realm of more strictly political beliefs. In the educational context, it would appear promising to adopt, with some modifications, the notion of the "open classroom climate" as used by Ehman;[49] the key factor in measuring this variable, which was shown to have a substantial effect on such attitudes as political efficacy, participation, and cynicism, was the relative frequency with which teachers discussed controversial issues in the classroom, illustrative examples of such issues being the Vietnam War, minority group relations, etc. It should be possible to expand this measure to obtain additional information on the range of positions taken in such discussions, the intensity of disagreement, and the prevailing modes of managing such conflicts as the discussion may have generated.[50] If, moreover, experiences of this kind could be generated and systematically varied in an experimental or quasi-experimental design so as to maintain some degree of control over demographic as well as other experiential variables, it should be possible to test whether, and under what conditions, our assumptions about the experiential source of attitudes towards dissent hold true.

On a different level of analysis, there seems to be a case for going back to the substantive framework for formal learning about politics provided in the codifications of civics textbooks and similar material. To be sure, political socialization research to date has not yet produced any convincing results on the ways in which the content of civic instruction, regardless of such intervening factors as modes of teaching, teacher personality, etc., may influence the process and direction of political learning, especially in terms of the acquisition of normative orientations to the political system.[51] This is, of course, at least in part due to the tremendous difficulties in operationalizing instructional content as a truly independent variable—a difficulty which in turn would account for the relative reluctance to study it systematically. With regard to the question of dissent toleration, or the formation of different latitudes in accepting nonconformist behavior, we may have a slightly less ambiguous situation than in the case of other attitudes for which it may be more difficult to find clearly commensurate precepts in instructional materials. There is no question but that most civics textbooks in this country as well as in other Western democracies place heavy emphasis on the importance and the desirability of consensus and harmony in democratic systems; instances of cleavage, dissent, or conflict are generally relegated to the realm of the extraordinary, deviant, or marginal.[52] However, there are also variations in this pattern, and it seems that concern among social studies teachers and curriculum experts with the more genuine role of conflict in democracies is becoming more widespread and serious.[53] Thus, if our expectation of a considerable range in the treatment of dissent and conflict in instructional materials could be substantiated, a case could be made for analyzing the differential effects of being exposed to differently oriented instructional content. From the results of such gross yet probably rather instructive types of analysis more refined approaches could be designed which would probably have to rely very heavily on some of the theoretical and methodological developments in the field of curriculum research and evaluation.

**Students' Status Expectations**

A third approach to studying the role of formal schooling in the formation of attitudes towards dissent and conflict has relatively little to do with instructional or other "internal" characteristics of the school, but more with the external "social definition" of the school's product, and with the students' perception of that definition. The notion that the school's perceived ability to confer future adult status is an important factor in the social and political learning process of the students has been recently advanced by John W. Meyer,[54] and has already shown its analytical usefulness in several political socialization studies.[55] Without going into a lengthy discussion of the full theoretical and methodological implications and possibilities of such an approach, it seems reasonable to assume that students' status expectations, as a function of their school's "charter," or externally accepted ability to confer status, may form an important source for that specific learning process leading to differential latitudes in the acceptance of nonconformity and dissent: high status expectations, we would argue, especially if they are reinforced by an empirically verified perception of the school's ability to guarantee the fulfillment of such expectations, may well result in a view of one's anticipated role in the social and polilitcal system which is considered to be much less threatened by dissent and cleavage than would be the case if the anticipation of one's future status were beset by a good deal more uncertainty. This may be a particularly tenuous and tentative proposition in the absence of hard empirical evidence to document its explanatory utility; nevertheless, it appears to offer a most promising way for moving beyond a strictly "intra-educational" conception of the role of formal schooling in the social and political learning process.

## Conclusion

The study of political socialization has become one of the most favorite meeting grounds for politically interested students of education and educationally interested political scientists. Professional meetings, journals, symposia abound with contributions to the subject, and a legion of graduate students in both education and political science are busy collecting, analyzing, and interpreting empirical data of widely varying quality. In view of this proliferation, the need for a critical examination of some of the basic premises and assumptions on the linkage between political socialization and the political system becomes ever more imperative. Contending that this linkage has so far been largely conceived in terms of maintenance, continuity, and consensus, we have argued for a reorientation in our concerns with political learning in such a way as to acknowledge not only the possibility, but the probability of conflictual elements in the relationship between political socialization and the political system. It will be a matter of further conceptual clarification and differentiation, of a good deal of labor on the design and validation of appropriate measurements and, above all, of careful empirical testing to fully realize the potential of this broader and more balanced notion of political learning.

## Notes

1. A good example of the contributions to this discussion is Jack Dennis, "Major Problems of Political Socialization Research," *Midwest Journal of Political Science* 12 (1968), 85-114.

2. Some of the more notable methodological improvements in political socialization research are represented by such works as Lee H. Ehman, "An Analysis of the Relationships of Selected Educational Variables with the Political Socialization of High School Students," *American Educational Research Journal* 6 (1969), 559-580; Kenneth P. Langton, *Political Socialization* (New York: Oxford University Press, 1969). See also Robert Dreeben's stimulating essay, *On What Is Learned in School* (Reading, Mass.: Addison-Wesley, 1968).

3. See, *inter alia*, David Easton, *A Framework for Political Analysis* (Englewood Cliffs, N.J.: Prentice-Hall, 1965).

4. See, for example, Kenneth Prewitt's contribution to this volume.

5. Orville G. Brim, Jr., and Stanton Wheeler, *Socialization After Childhood* (New York: Wiley, 1966); Harvard Educational Review, *Political Socialization (A Special Issue)* 38 (1968), No. 3.

6. See, for example, Philip E. Converse, "The Nature of Belief Systems in Mass Publics," David E. Apter, ed., *Ideology and Discontent* (Glencoe: The Free Press, 1964), 206-261; V.O. Key, Jr., *Public Opinion and American Democracy* (New York: Knopf, 1961); Herbert McClosky, "Consensus and Ideology in American Politics," *American Political Science Review* 58 (1964), 361-382.

7. Harmon Zeigler and Wayne Peak, "The Political Functions of the Educational System," *Sociology of Education* 43 (1970), 115-142; Robert D. Hess, "Political Socialization in the Schools," *Harvard Educational Review*, op. cit., 528-536; Michael Mann, "The Social Cohesion of Liberal Democracy," *American Sociological Review* 35 (1970), 423-439.

8. Jack Dennis, op. cit., 89.

9. David Easton, op. cit., 125.

10. David Easton and Jack Dennis, *Children in the Political System: Origins of Political Legitimacy* (New York: McGraw-Hill, 1969), p. 24.

11. Roberta Sigel, "Assumptions about the Learning of Political Values," *The Annals* 361 (September 1965), 2.

12. Richard E. Dawson and Kenneth Prewitt, *Political Socialization* (Boston: Little, Brown & Co., 1969), 213 and passim.

13. Ibid., 218.

14. Easton and Dennis, op. cit., 24.

15. Ibid., 42.

16. Ibid., 66.

17. See, for example, Roberta Sigel, op. cit.

18. "Just as socialization pertains to an individual's conformity to his society's culture, so political socialization refers to an individual's adaptation to his society's political culture." John J. Patrick, *Political Socialization of American Youth* (Washington, D.C.: National Council for the Social Studies, 1967, 1.

19. Zeigler and Peak, op. cit., 122.

20. Seymour Martin Lipset, *Political Man: The Social Bases of Politics* (Garden City, N.Y.: Doubleday, 1960), quoted from Anchor Books edition, 1963, 4.

21. Ibid., 2.

22. Ralf Dahrendorf, *Class and Class Conflict in Industrial Society* (Stanford, Calif.: Stanford University Press, 1959), 115.

23. Ralf Dahrendorf, *Conflict After Class: New Perspectives on the Theory of Social and Political Conflict* (London: Longmans for the University of Essex, 1967), 8. For an excellent application of Dahrendorf's concept of social and political conflict, see his *Society and Democracy in Germany* (Garden City, N.Y.: Doubleday, 1967).

24. E.E. Schattschneider, *The Semi-Sovereign People* (New York: Holt, Rinehart and Winston, 1960).

25. Lewis Coser, *The Functions of Social Conflict* (New York: The Free Press, 1956); *Continuities in the Study of Social Conflict* (New York: The Free Press, 1967); The Functions of Dissent, *The Dynamics of Dissent: Scientific Proceedings of the American Academy of Psychoanalysis* (*Science and Psychoanalysis*, Vol. 13), (New York: Grune and Stratton, 1968), 158-168.

26. Among the outstanding contributions is the work by Herbert McClosky and his associates: Herbert McClosky, "Consensus and Ideology," op. cit.; Herbert McClosky and John Schaar, "Psychological Dimensions of Anomy," *American Sociological Review* 30 (1965), 14-39; Herbert McClosky, Paul J. Hoffmann, and Rosemary O'Hara, "Issue Conflict and Consensus Among Party Leaders and Followers," *American Political Science Review* 54 (1960), 406-427. See also James W. Prothro and Charles M. Grigg, "Fundamental Principles of Democracy: Bases of Agreement and Disagreement," *Journal of Politics* 22 (1960), 276-294.

27. Dahrendorf, *Society and Democracy*, op. cit., 145.

28. See, *inter alia*, Lipset, op. cit.; for a stimulating recent discussion of the empirical utility of consensual and conflictual theories in explaining social cohesion in liberal democracies, see Michael Mann, op. cit.

29. Mann, op. cit., 423.

30. Ibid., passim.

31. V.O. Key, op. cit., 54-56 and passim.

32. Milton Rokeach, *The Open and Closed Mind: Investigations into the Nature of Belief Systems and Personality Systems* (New York: Basic Books, 1960).

33. See, for example, Marie Jahoda's conformance vs. non-conformance model ("Psychological Issues in Civil Liberties," *American Psychologist* 11 (1956), 234-240), or Muzafer Sherif's extensive explorations of intergroup conflict in his, *inter alia, In Common Predicament: Social Psychology of Inter-group Conflict and Cooperation* (Boston: Houghton Mifflin, 1966).

34. Milton Rokeach, "The Nature and Meaning of Dogmatism," *Psychological Review* 61 (1954), 194-205.

35. Rokeach, *The Open and Closed Mind*, op. cit., 15-16.

36. Ibid., 15.

37. Muzafer Sherif and Carolyn W. Sherif, *Reference Groups: Exploration into Conformity and Deviation of Adolescents* (New York: Harper and Row, 1964), 61-64 and passim.

38. Ibid., 62.

39. For various dimensions of social behavior, such measures have been successfully developed; see, *inter alia*, Muzafer Sherif, "Conformity-deviation, norms, and group relations," I. Berg and B.M. Bass, eds., *Conformity and Deviation* (New York: Harper and Row, 1961); Muzafer Sherif and Carl I. Hovland, *Social Judgments: Assimilation and Contrast Effects in Communication and Attitude Change* (New Haven, Conn.: Yale University Press, 1961).

40. In a recent study, the author has used measures of this kind to investigate levels of dissent toleration among West German youths; see his *Correlates of Dissent Toleration Among West German Youths* (Stanford: Institute of Political Studies, 1970), mimeo.

41. In the author's own study of West German Youths (see note 40), a strong relationship of this kind is, indeed, shown to exist.

42. D.E. Berlyne, *Conflict, Arousal, and Curiosity* (New York: McGraw-Hill, 1960).

43. For a detailed discussion of some of these hypotheses, see Sherif and Sherif, op. cit., 88-95, 178-180.

44. Ibid., 178.

45. See, *inter alia,* Jürg Steiner, "Nonviolent Conflict Resolution in Democratic Systems: Switzerland," *The Journal of Conflict Resolution* 13 (1969), 295-304.

46. Here again, the author's Germany data (see note 40) bear out the significance of the relationship between certain interaction experiences and the development of dissent toleration.

47. The methodological implications of this problem have most recently been summarized by John Harp and Stephen Richter, "Sociology of Education," *Review of Educational Research*, 39 (1969), 671-694; for an imaginative overview of the problems in identifying the specific outcome of schooling, see Robert Dreeben, op. cit.

48. Gabriel A. Almond and Sidney Verba, *The Civic Culture: Political Attitudes and Democracy in Five Nations* (Princeton: Princeton University Press, 1963).

49. Lee H. Ehman, op. cit.

50. The author's study of toleration among German youths (see note 40) has explored the feasibility of several ways to obtain this kind of information, and has shown that most of it can indeed be obtained through appropriate survey methods.

51. One of the few attempts in this direction is Kenneth P. Langton and M. Kent Jennings, "Political Socialization and the High School Civics Curriculum in the United States," *American Political Science Review* 62 (1968), 852-867, which comes to the somewhat guarded conclusion that "under special conditions exposure to government and politics courses does have an impact at the secondary school level" (866).

52. One widely used civics textbook—to give but one example—concludes its chapter on "To Insure Domestic Tranquility" by saying: "There are many provisions in the Constitution which help to create and preserve harmony. Without harmony no nation can progress, no people can be happy. Harmony within the nation has helped the United States become a world power. It has helped the people work together to build a better future. The men who wrote the Constitution were wise in their choice of goals. To insure domestic tranquility is one of

the most important goals mentioned in the preamble." Richard E. Gross and Vanza Devereaux, *Civics in Action* (San Francisco: Harr Wagner, 1966).

53. See, for instance, Seymour J. Mandelbaum, *The Social Setting of Intolerance* (Chicago: Scott, Foresman & Co., 1964); Stanley P. Wronski, "Implementing Change in Social Studies Programs: Basic Considerations," Dorothy McClure Fraser, ed., *Social Studies Curriculum Development: Prospects and Problems* (39th Yearbook of the National Council for the Social Studies), (Washington, D.C.: National Council for the Social Studies, 1969), 277-304.

54. John W. Meyer, "The Charter: Conditions of Diffuse Socialization in Schools," W. Richard Scott, ed., *Social Processes and Social Structures* (New York: Holt, Rinehart and Winston, 1970).

55. See, for instance, John C. Bock, *Education and Nation-Building in Malaysia: A Study of Institutional Effect in Thirty-Four Malaysian Secondary Schools* (Princeton: Princeton University Press (forthcoming)).

# 6 Sustaining Public Commitment Among the Young: Experiential Political Learning

EDGAR LITT

## The Research Agenda: Education and Politics After the Deluge

There is an old Yiddish tale about a gatekeeper in an Eastern European village whose job it was to wait for the coming of the Messiah. After many years of faithful duty, he complained to the village elders about the meager pay. "Yes, we know that the pay is meager," replied the elders, "but consider that the work is steady." The job of studying American education has also become steady, if a bit dangerous. For the political scientist, it has also become exceedingly frustrating. Having at last rediscovered that education is highly politicized, we became enchanted with the study of political socialization and then shocked by the extent to which our research failed to account for the waves of stress, conflict, and confrontation throughout the educational system. In his introduction to this volume Professor Kirst reminds us that educational systems are often closed to innovation, especially those involving political relationships. The same point can be made with regard to prevailing modes of professional research on education and student activism. It is true that terms such as "deauthorization" and "desocialization" are now being used to describe behavior and attitudes dissonant with the adjustment model that has dominated political science for more than a decade. It is also true that new winds of "relevance," "criticism" and "research involvement" are blowing through the meeting rooms of the social science fraternities.

The rub comes in continuing to regard education, in particular political education, as distinct in context, research orientation, and anticipated results. Too often paradigms and research methods tapped student responses within closed educational systems as if political learning was equated with cognitive learning within formal educational systems.[1] Furthermore, most of us continue to regard political learning research in conventional ways. In his otherwise excellent presidential address to the American Political Science Association (1969), David Easton, after taking a fresh and sympathetic look at the "post-behavioral" genre of emerging political science professionals, proposes that we devote more re-

Revision of a paper prepared for a Conference on Education and Politics, Stanford University, September 10-14, 1970. The applied phase of my proposal is guided by the efforts of Fred Wallace, a graduate student at the University of Connecticut.

sources to "applied research" designed to yield relatively quick policy-related conclusions, while continuing to pursue our normal scholarly endeavors—this under the distinct rubric and methodologies of "basic research." Now the split between cognition and action has plagued the social sciences since Descartes. The balance is not easy to secure. Hence, one finds irony in Gouldner's recent book in which he claims that radical sociologists have been exceedingly conservative in their intellectual formulations; the cries of "social relevance" retard opportunities to be intellectually innovative in what Gouldner calls "the crisis of Western Sociology," which by extension becomes the crisis of Western science and education itself.

In my view, experimental political learning, in which the young cope with the realities of politics in America, becomes the only way of breaking the double-bind that has gripped us. Teaching and research are themselves distributive values and resource capable of influencing both human development and the distribution of values and resources in the larger polity. Political learning includes the synthesis of cognitive, affective, and behavioral activities in a purposive way. It has an impact upon human beings, dominant institutions with which they deal, and the distribution of power, esteem, respect, enlightenment and other public goods. Purposive political learning—and any research designed to understand it—always involves elements of striving, negotiation, protest, and tactical formulation that adequately reflects the efforts of a sensitive and less powerful strata, such as adolescents or young adults, to secure some of their claims for life space and resist the containment policies of the authoritative political state. This means a return to the idea of experience as the prime teacher, with organized bodies of knowledge considered as sources of material which can only be useful once the student has already learned how to gain from it what he needs in order better to understand how to cope with his political culture.

One of the most obvious characteristics of those who come to college from the American high school is the extent to which the entrants are conditioned by the external stimuli and cultural phenomena of the society in which they have been living. The style of life in the high school and the community reinforce each other and conditions. The entrants have not extracted meaning from their experiences, not related it to the ongoing political realm, and it is precisely this prefabricated gestalt that has been tapped by much of our extant research.

It is for this reason that the radical view, and the one taken by student activists, is that personal action, intellectual and political, must precede and become part of any serious political learning projects involving the educational system. As far as education itself is concerned, the radical view turns in many ways on the kind of radical empiricism supported by William James and his concept of the stream of consciousness, and in many other ways on the kind of thinking about psychic behavior which stems from Freud and the psychoanalytic movement. From both sources and recent studies of student activists at all educational levels comes clear evidence that the intellect, emotions, and political realm are so closely intermingled in function that they cannot be dealt with in an inappropriate research context. It is not possible to do this in an atmosphere of distrust or in an atmosphere of authoritarian control since defense mechanisms are readily called into play. On this score, I can mention one study of black adolescents I conducted that would never have been so richly affirmative were it not for the fact that we traded political information for responsiveness—the credentials that mattered to these young men were our knowledge about the poverty program, welfare mechanism, and political structure of their city.

We are back then to the double problem of creating a free environment in which the student may act as a member of a cooperating political community and an agent of his own growth, and of systematically studying the consequences of such endeavors. In any event, it is clear that when purposive striving is involved the young—and not only the young—create their own alternative systems. It is true that these systems may be episodic and sporadic, but whether in a Vietnam summer project or a computer network linking Dartmouth to Princeton to Capital Hill, it is here that the raw materials of political learning research are to be found.

The key substantive problem for us is the absence of an alternative research system that deals with experiential political learning and that combines some qualities of scholarly inquiry with ongoing efforts to bring about substantive changes in the political world. Let me say again that I regard this as the only way to act effectively as political educators and to learn more about the sources of political commitment amidst the reality of stress, confrontation, negotiation, avoidance, and passion that are the stuff of politics. This requires a more activist orientation to research than most of us are accustomed to. It also requires a more active engagement of students utilizing their interests, concerns, and skills. (In this connection, the new National Science Foundation program to support Student-Run Environmental Research is a belated, but welcome recognition of student concerns.) As for the role of political scientists—a subject that has now received endless debate—I can but quote my friend Paul Kress in anticipating weary disclaimers about our objective professional stance:

Today's political scientist is more likely to take the view that whenever, and on whatever level, he acts or speaks as scientist, he must seek to sterilize himself of all taints of values. He will argue that he may hold values and engage in political action, but when he does so it is as 'citizen' and not as scientist. This position sometimes involves some rather bizarre claims. We are asked, for example to accept that a man whose business in life is acquiring superior scientific knowledge about politics *abandons* that status when he acts. The separation of science and practice, or in this case, thought and action, takes a curious revenge, for knowledge can retain its superior status only so long as it is not implemented.[2]

### The Research Proposal: A Regenerative System

If our concern is to synthesize political learning among the young and to develop appropriate feedback mechanisms that have research value, it is necessary to think in terms of a contextual perspective that accomplishes these objectives. I propose the creation of a regenerative system, regenerative in the sense that it fundamentally unites intellect and emotion on the one hand, and research and action on the other. What would the components of this system look like on a national level or at the level of discrete research projects? First, we must inventory the *psychosocial* resources of the student participants. Here we are on familiar ground with a plethora of findings about ego strength, self-esteem, anomie, and other variables. Of greater consequence, psychosocial resources have now been explicitly linked to political activity and to the probable contextual politics by which the young advance or frustrate their commitments. In his intellectual tour de force, *Radical Political Man,*[3] Hampden-Turner investigates data about student "radicals" within a rich model of synoptic behavior. He finds, among other things, that radical students cluster near opposite ends of the Kohlberg scale of moral values, a scale that reveals much about the level of psychosocial development of students. While most "radicals" have developed a high level of commitment beyond normal civic levels of duty and contract, a significant minority are operating at the impulse, self-gratification level. Hence, an insight that personal resources of activists are likely to be influential in contextual politics, influencing their perceptions of adult institutions, strategies, tactics, and ideologies employed to cope with the authority and distributive systems of our complex society. We now have the opportunity to utilize reliable affective knowledge *before* participants engage in overt political activity.

A second dimension of a regenerative system designed to explore the uses of political commitment includes cognitive knowledge about an aspect of the American polity. I propose that the researcher prepare a "short course" or working curriculum designed to inform students about the project in which they will be engaged. Emphasis on the distribution of power, sanctions, resources, and benefits available to an institution would be key items in the curriculum.

Third, the participants would develop a program designed to influence specific aspects of the system. The sources of concern would be concrete grievances with the administration of justice, allocation of educational opportunities, composition of the agencies designed to deal with urban poverty. Hence, the scope of the project is flexible, ranging from an examination of several institutions in an urban polity to a single agency such as the relationship of sanctioning authorities to varieties of student protests, movement, and so-called social behavior that is fundamentally political in nature.

The "field project" presents the area of greatest difficulty. I suppose the backlog of experience among political scientists here includes intern programs, Congressional fellowships, and the once useful National Center for Education in Politics. None of these programs premised some fundamental differences in outlook, interest, and behavior between the generations, students, and institutions, as the case may be. There is risk as well as uncertainty here. It is not our wish, in the name of science, research, or sympathy with some demands of student protesters to produce more "Milgram traumas" (I refer to the psychological "stud-ies" conducted at Yale designed to induce subjects to administer shocks on authoritative command). Relationships with police departments are often very sticky in many communities, yet we know enough about them and the signifi-cance of what used to be called "the state's instruments of violence" by Weber. The concern about authority models and authoritative institutions among the transitory "youth culture" is well established in the depth studies of Erickson, Kenniston, Lane, Hampden-Turner, Friedenberg, and others.[a]

The research problem—and it is the critical one—is that of establishing the contextual environment of experiential knowledge, relations between the partici-pating parties, and a sense of known differences in role, values, interests that are potentially the subject of some modification. The point is that in this matter of authority, at one end stand the police of the police state, ready to beat the citi-zen into submission to the state's conception of law and order as defined by the abstract will of the state and carried out by a constellation of enforcement agen-cies. At the other end, stands the teacher-activist-researcher ready to help create a situation in which his students may act in freedom, secure in the faith that in an atmosphere of trust, acts will turn themselves away from destructiveness, ag-gression, and hostility toward cooperation, mutual respect, and affection. And this is the prerequisite to political efforts to alter unduly sanction-prone behav-ior. In between these two poles stands the conventional educational system, and conventional educational research, sometimes moving toward the police, at other times toward intrinsic uses of political knowledge, but in general unaware of the psychological or political meaning of its own actions. The effort to initiate such awareness in students, researchers, and political agencies is the core premise of experiential political learning, that is to explore the often unknown realm of differences and selective perceptions in an effort to make ameliorative changes in concrete, public relationships.

Having developed models of change, the core of the study is an examination of the effectiveness of strategies and tactics designed to produce change, more specifically those designed to enhance key values among the young. I view these activities as tangential in the sense that they occur between the formal educa-tional system and one or more of the outside agencies mentioned. This vantage point also provides the opportunity to assess the political responses of educa-tional administrators, teachers, and other students on the margin as it were. How supportive are elements in the formal educational system? How freely or restric-tively does the high school, for example, make resources such as influence, facil-ities, information available to the participants? The contextual activities can be measured, for instance along a continuum from system-oriented ways of bringing about change, such as informal negotiation with institutional leaders, to student-

[a]In particular, Hampden-Turner's *Radical Man* is an important intellectual contribution to a dynamic, substantive political science because it is not based on the static and conservative assumptions about political life that so often pervade "political socialization" research.

oriented ways of bringing about change, namely using the resources of protest available to the outsider.

In addition, the research team has the difficult task of providing support to the project's goals and maintaining sufficient intellectual distance in order to report accurately the varieties of politics that occur and the effectiveness or ineffectiveness of varied ways of influencing responses by the system. There ought not be any overarching problem here with the aid of division of labor, evaluation sessions with students and the "significant others," and whatever sense of neutral ground for the discussion of ideas and proposals still obtains to those who work in American universities. The yield here is that we can learn much about the independent impact of the forum of political activity. What responses follow a series of formal conferences with the police department as compared with responses following encounter sessions on the campus, sessions in which the police can freely vent their feelings about long-haired hippies, privileged, irresponsible middle-class students and the rest. Indeed without the elements of measured stress and disagreement, the project becomes yet another game, another way of playing at pseudo-politics divorced from any sense of power, disagreement, conflict, and interests.

Another source of "data" is the continued flow of project reports both by participating students and by representatives of the participating agencies. (Incidentally, the project obviously requires some political finesse on the part of the researcher in securing at least the reluctant cooperation of all parties.) Moreover, I am persuaded that these varied techniques can tell us more about how effective negotiated change under pressure is in fact. The microcosm to be created in this proposal, after all, reflects the core problem of American society, namely our inability to find alternative ways of producing productive responses by both institutions and individuals who deal with them. Value research has always been a loose term in the social sciences. Hence, experiential research carried on in the kind of context I have sketched provides a way of finding out what values are capable of being changed by politics and which, as some of the young suspect, are simply incapable of being negotiated, modified, or changed in any fundamental way.

A proposal of this kind does not guarantee the kind of significant change in institutional response desired by the young in the educational, police, or other spheres. It does open up, or so it seems to me, the critical uses of political knowledge, the ability of the social scientist to study induced efforts at social change, and the utility of findings about the uses of politics itself as an instrument of persuasion and influence. In other words, the contextually based political learning project will, in the final analysis, enable the young to know the nature of the "social contract" they have with the administrators of their schools, police, and governmental agencies. And more importantly it will enable them to test out their preconceived notions as to how the system works, how tractable the "Establishment" is in its professed positions, and how viable are the inherited tools of democratic politics which, after all, form the basis of any regenerative efforts directed against repression and toward the fulfillment of human needs that depend markedly on institutions capable of adaptation and change.

## A Specific Focus: The Development of Radical Attitudes

This general approach described above can now be refined into a specific research foci on the radical youth. In the growing literature on the student activist, whether polemical or scholarly, there has been no indication that these radical students differed markedly from their peers as young children. The people who are now so open and adamant in their opposition to the government probably possessed a strong emotional attachment to it as children. Much of the opposition can be explained by the activist's ultimate politization, however, a critical difference in their early political socialization is indicated. People do not acquire or change their entire perception of the world without an underlying predisposition capable of sustaining the perception. What is needed is a model of early political socialization which can account for the development of both the activists and their nonactivist peers. The model, therefore, must serve as the basis for subsequent relevant politization.

To account for the simultaneous development of the student activist and his nonradical peers we must begin in earliest childhood. The basic political socialization process in the United States, as in most nations, starts with an appeal to youthful idealism. The child learns to identify the elements of the nation's political credo with the nation itself. Abstractions such as freedom, liberty, and justice quickly become synonymous with the concept America. Both the abstractions and the idea of the nation are extremely vague at this time. As the child's cognitive capacity increases the concept America undergoes coalescence. As it does so, it is defined in terms of the institutions and structures of our political system. The child no longer conceives of America in terms of its myths or political credo, but in terms of Congress, the presidency, the policeman, the mayor, and the states. At this time the child views all these institutions as "good." He does so because they are part of the concept "America" which is the embodiment of the idealistic abstractions learned in early childhood.

The process described above accounts for the positive feeling children have toward their government. The initial appeal to ideals and the identification of the ideals with the vague concept "America" is the prelude to the definition of America in terms of its political institutions and structures. This phase of the first period of the process encompasses the first two steps of our model: (1) the appeal to ideals and the learning of these ideals, and (2) the subsequent transference of the ideals to the concept of America and the redefinition of America in terms of its political institutions and structures.

The radical and the nonradical are probably indistinguishable at this early age. We feel, however, that the beginnings of the differences which will some day divide these groups is already present. The division is imperceptible and would probably evade the notice of the most skillful observer. Both groups manifest their positive feeling toward the government in the same manner. We theorize that for the future radical "America" is still defined more in terms of the idealistic abstractions in its political credo than in terms of the constituent parts of the political system. The transference of America the ideal, to America the political system did not occur completely. We are using theory here as a microscope to look inside the mind of the child. In theorizing this difference, we are not saying that the nonradical child does not still possess the belief in, and we should add, faith in America in terms of the ideals and myths. But his view of America is more in terms of the institutions than the abstract concepts.

At this young age both groups still possess a romantic vision of the United States and hold a strong emotional attachment to it. This sets the stage for the third step in our model: a conflict of value sets. We perceive, however, a second set of values coming gradually into conflict with the political values of the young. Although these are not explicitly political there are very definite political ramifications involved in their acceptance. We have labeled the second set as secular values. They include the drive for security, the urge for competition, and concomitantly the desire to "get ahead." Moreover this would also include political realism. It is the realist's vision of the world coming into conflict with the idealistic vision. Through the conflict of value sets, the child loses the innocence of youth and replaces it with a realistic positive attachment to the government. The process through which he becomes a political realist is very gradual. A major study of children from second through eighth grade finds a gradual decline in their idealistic view of government.[4] It was slowly replaced by a more realistic view, which means one that is more appropriate to the role of the adult citizen. This is the result of both increasing knowledge and the acquisition of the secular set of values.

Within our model we consider the gradual loss of idealism the result of a conflict of value sets. During his early life the young child is appealed to through ideals. As he becomes older he is presented with a second set of values. The child finds that these secular values are continually reinforced and emphasized in the adult world into which he is quickly entering. Gradually these values become the basic set for youth as it is for most Americans. The earlier idealistic political values are incorporated and subsumed by this pervasive secular value system.

The student radical goes through the same process, but at a different stage of the maturation cycle. It follows that the conflict with the secular value system is much sharper for the radical. In fact, it appears from our previous interviews that the radical loses his political innocence at a much later stage in life than do nonradicals. This is possible because the future radical grew up in an environment which reinforced the idealized set of values. This is consistent with our knowledge of the background of the radical. The major literature which discusses the home life of the activists emphasizes that they grew up in upper middle class families. In these homes there is a constant stress on the quality of life; success was assumed. We also discovered that the radical activists we interviewed were religious as children and also that they participated in many youth groups. This type of youthful involvement also serves to reinforce ideals. The merging of these factors may well account for the prolonging of childhood idealism through adolescence into early adulthood. At some point this protected individual is confronted with reality. He cannot accept its imperfections and problems because the idealistic set of values have taken on a moral strain as well as political orientation, and rest at the heart of the person's perception of the world. A person in this position has three alternatives: (1) change his perception of the world to match reality; (2) ignore the existence of reality; and (3) confront reality armed with his ideals and attempt to change it to match his ideals.[5] The student radical opts for the third alternative. Although we question whether only children of upper middle class families hold to the idealistic value sets, we assert that this is the basic manner in which the radical activist is politically socialized in the first period of this process. Thus he completes the first period in a state of unresolved conflict between the two basic value systems which constitute the political culture of the United States.

During the second period of the socialization process the individual acquires the political orientations which have overt meaning for the political system. These orientations should be consistent with the basic political perceptions and values learned during childhood. The young person gains his position in relation to the political community through a series of attachments including political parties, ethnic, religious, professional, and regional affiliations. The key here is that there are intermediary groups between the government and the individual. Robert Lane points out that the common man sees himself as distant from the government.[6] The early attachment to the government slowly wears off. It is diverted to these secondary groups. The individual becomes detached from the government and his motivation for political action, other than voting, can be understood in terms of self-interest. The influence of these secondary groups plus the self-interest derived from the secular values are the keys to understanding the crystalization of the political self. Once this political self is formed it is extremely hard to change. A person's role in life may change and his political interest may be altered to fit this new role, but his basic political self remains.

The student radical has an extremely difficult task in acquiring a political self. We call the process he goes through radicalization. In attaining this new self-concept he alters his basic position in relation to the larger society by placing himself outside of society. He does this by relying on his root values. Here no simple model can be constructed. However, some key elements of the process can be placed together to form a sequential ordering of events in the individual's radicalization. Some of these concepts are the following: alienation, rebellion, identification, acceptance, rejection, and reinforcement. One possible sequential chain is:

1. Sense of being different
2. Isolation from early peer group
3. Attraction to new friends based on similar value sets
4. New peer group pressure to be involved
5. Involvement leads to conflict with "establishment"
6. We-They distinction develops
7. Escalation of activity
8. Radical critique of society
9. Steps 4 through 8 repeat themselves and the individual finds himself in greater and greater conflict with society.

This particular ordering of events holds for most of the young people Kenneth Keniston studied in his book, *The Young Radicals*.[7] The actual process from the time a young person becomes aware of being different to the time he is sitting-in at Harvard or provoking the police in Chicago is unique for each individual. The person goes through this process under extreme stress and basically alone. There are few, if any, intermediary groups besides his newly acquired peer group which serve to reinforce his new position. Because he is alone, he sees himself in direct personal conflict with "the government." His emotional drives are not siphoned off but are maintained as a source of strength in his personal confrontations. The student radical is operating from idealistic motives, hence every decision to him is a moral decision. There are times when a rational choice would demand one action, yet the radical chooses the alternative. This combination of factors (idealism, morality, and emotionalism) continually leads the individual into conflict with society.[8] They also guarantee the uniqueness of the radicalization process for each individual.

### The Proposed Study: An Overview of Objectives and Methods

The central concern of the planned study is a thorough analysis of the nature and causes of student unrest. To this end we are primarily interested in developing a meaningful understanding of the student activist who is the principal actor in campus turmoil. Our objective involves more than knowledge of the few radicals who make headlines or conduct dramatic confrontations. Our concern is with the generation of idealistic youth who are now, or who have recently been participants in campus agitation. In pursuance of the central concern of the study we are cognizant of the fact that the political milieu, both immediately surrounding the individual and the more general environment, are important determinants of unrest. Such an approach should be pilot tested in one university setting and if successful extended to others.

The interviews we conducted in 1970 yielded important information with regard to the nature of student activism on various campuses. Based on this knowledge we have derived a series of general propositions pertaining to the differences and similarities among campus radicals and the forms of their activity. There are basic similarities in the personal concerns of radicals: (1) how to act upon their ideals; (2) uncertainty about their futures; and (3) awareness of the moral consequences of decisions. They perceive the general political environment of the United States as hostile to change. Thus they do not expect significant changes as a resultant of their activity. They lack a Utopian vision, therefore most of their activity is manifested in negative terms. These activities evolve around situations which the radicals view as being the most overt examples in which the American creed is absent. Concomitantly, since they are idealists, they demand that the government live up to these ideals. Implicit in these demands is a basic romantic faith in the government as capable of curing all ills if only it were controlled by "honest and brave men." The student radicals are extremely individualistic in their activity, which accounts for the absence of permanent leadership as well as consistency of programs. This individuality is clearly manifest in the lack of concern between campuses for coordinated programs and actions, even in a state as small as Connecticut. The individual is a result of the radicalization process during which each person finds himself to be alone in the face of severe personal conflict. Lastly, there is a strong emotional content in all the activities of student radicals resulting in an emphasis on fraternity and community among themselves.

Despite these basic similarities, the manifestations of the radicals' underlying discontent is channeled into a wide variety of activity. Their individual political contexts define a gamut of possible behavior which varies from campus to campus and from individual to individual, as well as for any single individual over time. The problem, then, is to define the relevant factors which distinguish one political context from the next. We propose that there are nine significant factors which define the range of possible political activity on the part of student radicals: (1) the educational philosophy and purpose of the institution; (2) the nature of the student body; (3) the location of the campus; (4) the size of the radical student element; (5) the support for radical activity from within the institution; (6) the presence or absence of radical graduate students; (7) the presence of specific conflict provoking situations; (8) the directness with which the influence of the government is felt; and (9) the quality of the radicals' critique of society.

Most student radicals hold the same basic political and moral beliefs. They share the same personal visions and feelings, acquiring much of their identity from "the movement." Although similar in these ways their activity varies in accordance with the political context of their immediate environment as it is defined by the above mentioned factors. Some student radicals rise above their milieu and ferment activity which can be considered unexpected. The majority, however, act within a limited range and this range changes as the context of the situation is altered. Thus, when students from campuses untouched by protest found themselves in front of the Pentagon in 1968 or at Grant Park in Chicago during the 1968 Democratic National Convention the overt manifestations of their beliefs and feelings found a different mode of expression.

*Interview Guidelines*

The specific questions contained in the format below cannot be considered exhaustive or even definitive. They have been included to indicate the direction being taken under each of the general rubrics.

*Part I—Early Political Socialization*

**A. Personal History through Elementary School**: Where did the respondent live as a youth? What was the school like that he attended? Did he like the school? How well did he do grade-wise? What role did religion have in his life during this period? What type of peer groups did he belong to? Was he looked upon as a leader or a follower in these groups? Who were his heroes? What did he want to be? How would he define his relationship to his family? Was he shown respect in his home?

**B. Political Development through Elementary School**: What political events does the respondent remember from this period? How did they make him feel? What were his feelings toward the United States, the presidency, Congress, the police, etc.? Did he discuss politics at home or with his friends? Were there any major events during this period which affected his life? These may have absolutely nothing to do with politics. If yes, what were they and what was the effect believed to be?

**C. Family History**: Who are the radical's parents? What is their background? How far did they go in their education? What are their occupations? What social class do they move in? What part does religion play in their lives? Has it changed since the respondent was young? How many brothers and sisters were there in the family? What is the respondent's attitude toward them now and how has it changed, if it has? What did the respondent like most (least) about his home? How much pressure was put upon him to do well so that he could better himself? How much emphasis was there on money in family discussions? Did the mother or father make the important decisions in the house? Did the radical favor one parent over the other? Does he now? Taking advantage of hindsight, what are the qualities that the respondent admires most (least) about his father (mother)? Did any of their values influence the respondent to be what he is today? What values did he acquire directly from his parents?

**D. Personal History through High School**: The questions in this section will be similar to those included in the earlier personal history. There will be, however, additional questions. Was the respondent active in high school? If yes, in what ways? What organizations did he belong to outside of high school? What was his self-image? Did he feel different or separate from his classmates? If yes, why? What were his visions of college? When did he decide to go to college? Did he care where he pursued his education? Was the respondent money conscious? Did he thrive on competition? Did he have a compulsion to be first in whatever he did? Did he take pride in his work no matter how others judged it? Did the respondent ever feel that he had been treated unfairly in school or elsewhere?

**E. Political Development through High School**: What are the political events which the respondent remembers most clearly from this period? Which were the most important to the respondent personally? Why? How did he react to them? What did he think of student radicals? What did he think about the civil rights movement? Did the respondent doubt that the United States government was doing all that it could in this area? When did he become aware of the black problem in this country? Poverty? The war in Vietnam? What did he think about these issues? Did he see himself as different from his friends or parents on these issues? Was the respondent active politically in any manner while in high school? Did he discuss politics with his parents or friends? What were the respondent's general feelings toward the government? Towards Russia? China? Germany? Hungary? If he had been given a large sum of money to be given away to poor or starving people, where would he have sent the money?

*Part II – The Radicalization Process*

**A. Present Image of the United States**: What does the radical see as the defining characteristics of this country? Who are the people (individuals and/or groups) the respondent admires most (least)? In this nation? Outside of the nation? What is his attitude toward governments in general? To authority?

**B. Present Values**: What are the most important values that the respondent is fighting for? Why are these so important to him? Where did he learn them? Is violence compatible with these values? What is the end that the respondent is attempting to achieve? Do any tactics justify the attainment of these ends?

**C. Motivation for Activity**: Why does the respondent demonstrate in general? What does he hope to accomplish? Is there a serious pressure from his peer group to participate? These questions will be followed up with specific questions about the respondent's activity at protests on his particular campus.

**D. Image of World Prior to Becoming a Radical**: What were the respondent's attitudes toward the United States before he became a radical? How did the individual define himself politically? What were his major concerns? Was he active in politics? What did he anticipate he would do after finishing college? Did he feel that he had complete control over his life or did he feel that he just accepted what came along? Were there any values he used in guiding his actions?

**E. The Radicalization Process Itself**: How did the respondent become a radical activist? How different does he see his beliefs and values from before the change? Has it affected his personality and self-image? How does he define himself politically? Has the respondent's vision of human nature changed?

*Part III—Major Problems Facing the Radical*

**A. Personal**: What are the major problems facing the radical in his personal life? Does he act consistent with the values he espouses? Is he basically an optimist or pessimist? Does he feel discriminated against because he is a radical?

**B. Political**: What are the chances of the respondent creating a better society? Does he feel that a society can exist based on his values? How will the change come about?

*Part IV—Personal Aspirations: The Future*

What does the future hold for the respondent? Where will he go from where he is now? What will he do? Can he find peace within himself or will he always have a compulsion for political activity? Does he see an inevitable retreat from his values as he becomes more and more immersed in the problems confronting the working individual?

**Notes**

1. The point is eloquently made by David Sears in his review of the David Easton, et al. study of children and politics, *Children and Political Attitudes* (Chicago: University of Chicago, 1969). See David Sears, "Political Socializa-

tion," *Harvard Educational Review*, 37 (Summer, 1969). See also Edgar Litt, "Public Knowledge and Private Men," *Harvard Educational Review*, 38 (Summer, 1968), esp. pp. 500-501.

2. Paul Kress, "Politics and Science: A Contemporary View of an Ancient Association," *Polity* (Fall, 1969), p. 12.

3. Charles Hampden-Turner, *Radical Man* (Cambridge, Mass.: Schenkman, 1970).

4. David Easton and Jack Dennis, "The Child's Image of Government," *The Annals of the American Academy of Political and Social Science*, 361 (September, 1965), pp. 40-57.

5. Gary C. Byrne, "Minority Problems, Value Inconsistency, and Student Protest Behavior." Paper presented to the American Political Science Association Convention, New York, 1969 (Mimeo.).

6. Robert E. Lane, *Political Ideology* (New York: The Free Press of Glencoe, 1962), esp. Chap. 10, "The Alienated and the Allegiant," and Chap. 24, "Identity Diffusion and Ideological Caution."

7. Kenneth Keniston, *Young Radicals* (New York: Harcourt, Brace & World, Inc., 1968), esp. Chap. 4, "Becoming a Radical."

8. Richard Flacks, "The Liberated Generation: An Exploration of the Roots of Student Protest," *Journal of Social Issues*, 23 (July, 1967), pp. 52-75.

## Bibliography

*Books*

Almond, Gabriel and Verba, Sidney. *The Civic Culture*. Princeton: Princeton University Press, 1963.

American Council on Education. *American Universities and Colleges*. 10th edition, Washington, D.C., 1968.

Axelrod, J.; Freedman, M.; Batch, W.; Katz, J.; and Sanford, N. *Search for Relevance: The Campus in Crisis*. San Francisco: Jossy-Bass, 1968.

Barzum, Jacques. *The American University: How It Runs, Where It Is Going*. New York: Harper and Row, 1968.

Cohen, Mitchell, and Hale, Dennis. eds. *The New Student Left*, Boston: Beacon Press, 1967.

Cox Commission Report. *Crisis at Columbia*. New York: Vintage Books, 1968.

Dawsen, Richard E., and Prewitt, Kenneth. *Political Socialization*. Boston: Little, Brown, and Co., 1968.

Erickson, Eric. ed. *The Challenge of Youth*. New York: Anchor, 1965.

Erickson, Eric. *Childhood and Society*, New York: Norton, 1950.

Eistenstadt, S.N. *From Generation to Generation: Age Groups and Social Structure*, New York: Free Press, 1956.

88

Feuer, Lewis S. *The Conflict of Generations: Character and Significance of Student Movements.* New York: Basic Books, 1969.

Gouldner, Alan. *The Coming Crisis of Western Sociology.* New York: Basic Books, 1967.

Greenstein, Fred. *Children and Politics.* New Haven: Yale University, 1965.

Hess, Robert, and Torney, Judith. *The Development of Political Attitudes in Children,* Chicago: Aldine Publishing Co., 1967.

Hyman, Herbert. *Political Socialization: A Study in the Characteristics of Political Behavior,* Glencoe, Illinois: Free Press, 1959.

Jencks, Christopher and Reisman, David. *The Academic Revolution.* Garden City, N.Y.: Doubleday, 1968.

Kennan, George F. *Democracy and the New Student Left.* Boston: Atlantic-Little, Brown, 1968.

Kenniston, Kenneth. *The Uncommitted.* New York: Harcourt, Brace & World, Inc., 1960.

Kenniston, Kenneth. *Young Radicals.* New York: Harcourt, Brace & World, Inc., 1968.

Key, V.O., Jr. *Public Opinion and American Democracy.* New York: Alfred A. Knopf, 1961.

Lane, Robert. *Political Ideology.* New York: The Free Press of Glencoe, 1962.

Lipset, Seymour Martin. *Political Man.* Garden City, N.Y.: Doubleday, 1960.

Lipset, Seymour Martin, and Lowenthall, Leo. *Culture and Social Character: The Work of David Riesman Reviewed.* Glencoe: Free Press, 1967.

Lipset, Seymour Martin, and Wolin, Sheldon S., eds. *The Berkeley Student Revolt.* Garden City, N.Y.: Doubleday, 1965.

Litt, Edgar. ed. *The Political Imagination.* Glenview, Illinois: Scott, Foresman and Company, 1966.

Lynd, Alice. ed. *We Won't Go.* Boston: Beacon Press, 1968.

Mead, George H. *Mind, Self and Society.* Chicago: The University of Chicago Press, 1934.

Newfield, Jack. *A Prophetic Minority.* New York: Signet, 1966.

Riesman, David; Glazer, Nathan; and Denney, Reuel. *The Lonely Crowd.* New Haven: Yale University Press, 1950.

Remmers, H.H., and Radler, D.H. *The American Teenager.* Indianapolis: Bobbs-Merrill, 1957.

Rosenberg, Morris. *Society and the Adolescent Self-Image.* Princeton: Princeton University Press, 1965.

Whyte, William H., Jr. *The Organization Man.* New York: Anchor Books Edition, 1957.

Wolfenstein, Martha, and Eliman, Gilbert. *Children and the Death of a President.* New York: Doubleday, 1966.

Wood, Robert C. *Suburbia, Its People and Their Politics.* Boston: Houghton-Mifflin, 1958.

Zeigler, Harmon. *The Political World of the High School Teacher*. Center for the Advanced Study of Educational Administration, University of Oregon, 1966.
Zinn, Howard. *S.N.C.C.–The New Abolitionists*. Boston: Beacon Press, 1964.


*Articles and Periodicals*


*The Annals of the American Academy of Political and Social Science*. Special Issue: "Political Socialization: Its Role in the Political Process." 361 (September, 1965).
————. Special Issue: "Protest in the Sixties." 382 (March, 1969).
Almond, Gabriel. "Comparative Political Systems." *Journal of Politics*. 18 (1956), 391-409.
Bernstein, Basil. "Some Sociological Determinants of Perception: An Inquiry into Sub-Cultural Differences." *British Journal of Sociology*, 9 (June, 1958), 159-174.
Bronfenbrenner, U. "Soviet Methods of Character Education." *American Psychologist*, 17 (1962), 550-564.
*Daedalus*. "Students and Politics." 97 (Winter, 1968).
Dodge, R.W., and Uyeki, E.S. "Political Affiliation and Imagery Across Two Related Generations." *Midwest Journal of Politics*, 6 (August, 1962), 266-276.
Easton, David. "The Function of Formal Education in a Political System." *The School Review* (1957), 304-316.
Edelstein, Allen S. "Since Bennington: Evidence of Change in Student Political Behavior." *Public Opinion Quarterly*, 26 (1962), 564-577.
Flacks, Richard. "The Liberated Generation: An Exploration of the Roots of Student Protest." *Journal of Social Issues*, 23 (July, 1966), 52-75.
Greenstein, Fred I. "The Benevolent Leader: Children's Images of Political Authority." *American Political Science Review*, 54 (December, 1960), 934-943.
*Harvard Educational Review*. Special Issue: "Political Socialization," 38, No. 3 (1968).
Jahoda, Maire, and Warren, Neil. "The Myth of Youth," *Sociology of Education*, 38 (Winter, 1965), 138-150.
Kenniston, Kenneth. "American Students and the Political Revival." *The American Scholar*, 32 (1963), 40-64.
————. "The Sources of Student Dissent." *Journal of Social Issues*, 22 (July, 1967), 108-137.
————. "You Have to Grow Up in Scarsdale to Know How Bad Things Really Are." *The New York Times Magazine* (April 27, 1969), 27 ff.
Lane, Robert. "Fathers and Sons: Foundations of Political Belief." *American Sociological Review* (1959), 502-511.
Langston, Kenneth. "Peers, Schools, and Political Socialization." *American Political Science Review*, 61 (September, 1961), 751-758.

Litt, Edgar. "Civic Education, Community Norms, and Political Indoctrination." *American Sociological Review*, 28 (1963), 69-75.

Maccoby, Eleanor E., Morton, Anton S., and Matthews, Richard E. "Youth and Political Change." *Public Opinion Quarterly*, 18 (Spring, 1954), 23-39.

McClintock, C.G., and Turner, H.A. "The Impact of College Upon Political Knowledge, Participation, and Values." *Human Relations*, 15 (1962), 163-176.

Middleton, Russell, and Putney, Snell. 'Political Expression of Adolescent Rebellion." *American Journal Of Sociology*, 48 (1963), 527-535.

Schick, Marvin, and Somit, Albert. "The Failure to Teach Political Activity." *The American Behavioral Scientist*, 6 (January, 1963), 5-7.

Spender, Stephen. "What the Rebellious Students Want." *The New York Times Magazine* (March 30, 1969), 56 ff.

Vaughan, Roger. "The Defiant Voices of S.D.S." *Life Magazine*. (October 18, 1968), 80 ff.

# 7 Schooling, Stratification, Equality: Notes for Research

KENNETH PREWITT

This paper attempts to draw together well-known facts about schooling in Africa in such a way as to formulate a broad research problem and to suggest several specific research questions. The argument rests upon two propositions, one about schooling and stratification and one about schooling and equality.

Schooling and stratification are everywhere associated. This is true whichever of the Weberian dimensions of stratification are under discussion. Power and education are associated through the tendency of the educated to monopolize recruitment channels into the ruling groups; wealth and education are associated through the ability of the educated to monopolize the skills and positions which are disproportionately rewarded in society; deference and education are associated through the access of the educated to the cultural system which stands at the center of society and which is held in high esteem.

These associations are nowhere perfect; there are cross-national variations, historical variations, and variations from one form of stratification to the next. Nevertheless, data from societies around the world and throughout history show the associations always to be positive and always to be significantly higher than chance alone would predict.[1]

The association between schooling and equality is nearly as universal and persistent as the association between schooling and stratification. The spread of egalitarian ideologies has been accompanied by the spread of formal schooling. The association is partly to be explained by reference to the universalization of citizenship on which rests the modern state.[2] Citizenship connects schooling and egalitarian ideals in two ways, one of which results from liberal motives and one of which results from conservative motives. To liberals, schooling is social justice; it is part of and helps establish the equality of opportunity so necessary to the assault on special privilege. Schooling is a social service which the state is responsible to provide on an equal basis for all citizens. Education is a means for "equalizing the capacity of all citizens to avail themselves of the rights to which

The author is a staff member of the Institute for Development Studies, University of Nairobi, 1970-72, on leave from the University of Chicago. The points of view expressed in this paper in no manner reflect official positions of either of these institutions. Various people provided critical comments on earlier drafts of this paper, including participants of the "Research Workshop on The Politics of Elementary and Secondary Education," Stanford, California, September, 1970, as well as colleagues at the University of Nairobi. I express my appreciation to them and also, especially, to Arnold Anderson of the University of Chicago.

they are entitled."[3] To conservatives, schooling is social insurance. If, as conservatives often believed, "mobocracy" lurked behind every extension of democracy, then at least universal education could socialize the newly enfranchised and thereby insure their loyalty and orderliness.[4] Thus schooling and egalitarian thinking are associated because schools were (and are) expected to diffuse the norms of citizenship throughout the modern state. And schooling is associated with actual equalities because universalizing citizenship led to the demand for social services, with public education being primary among these.

The two propositions are little more than restatements of conventional knowledge, but they do serve to underscore what will shortly be conceptualized as a research problem. Both stratification and equality can be studied from the vantage point of formal schooling; such a study should reveal something about the social processes and arrangements which allow widespread egalitarian thinking to stand side-by-side with obvious inequalities of power, wealth, and esteem.

The research sites are two East African countries, Kenya and Tanzania. There are two reasons for this choice. Both countries are far from settled with respect to the institutions of schooling, the crystallization of stratification systems, or the ideologies of egalitarianism. This unsettledness can be turned to advantage if research questions are posed with an eye to likely trends, for the future is being visibly shaped by present decisions. Secondly, Kenya and Tanzania share many common features, including educational practices inherited from colonial rule, but differ along one very significant dimension. Though the national leaders of both nations profess a commitment to universal citizenship and the equalities this implies, Tanzania's route is self-consciously socialistic whereas Kenya's route is capitalistic. Comparison therefore should be particularly useful, especially with respect to issues such as stratification and equality.

## Schooling and Stratification

My usage of stratification is derived from Weber, which is to say that members of society are stratified along the three dimensions of power, wealth, and esteem.[5] The choice to follow Weber means that different amounts of education do not in themselves constitute a form of stratification. There have been suggestions that members of society can be stratified according to the amount of information or knowledge they possess; this suggestion makes education itself a fourth dimension of stratification. In rejecting this notion, I share with others the position that education locates individuals in the power, wealth, esteem hierarchies but does not itself constitute a separate hierarchy. The point has recently been summarized by Runciman when he observes that if knowledge constitutes an advantage in society "this is precisely because it constitutes an advantage in the hierarchies of either class, status, or power."[6] Runciman bases his argument on the sound proposition that education does not stratify society, it only differentiates it. "Where education does stratify rather than differentiate, this is because of its contingent association with economic *Lebenschancen*, or social prestige, or influence and authority, or possibly all three."[7]

By maintaining the analytic distinction between education and stratification it is possible to ask about the empirical association between them. Two specific questions suggest themselves: How close is the association between education and each of the three forms of stratification? What social processes bring about the associations; and, conversely, what social processes work counter to the associations? The second part of this latter question is to ask why higher positions are sometimes filled by the uneducated and lower positions sometimes filled by the educated.

Because these questions are part of the suggested agenda for research it would not do to attempt systematic answers at this point. Yet it might be useful to note why there is cause for expecting a close association between education and each form of stratification, though the account must necessarily be extremely brief and incomplete.

## Schooling and Political Power

Though a few Africans in positions of authority are "uneducated," the new ruling groups are overwhelmingly drawn from the better educated sectors of society.[8] Partly this is a result of the colonial past. For an African to be absorbed into the pre-independence administrative infrastructure it was necessary that he be educated (which usually implied "Christian" as well). There then was a group of educated clerks and administrative functionaries who were in a position to move rapidly into elite positions with the advent of independence. An old-boy network which evolved among graduates of the few prestigious schools helped perpetuate the practice of recruiting from narrow though well-educated circles. The introduction of elections and parliaments did little to alter the unwritten but widely heeded norm that the uneducated were disqualified from high political position. Voters choose the educated to represent them in Parliament and other councils of government, partly because the educated select themselves for candidacy and partly because voters consider education a qualification for managing the affairs of society.[9] Finally, at various levels of the civil service it is evident that some of the skills necessary to the political management of society are acquired through formal schooling. Management tasks often require familiarity with the language of economists and perhaps skills at accounting as well; they may depend on knowledge of import-export regulations and other legal intricacies; they frequently involve decisions about materials such as fertilizer, machinery, and so forth; they require abilities in the recruitment and deployment of personnel; and, still true to a large extent, they may depend on the self-confidence which enables one to work and play in circles influenced by very highly trained expatriate staffs. Formal education cannot teach all of these skills, but the uneducated are put at a crippling disadvantage.

There are factors working counter to the dominant trend for positions of authority to be monopolized exclusively by the educated. The political party when well organized and linked to the rural sectors is an avenue of political mobility less influenced by educational achievements. T.A.N.U., the ruling party of Tanzania, is a case in point. Activity in the service of the party and loyalty to the dominant ideology is weighed along with education in promotions. Perhaps it is true, as one commentator notes, that the political party "is an avenue most likely to be utilized by those who have been frustrated, by lack of ability or finance, in educational achievement."[10] Another factor accounting for the less than perfect correspondence between education and political influence is the residue of traditional elites. Though the power of chiefs and clan elders has been substantially diminished by the growth of a national political apparatus manned by an urban-based and educated elite, traditional tribal authorities continue to exercise some authority.

The degree of fit between educational attainment and position in the political hierarchy is affected as well by processes within the ruling group. Although education may be a reliable predictor of entry into the ruling group, this does not mean that the most educated will monopolize the most influential positions. Allocation of positions proceeds according to many criteria, including talent, ambition, and skill as well as ethnicity, friendship patterns, and personal relationships. Seniority also plays a role. Internal promotion according to seniority protects the less-educated, many of whom reached the elite shortly after or even before Independence, from the challenge of newer recruits now graduating from the universities. It is likely that the association between education and political position within the ruling group will be significantly less than the association between education and entry into the group.[11]

Nevertheless, it is correct to say, as many have, that higher education tends to be necessary for a position of authority in the society.

*Schooling and Wealth*

There is a high positive association in East Africa between educational attainment and access to wealth. The observations of the previous section provide part of the explanation. If education and power covary, then education and wealth covary. This follows from the fact that political elites appropriate some of the surplus produced by the economy for personal use. The appropriation is accomplished in many ways: high salaries, emoluments and expense accounts, commercial ventures (which are particularly attractive when the economy and polity are as closely intertwined as they are in East Africa), and unabashed corruption. The complex and clever arrangements which so disproportionately reward the educated political elite have been well chartered by Dumont, among others.[12]

Entry into the wage sector, and point of entry, is almost entirely dependent on amount of schooling completed. Great respect is paid to certification and even level of pass in awarding scarce jobs in the public and private sectors. No advertisement of a job opening is without stipulation as to minimum schooling necessary for applicants. Schools and the associated examinations, degrees, diplomas, and certifications have assumed much of the responsibility for sifting, sorting, and selecting youth into occupational slots. The pattern in Kenya and Tanzania is similar to that of other nations, only more so.[13] It does not exaggerate to observe that occupational chances and even mobility are largely concentrated *within* the school years, for the point at which one steps off the educational ladder establishes the point at which one steps on the employment ladder, which in turn fairly well fixes career prospects.

There are factors which reduce the association between wealth and education. Entrepreneurial talents are not always associated with formal schooling. (They are most certainly not brought about by schooling. If anything, the stress on rote-learning and low risk-taking in schools tyrannized by an inflexible examination structure can kill innovativeness and initiative.) Persons with entrepreneurial talents and ambition can compensate for lack of education, the often discredited *Kulaks* among the peasantry are a case in point. The transfer of trading licenses from Asian (mostly) noncitizens to Africans in Kenya provides opportunities for the uneducated but enterprising to increase their wealth. As the wage economy spreads, the greater distribution of spending money throughout the population allows for the emergence of the "self-made" businessman who accumulates wealth irrespective of his formal schooling.

If it is true that not all of the wealthy are educated, it is even more true that not all of the poor are uneducated. The absorbtive capacities of African economies are limited, causing the well-known "unemployed school leaver" condition. The schools mediate very imperfectly between any given age-cohort and the employment opportunities provided by the society, partly because the educational bureaucracies are too inflexible to adjust to changing employment conditions but also because the time schedules influencing the production of school graduates and the production of different types of jobs are very dissimilar.

Taking into account the rates of upward and downward mobility which affect the distribution of wealth independently of the distribution of education, it is still true that economic life-chances are very significantly affected by educational attainments. Schooling and the stratification of the population by wealth are closely associated.

## Schooling and Social Esteem

There are three reasons for expecting a close fit between schooling and deference, or social esteem. First, though esteem is not identical with power or

96

wealth, it often covaries with one's position in these hierarchies. Thus the tendency for education to locate persons as to their power and wealth implies that education also locates persons as to their social esteem. However, the "overlap" proposition does not account for all the association between education and esteem because not all power and wealth are attributable to education and not all deference is attributable to power and wealth.

A second reason has to do with the close fit between occupational position and social esteem.[14] As Shils notes, "Occupational role is ordinarily thought of as one of the most significant entitlements to deference. The most esteemed occupations in societies, for which there are survey or impressionistic data, are those which are in their internal structure and in their function closest to the *centres*."[15] Evidence available in East Africa confirms the evaluative rankings of occupations reported for many other societies.[16] Perhaps it is unnecessary to add that entry into prestigious occupations is conditional on educational qualifications, and employment in the less prestigious occupations goes primarily to the uneducated.[17]

There is a third, and theoretically more interesting, reason for expecting a close association between deference received in society and educational degree displayed. The modern (largely urban) sectors of East African societies are characterized by a value-system along with an associated life-style (dress codes, leisure activities, consumption behavior, religious practices) that are very much intertwined with formal education. An alien though prestigious culture was first introduced through the mission schools. And though the culture is no longer so alien and though the school shares with other agencies in the diffusion of this culture, it is still widely accepted that the educated have more access to the "modern" culture than the uneducated. It should be stressed that the values and practices transported into East Africa by mission-educators and colonial administrators have been substantially modified through contact with local traditions and post-Independence ideologies; still, the synthesis itself puts Western modeled education at the center of the value-system and the value-system continues to be largely transmitted through the schools.[a]

The point I wish to make about education and social esteem owes much to Shils' writings about the charismatic center of society. His thesis is not easily summarized but, among other things, includes the notion that a pattern of social values and beliefs help establish society as a "significant cosmos from which members derive some of their significance to themselves and to others."[18] The relevance of this formulation here is suggested by his observation that "the educated person is one who has received the culture of beliefs and appreciations which are central in the society."[19] Education not only acquaints persons with

[a]In Tanzania, for instance, the political science department of the University of Dar es Salaam has recently been asked to prepare a course to teach educators how to teach civic consciousness and political values. The larger aim is to use the schools to create political consciousness among the mass of the population.

this culture, it also provides the skills "which prepare for participation in the centre of society through the exercise of authority, technological performance, the discovery and transmission of vital truths about the universe, man and society, in short for *creating* and *ordering*."[20]

This thesis is particularly applicable in nations such as Kenya and Tanzania where post-Independence values and practices are unavoidably implicated with formal schooling. Schools were the first major "modern" institutions, and they continue to be central in all discussions of nation-building.[21] The educated man is expected to acquaint himself with the content of post-Independence values and to pass them on to his uneducated fellow-citizens. The consequence is that the educated are "where it counts" and thus are held in esteem. If education and deference are associated, this is partly the result of (1) making formal education part of the central, charismatic values of society, and (2) using the educated to transmit these values, either specifically as teachers or more indirectly as role-models.

One major qualification should be appended to this discussion. There are sub-groups in Kenya and Tanzania comparatively isolated from the centers of the national society. For persons in these groups criteria other than formal schooling serve as bases for assigning social esteem. The witch-doctor, for example, has access to beliefs and values which remain highly salient to large parts of the population despite the inconsistency of these beliefs with modern educational values. The social position of the witch-doctor, which in some circumstances can be very high, as nothing to do with formal schooling. But the witch-doctor and what he illustrates is the recessive strain in these societies; the dominant strain clearly lies in the beliefs and values which hold modern education (and the educated) in esteem.

## Schooling: Allocation and Evaluation

The cursory overview of how education and stratification are related suggests two points: schooling *allocates* persons into different power, wealth, and esteem positions; it also *evaluates* these positions differently. This latter point was less explicit in the discussion and merits more attention.

When positions in society are rewarded differently, some justification of the rewards is likely. Otherwise holding society together requires a large amount of coercion, a costly alternative. Justification is usually provided by assigning moral worth or social significance to those positions which receive the highest rewards in the way of authority, wealth, and esteem. If members of society, those in lower as well as those in higher positions, come to believe that some tasks are more significant for social development than others, this will go a long way toward justifying inequalities.

Impressionistic evidence suggests that several interrelated beliefs are widely held by large parts of the East African populations: the well-educated are the more skilled and talented; the skilled and talented make a greater contribution to society; persons who contribute to society merit greater rewards.[22] The truth-value of these statements is less important to the present argument than the extent to which they are believed. It therefore is necessary to ask two empirical questions; how widely distributed are such beliefs? how do these beliefs come to be held?

I believe that research will show these beliefs to be widely held, and will indicate that schools are instrumental in promoting them.[23] The stress on the link between education and mobility, a link educators can hardly be faulted for promoting, cannot but carry with it the lesson that unequal social significance is attached to different social roles in society. For example, if the future is to be one where sickness is contained and health prevails, teachers will talk about what clinics, hospitals, medical colleges, and research laboratories will bring about, and probably stress how important doctors, nurses, medical professors and researchers, health officers, and dieticians are to realizing a healthier society. These positions of course require long years of education. Intended or not, the lesson taught is that certain positions are more socially significant than others. The current struggle to define farming as an important occupation to national development only recognizes how pervasive is the counter lesson.[24] Indeed, if national leaders and teachers take every opportunity to emphasize the abstract point that "education is critical to creating the future society we want," it should not surprise us to learn that the people interpret this as meaning that the educated individual is somehow critical. For there is no way to attach significance to education in the abstract without also attaching significance to the educated. If Kenyatta pronounces education as "perhaps the greatest single foundation of effective nation-building,"[25] his listeners will surely not be surprised to hear him also report that "it is to the universities that we look for the man and for the woman who will lead the nation to frontiers of knowledge and achievement."[26]

Recent work by John Meyer has provided theoretical underpinnings to the proposition that schooling attaches differential social worth to those roles in society which are filled by the educated.[27] Meyer stresses that schools have a charter from the society. This charter requires schools that they supply students with appropriate skills and attitudes, and it also expects of schools that they attach students to validated social statuses. A charter, then, is a general agreement that schools produce graduates fit to occupy very specific positions in society. The charter is the social definition given to schools and therefore *also* to the products of schooling. Public awareness, sometimes legally reinforced, establishes the presumption that school graduates will assume certain social responsibilities. The practice of bonding university students is an exaggerated instance of this.

The usefulness of Meyer's formulation is easily seen, even if applied in a less subtle manner than he himself would.[b] Each age-cohort in Kenya and Tanzania is progressively classified into different subgroups depending on amount of schooling completed. The group into which one is classified becomes part of the social identity of each member of the cohort, an identity real to the youth as well as to the larger society in which he seeks employment, recognition, opportunities, a marriage partner, political rights, in short, a livelihood and a way of life.

Consider the age group eligible for primary schooling in Tanganyika in 1961-62.[28] There were approximately 250 thousand youth aged seven or eight. Of these, 117 thousand (47%) did not enter school, therefore being classified throughout the remainder of their lives simply as the uneducated. Another one-third (81 thousand) of the age-cohort completed only four years of primary schooling, thereby being classified as literate but little more. Slightly more than half this many (45 thousand) finished primary schooling, henceforth to be known as the primary school leavers. The remaining 3 percent found places in secondary schools in 1968-69, though not all of them will graduate from these schools, and fewer yet will progress through higher schools into university education.

The purpose of these figures is not to show how narrow the educational pyramid is, though they do indicate this, but to emphasize that at each selection-elimination point members of the age-cohort are assigned very different social positions and life-chances depending into which classification they fall: uneducated, literate, primary school leaver, secondary school student, secondary school graduate, higher school graduate, university product. There is ample reason to expect that these classifications are internalized as components of self-identity, and that they therefore form the basis for patterns of social evaluation which attach differential social worth to the differently educated.[29]

## Schooling and Equalities

Following from the several points made about schooling and stratification is the simple summary statement that schools are major institutions for defining and justifying the stratification of the population into power, wealth, and deference groupings. This observation is the point of departure for outlining the research problem. The next step is to consider schooling and egalitarianism.

I indicated in the opening paragraphs that in two respects citizenship serves as a linkage between schooling and equality. First, schools are the locus of civic education and thus (presumably) provide instruction in the civil and political rights accorded equally to all citizens. Second, schooling itself is viewed as a

---

[b]Meyer's thesis includes distinctions between types of schools and even programs within schools, and thus in applying it to schooling in general I run roughshod over the subtlety of his thesis.

basic social service of the state and consequently educational opportunities should be equally available to all citizens.

Each of these points can be brought into focus by briefly reviewing T.H. Marshall's classic essay on the history of citizenship in England. Marshall's thesis holds that citizenship developed in three major stages, each more or less associated with a different century.

The eighteenth century was the formative period of civil or legal citizenship. "The civil element is composed of the rights necessary for individual freedom— liberty of the person, freedom of speech, thought and faith, the right to own property and to conclude valid contracts, and the right to justice. The last is of a different order from the others, because it is the right to defend and assert all one's rights on terms of equality with others and by due process of law. This shows us that the institutions most directly associated with civil rights are the courts of justice."[30] Legal protections, especially protections of contract, arose with the growing significance of the bourgeoisie.

During the nineteenth century, citizenship was extended to the political realm. "By the political element I mean the right to participate in the exercise of political power, as a member of a body invested with political authority or as an elector of the members of such a body. The corresponding institutions are parliament and councils of local government."[31] The political rights of citizenship are closely associated with demands of the working class.

Finally, and most clearly belonging to the twentieth century, there is the element of citizenship which Marshall labels the social rights. They range from "the right to a modicum of economic welfare and security to the right to share to the full in the social heritage and to live the life of a civilized being according to the standards prevailing in the society. The institutions most closely connected with it are the educational system and the social services."[32]

Citizenship has been universalized in Kenya and Tanzania, and extended into all three of the domains identified by Marshall. With regard to legal, political, and social rights, each member of society stands in a more or less equal relationship with all others. An account of how universal citizenship came to be established so quickly has yet to be written for Kenya and Tanzania. When it is, we undoubtedly will learn that a mixture of humanitarian and exploitative motives played a role. The leaders who came to power with Independence were schooled in the tradition which accepted universal citizenship as a natural and moral state of affairs. The struggle against colonialism was in part a struggle *for* citizenship, and it went unquestioned that principles of universal citizenship should be adopted as elements of the founding charters. Yet note should be taken that national citizenship was (is) necessary for the programs which aimed to unify separate peoples and to mobilize traditional groups, along with their resources, in the service of elite fashioned national goals (and perhaps in the service of the elites themselves). Bendix's comment on the expansion of citizenship in nineteenth century Europe is appropriate; the leaders, he writes, became fascinated "with the possibilities of strengthening the powers of the nation-state through the mobilization of the working class in its service."[33] One need only insert "peasants" for "working class" to see how this sentiment may have been operable in East Africa. Kenyatta possibly reveals more than he intends when he remarks, "I have been encouraged to learn that the Masai have now realized the value of land cultivation."[34] (Which is to say that nomadic people are giving up traditional practices in order to contribute to the surplus of an agricultural based economy.)

But whatever the reasons, and they are bound to be mixed, it is clear that a commitment to universal citizenship has been made, and along with it an acknowledgment of egalitarian imperatives. Although it is not possible to have universal citizenship without institutionalizing certain basic equalities, it is possible to institutionalize these equalities without implicating the schools. In holding this position I disagree with Bendix when he writes that "access to educational facilities appears as a precondition without which all other rights under the law remain of no avail to the uneducated."[35] The success with which Tanzania has carried out two national elections despite an adult population still largely illiterate (voters choose between two symbols, a hoe and a house) contradicts the deterministic thrust of Bendix's proposition. But if the point be stated in terms of probabilities, it is true that citizenship equalities are very unlikely to be institutionalized without implicating the schools, for the two reasons already cited and which can now be expanded.

Schools share major responsibilities for establishing the attitudinal and informational basis of civic and political citizenship. In this regard Bendix is correct to observe that providing "the rudiments of education to the illiterate appears as an act of liberation" and later, "The right and duty to receive an *elementary education* may be considered another way of equalizing the capacity of all citizens to avail themselves of the rights to which they are entitled."[36] More is involved here than the success or failure of specific civic education programs, though note should be taken that instruction in citizenship rights is expected to be transmitted through the curriculum.[37] Nyerere's "Education for Self-Reliance" is only the most visible of many documents and speeches which emphasize the civic component of education. But schooling and citizenship are intertwined in a more basic sense than that implied by political education programs. Schooling provides the tools for political action; it can also lead to greater political self-awareness and even to political assertiveness. Although citizenship as thus far interpreted in Kenya and Tanzania stresses the life of the citizen in nation-building, sooner or later citizens will realize that political activity also functions to achieve interests. The significance of citizenship will then take on new dimensions. And the spread of schooling will have played no small role in establishing a political consciousness which gives more substance to citizenship than is presently the case.

In a second way schooling and equality are intertwined. Equal opportunity to see one's children educated is a widely voiced aspiration. With respect to the

social rights of citizenship, no service is in such demand as are schools themselves. And the demand is loud, persistent, and nearly universal.[38] It has not
been lost on national leaders, as when Kenyatta remarks, "I am aware of the
great interest our people have in education. It took the British seventy years to
build 141 secondary schools in Kenya. In the three years since we came to
power the number of secondary schools has increased by 195, . . . Such expansion will continue each year."; or when Nyerere points proudly to the "very big
expansion of educational facilities available" since Independence.[39] Resources
have been repeatedly stretched in order to provide more school places.

The demand for educational opportunities has clear implications for the
spread of egalitarian values. In both the citizen demand and the government response, reference is continually made to the rights of *all* citizens to be educated.
The sentiment voiced by Marshall echoes often in East Africa: "The right to
education is a genuine social right of citizenship, because the aim of education
during childhood is to shape the future adult. Fundamentally it should be regarded, not as the right of the child to go to school, but as the right of the adult
citizen to have been educated."[40] The frequent repetition of this sentiment,
whatever words might express it, serves to legitimate the ideals of equality which
initially motivate and justify the quest for schooling.

*Summary*

Four specific questions have been raised and it will be well to repeat them before
formulating the research problem.

1. How close is the contingent association between the distribution of education, on the one hand, and the hierarchies of power, wealth, deference, on
   the other?
2. What social processes bring about the association, or prevent it from occurring? Specifically, how does schooling itself influence the association?
3. To what extent does schooling diffuse a definition of citizenship which
   stresses the equality of all members of society?
4. In that education is a widely felt aspiration, what are the implications for the
   content and spread of egalitarian ideals and for the institutionalization of
   actual equalities?

Although evidence is far from complete on these questions, enough is available to draw a tentative conclusion. Schools are simultaneously implicated in
defining and justifying systems of stratification *and* in defining and justifying
ideals and practices of egalitarianism.

## Reformulating a Familiar Question

If this conclusion has a familiar ring, it is intended to. It points toward a reformulated and more narrowly construed statement of an issue which has preoccupied students of society for well over a century. How is it that the inequalities implied by social stratification stand side-by-side with the equalities implied by universal citizenship? That they do coexist in the same societies is an undeniable historical fact, as evidenced by the experiences of such divergent nations as the United States and the Soviet Union, Yugoslavia and Mexico, or, if you will, Kenya and Tanzania. Moreover, this fact has such a persistent quality, having come to the fore whenever and wherever universal citizenship is adopted, that only the utopians continue to consider it a passing phase. Most serious observers have stopped asking when will stratification systems go away, and have begun to search for the social processes which allow these seemingly incompatible phenomenon to coexist.[41] Though it is surprising how inadequate are the social theories which would account for the persistence of inequalities despite the diffusion of universal citizenship.

One line of inquiry concerns inequalities of power. The expansion of suffrage was accompanied by an extension of representative forms of government, and together these political processes might account for the persistence of authority hierarchies despite the spread of citizenship. Parliaments, electoral accountability of political rulers, circulation of the elite, and access of citizens to authorities through organized pressure groups and mass-based political parties redress the power imbalance between governors and the governed. Elections, for instance, are interpreted as institutions which rearrange the power relationship, if only temporarily and infrequently, by making tenure in office dependent on electorate choices. The political rights of citizenship are seen as greatly moderating the actual inequalities of power.

A less sanguine, or more radical, interpretation of the same facts distills a different explanation, one which includes the following propositions. Democracy facilitates gradual reformism, and thus the harsh realities of power inequalities are tolerated by the powerless, perhaps on the assumption that history records the improvement of their lot. Moreover, citizenship has visibly "democratized" participation, and this disguises the fact that power remains stratified. Related to this, if the composition of the ruling class is continually undergoing modification, especially through absorbing prominent members of powerless groups, this suggests to the untutored that the structure of rule itself is being modified, perhaps in the direction of reduced power inequalities.

This latter interpretation holds that citizenship leads to mystification regarding the objective power conditions, and thus differs from the former interpretation which holds that citizenship actually does reduce power inequalities. I need not side with either interpretation to point out that they share one important conclusion: inequalities of power continue despite egalitarian ideologies.[c]

Writers more interested in the inequalities of wealth than the inequalities of power have invoked the famous trinity: equality of opportunity, norms of achievement, upward social mobility. These factors adjust egalitarian thinking with a superstructure of economic inequalities. In a guarded passage Marshall first admits that "the preservation of economic inequalities has been made more difficult by the enrichment of the status of citizenship. There is less room for them, and there is more and more likelihood of their being challenged." Nevertheless, his conclusion is that equality fostered by citizenship can coexist with economic inequalities; he reasons, "Status differences can receive the stamp of legitimacy in terms of democratic citizenship provided they do not cut too deep, but occur within a population united in a single civilization; and provided they are not an expression of hereditary privilege."[42] Elsewhere he observes that the Welfare State, though opposed to rigid class divisions and to distinctive culture patterns at different social levels, must "recognize some measure of economic inequality as legitimate and acceptable."[43] Similar themes can be found in the work of Lipset, especially when he interprets the basic value pattern in the United States as the interplay between equality of opportunity and norms of achievement.[44] Inequalities of wealth and income can be tolerated because any citizen has a chance to move up the hierarchy.

There is a revisionist interpretation analogous to that cited in connection with power inequalities. There is less equality of opportunity than there is belief in it; there is less achievement than there is faith in it; there is less upward mobility than there is hope for it. The belief, the faith, and the hope are components of a mystification which rationalize inequalities of wealth, but do not eliminate them.[45] In American history, Social Darwinism was a particularly acute form of mystification.[46]

The literature on inequalities of deference and citizenship is much less systematic, though an essay by Shils has the outlines of an argument. He makes three points. The first is premised on the assumption that deference hierarchies and power hierarchies overlap to some extent. Because citizenship implies a certain equality of relationship as regards the exercise of authority, it promotes the dispersion and therefore equalization of deference. Though, as Shils notes, "The sharing of power and the attendant equalization of deference through citizenship does not abolish the inequality of power and thus the inequality of deference associated with unequal distribution of authoritative occupational roles. It does, however, offset it and in some situations to a very considerable extent."[47] Second, ethnicity can assign persons to lower or higher deference positions, as has long held regarding race relations in the United States. If national citizenship

[c]Neither interpretation, I believe, serves as an adequate theory of this fact. It is likely that when the theoretical work necessary has been completed, it will turn out that as yet unrecognized factors work to hold together citizenship equalities and power inequalities in the same social systems.

is taken seriously, this can neutralize the inferior-superior relationships which otherwise govern the view ethnic groups have of themselves and of others. Finally, citizenship brings about an attenuation of deference because egalitarian tendencies lead to the diminution of ruling classes and the pluralization of the elite. Elaborate ceremonies, rituals, and symbols of deference are accordingly diminished in scope and significance, and this sends ripples throughout the society. Elites, being less imposing in democratic societies, no longer symbolize or hold together an order in which deference plays a major role. Shils would not conclude that deference hierarchies will disappear, but does, in the following observation, acknowledge their variability: "It is one of the features of modern Western societies that they are moving in the direction of deference-indifference and attenuation."[48] And this movement seems strongest where egalitarian outlooks are most pronounced, though even relationships of equals "can and do at present contain considerable elements of attenuated deference and can indeed not dispense with them."[49]

## Schooling: Lessons of Equality and Inequality

The foregoing cursory review of broad themes about citizenship and stratification intend only to emphasize that the problem as I formulate it is but an instance of a broader social phenomenon. This phenomenon has received considerable if not altogether satisfactory attention by social scientists. In isolating the institutions of schooling as a perspective for exploring the coexistence of citizenship equalities and power, wealth, deference inequalities, I exercise no small amount of arbitrariness. It is too early to determine whether this arbitrariness means also artificiality of explanation, but this possibility should be reckoned with whenever an instance of a phenomenon rather than the full pattern of events is investigated.

How is it that the inequalities implied by social stratification stand side-by-side with the equalities implied by universal citizenship when the schools are so clearly linked to the systems of inequality as well as the principles of equality? This formulation of the question sharpens the issue for my purposes, and also contains hints regarding an answer. Is it possible that schooling, in its organization and structure and through the explicit as well as implicit content of its instructional program, itself is a major process for adjusting egalitarian values and persistent inequalities?

A profitable way to organize research about these questions, at least in Kenya and Tanzania, is to separate two aspects of schooling. One aspect has to do with entry into schools and promotion from one level to the next. The other aspect refers to the scope of privileges which the educated are able to command once schooling has been completed.

*Selection: School Entry and
Promotion Criteria*

Evidence about Tanzania presented earlier shows that the youth of that nation face a sharply pyramidical structure of educational opportunities. Data from Kenya are similar, though the proportions are slightly higher at all but the highest levels. Approximately two-thirds of the primary school age group is presently enrolled in school, and secondary school places are available for about one-third of all primary school leavers.[50] Even when other educational opportunities are added in, such as technical training and teacher colleges, the number of school positions are many fewer than the size of the age-cohort group eligible for any given level of education. The ratio of positions to population is successively smaller, sharply so, the more advanced the schooling.

Entry into schooling and promotion through the various ranks are selective. This is unavoidable given the present structure of opportunities. But even if some miracle of financing could create places and instruction on a mass basis, this would not eliminate the selective function of schools. Schools would be differentiated by quality of instruction, materials, and equipment, just as they are in the mass education system of the United States, and it would be necessary to select entrants for the superior (and more prestigious) schools. Moreover, it is likely that those who teach will always receive more education than those who are taught, as Nyerere recognizes when he observes that "The teacher in a seven-year primary school system needs an education which goes beyond seven years; the extension officer who will help a population with a seven-years' education needs a lot more himself. Other essential services need higher education—for example, doctors and engineers need long and careful training."[51]

The unavoidable fact that schooling is selective, preventing some and allowing others to be educated, underlines the importance of selection criteria. A major proposition for explaining the coexistence of inequalities and egalitarian ideals takes as its starting point the selection criteria of schools. The proposition has been forcefully put by Talcott Parsons.[52] He first notes that social differentiation always presents a problem for society because higher rewards and privileges are conferred on particular groups, and I would add that the problem is likely to be accentuated in proportion to the acceptance of egalitarian ideologies. For Parsons, the problem is muted, at least in the American case, by socialization processes which lead the loser in the competition to accept stratification and his own location in it which derive from the selective activities of schools.

It is the high value placed on achievement, by parents as well as children, which reduces the strain inherent in the differentiating activities of schools. Members of society believe that schools selectively reward and punish on the basis of individual achievement. They believe there to be a realistic opportunity for all and a fair application of selective criteria. The application of these criteria do not reward children from particular social groups, and thus the achievement norm in the classroom compensates for the ascriptive advantages of some children.[d] The common valuation of achievement "helps make possible the acceptance of the crucial differentiation, especially by the losers in the competition. Here it is an essential point that this *common* value on achievement is shared by units with different statuses in the system. It cuts across the differentiation of families by socio-economic status."[53]

A similar theme is sounded by Marshall when he writes that school selectivity need not conflict with egalitarian principles if achievement criteria prevail over ascriptive advantages. To be protected is the principle "that all should be judged by the same procedure, as impartially and impersonally as possible, that favoritism and privilege must be eradicated, and also the effects of differing social environments on the critical turning-points of life."[54]

The Marshall-Parsons proposition is important in several respects. It is a major attempt to treat theoretically the issue of how egalitarian principles and structures of inequality are adjusted in society. It identifies specific values and processes which might account for the adjustment. Relevant to present interests, it singles out schools as central institutions in facilitating these values and processes. Finally, it can be stated as a series of specific research questions, the answers to which permit valuation regarding the utility of the proposition. The derivative research questions are particularly important because they indicate points of comparison between Kenya and Tanzania, and between subgroups within each of these societies. The core questions are as follows:

1. To what extent is there a common valuation on achievement and mobility which does cut across major social groupings, including ethnic and regional as well as economic?

Answering this question partly depends on what we learn from historical studies, especially social-anthropological investigations of how traditional cultures treated the issues of achievement and mobility. The relevant literature cannot be reviewed here, but it does show enormous variation between different tribal cultures as regards the valuation on achievement, especially the individualistic achievement as indicated in Parson's formulation. There is then certain "within-society" variations regarding a major variable in the proposition. Insofar as traditional cultures persist, these variations should relate to different tolerance levels for the inequalities fostered by schooling in the modern sectors of the society.

A further answer to the question will be provided by careful comparison of the two countries. At least with respect to political and economic ideology, it is evident that Kenya and Tanzania differ in the emphasis to be placed on individ-

---

[d]My immediate purpose is not to argue with Parsons, though it should be noted that as regards the facts in the United States patterns of personal prejudice as well as institutional practices do systematically benefit children fortunate enough to be born into certain ascriptive groups, and penalize others whose ascriptive traits are held in low esteem by the society.

ual achievement. Tanzania has quite explicitly adopted an ideology which insists that schools are to stress cooperative endeavors rather than individual achievements.[55] Attempts are currently being made to institutionalize an "anti-individual achievement" ethic, with schools themselves being the first targets of reform. Kenya leaders pay homage to the cooperative spirit, but it is apparent that blessing is also given to individual achievement. Individuals will go as far as their talents and ambitions (and contacts) will take them, with school success itself helping to define personal mobility.

2. To what extent are selection and promotion criteria in schools based on achievement?

Even if the Marshall-Parsons proposition is sound and in principle is applicable in Kenya and Tanzania, it still is necessary to determine the facts of the matter. In no social system will there be perfect equality of educational opportunity, completely unbiased application of achievement criteria, and mobility determined only by talent, effort, and merit. Certainly many factors other than ability and achievement affect mobility through the schools of Kenya and Tanzania, though in both cases the commitment is to eliminate ascriptive advantages.

In the first place, schools are not equally distributed geographically. One province in Kenya registers 90 percent of the appropriate age-cohort in primary schools; another registers well under 10 percent. Even where school places are available, the quality of instruction and facilities varies enormously with the prestigious schools primarily located in urban centers where they educate the children of the already educated. Schools across both countries have very uneven examination records, not all of which can be attributed to quality of students who are enrolled.[56] School location and quality are not the only factors biasing selection in favor of particular families and groups, usually the educated and better-off. School fees are less of a hardship in families which include persons already educated than they are in the completely uneducated family. The educated father, uncle, or older sibling is likely to be a wage-earner, and from wages come school fees. The home environment is also significant, especially when schooling is organized around regularized, formalized, and formidable examinations. Educated and wealthier parents who purchase books and educational toys, who speak English in the home, who can afford private schools for their children, and who otherwise use their resources to create an environment conducive to successful performance in school, provide advantages difficult to match in the poor, uneducated, and usually rural home.[57]

If there is always some bias in the selection and promotion criteria applied in schools, this raises an important theoretical issue. How much gap can there be between promise and practice before this reverberates through the social system in a way which alters the adjustment between egalitarianism and inequalities? It should be stressed that this question does not ask how much inequality is toler-

able, a very different question. and one to be raised shortly. Here I wish to underscore that the Marshall-Parsons proposition rests upon the assumption that
equality of opportunity and mobility through achievement are critical factors if
a society is committed to egalitarian thinking yet sustains inequalities. Because
the objective conditions of opportunity, achievement, mobility exist always in
some measure short of perfection it is necessary to ask what measure of short-
ness has what implications for the social phenomenon we are trying to explain. I
fully appreciate the measurement and definition problems raised by this question; yet I feel the question is unavoidable if the Marshall-Parsons formulation is
to be used in analyzing historical cases.

There are other implications of the proposition about equality of opportunity, but enough has been said to reinforce an earlier point. The proposition
under discussion has the very great merit of identifying social processes which
might account for a phenomenon which has long perplexed students of society,
the persistence of inequalities despite the universalization of citizenship equalities. It has the additional merit, for us in particular, of direct application to
schooling. In drawing attention to what is happening within the school and during the school years, the proposition identifies things which affect the socialization of the students and which influence the pattern of expectations and social
values held by parents.

## The Distribution of Privileges
## and Benefits

There is a second cluster of ideas which move toward a theoretical statement
about the coexistence of citizenship equality and stratification systems. These
ideas have to do with the distribution of privileges and benefits in society. The
basic proposition seems to be that inequalities should not be too severe. That is,
even if equality of opportunity and mobility through achievement were to operate perfectly, this would not justify the better-off being very much better-off,
nor justify their being better-off as regards all the socially desired values.

In introducing this issue I quickly emphasize that an exceedingly complex
topic about which a great deal has been said will here be treated in a brief, super-
ficial manner. Moreover, in order to formulate research questions I will take
liberties which thus far have been avoided. I cannot easily develop the remainder
of the argument without relaxing the distinction between education, on the one
hand, and the three forms of stratification, on the other. Although this relaxa-
tion is not strictly necessary, without it the argument would require so many
qualifications and cumbersome detours that for present purposes I take the
easier route. The concluding section of this paper is not about differences in
levels of schooling so much as about differences in general social status. In order
to emphasize this, I will refer to the better-off and the worse-off, terms which

distinguish between those generally powerful, wealthier, and esteemed, and those generally powerless, poor, and ignored.[e] Because level of schooling is associated with being worse-off or better-off, this shift represents less of a sacrifice in the argument than might be thought. Still, it is necessary to underline that the final point is not strictly speaking about *schooling*, stratification, and equality, though it is about stratification and equality.

The proposition that coexistence of egalitarian ideals and social inequalities occurs if tolerable limits are set to inequalities can be studied by turning the issue on its head. What are the tolerable limits of equality? It often is observed that there are limits beyond which equalization of condition and of opportunity cannot go.[f] This observation is seldom formulated in a theoretically rigorous manner, which would require attention to the structural, cultural, and psychological factors which affect these limits and to how they vary historically and across societies. But the observation has so often been repeated that its main propositions are well known. I will briefly note three of the propositions and indicate the research areas suggested by them.

**1. Limits to egalitarianism are imposed by what is acceptable to those in positions to resist policies which promote equality.** If, as Dahrendorf tells us, societies are held together by coercion as much as anything else, then those with powers of coercion, who tend also to be the better-off, minimize the consequences of egalitarian programs. This is especially likely if the programs are construed as a direct attack on their own privileges. The ability to block such programs is limited and is affected by many factors, including the intensity of public pressures, the institutions by which leaders come to power and are legitimated, and the force with which the egalitarian ideology has been articulated. But it is never absent. One observer of Tanzania, though sympathetic to its socialist goals, recognizes this in the following words, "Perhaps the most serious doubts about the chances of socialist policies generally, and particularly in education, stem from the lack of commitment to, or understanding of, socialist principles on the part of those charged with translating these aims into concrete programmes. Generally, President Nyerere has had to contend with the fact that

---

[e]I am also skipping over the issue of intercorrelation among the three dimensions of stratification, an important question but not one central to the present argument.

[f]I am aware that many sociologists prefer to hold to the distinction between equality of condition and equality of opportunity whereas in the present discussion I ignore this distinction. My muddling of the distinction is deliberate. If there are inequalities of condition there will always be inequalities of opportunity, for essential to the meaning of privilege is the ability to pass along at least some of your privileges to those you choose, normally your immediate offspring. Inheritance taxes affect only one aspect, and that not always the most important, of the many ways in which parents affect the life-chances of their children. To say that opportunities can be equalized while permitting objective conditions to be very unequal is not completely incorrect, but the statement overlooks so many critical factors that its usefulness in analysis is very limited.

most of his programmes are in some way curbing the interests and privileges of the elites who have to implement these policies . . . "[58]

One research question is to ask how widely spread is the commitment to egalitarian principles among the power-holders in society; and related to this, what socialization processes affect the balance between willingness to promote egalitarian programs and resistence to having one's own privileges curbed. A second research question would simply investigate the political resources available to those who resist egalitarian policies and the resources available to those who promote them.[59]

**2. Limits to egalitarianism are imposed by the requirements of incentive systems in society.** Some measure of inequality is implied by incentive systems designed to raise productivity, to insure that socially useful positions are filled, and to motivate the talented to also be the hard-working. It is possible to recognize the truth in this statement without adopting the functionalist thesis that inequality is necessary for social survival and therefore essentially benign in consequences. It has already been pointed out that incentive systems can work as much to benefit those who manage them, the ruling class, as they do to benefit something called the public welfare.[60] But it does not serve sociological analysis to ignore the function which incentive systems everywhere play in getting the job done, whatever the job is and whoever benefits from its performance. The most prominent socialist in East Africa, Julius Nyerere, comments that complete equality of income is a "wrong" goal, reasoning as follows "Incomes must depend upon work and output too; there must be an incentive for everyone to work a little harder. The central point about our wages policy must be that, while it prevents gross inequalities, it creates a direct link between productivity and income. Wherever appropriate piece-rates should be employed, or bonuses paid for increased output. And where this is not possible—for example, in jobs like teaching or nursing—we should take account of the social usefulness of the work, and its relative attractiveness in comparison with other opportunities for earning a living . . . We must recognize that the way to increase our members' standard of living is by helping them to become more productive at whatever job they are doing."[61]

The persistent association between education and inequalities is partly because societies everywhere take advantage of the assumption that skills and abilities correspond to schooling completed, and therefore peg beginning salaries and even promotion rates to level of formal education. As already noted, Kenya and Tanzania are not exceptions in this regard.

If equalities are limited by incentive systems then the relevant research is to study what gradations in the incentive systems are necessary to accomplish social goals, and to study how many sectors of economic and social life are to be regulated by incentive systems. Comparison of Kenya and Tanzania is useful in both respects. The latter is embarked on a route which insists that the distance between the bottom and the top should be held within moderate bounds, and which envisions a limited role for incentive systems in general. Similar constraints are not apparent in current Kenyan policy; thus, for instance, Members of Parliament in Kenya earn more than twice what they do in Tanzania.

**3. Limits to egalitarianism are imposed by the principle which allows for the equal right to be different.** Complex normative, epistemological, and empirical issues are raised by the phrase the "equal right to be different." These issues are well beyond my ability to explain, and I offer only the commonsense observation that the ethics of equality always cut in two ways. Education provides a useful illustration. Equality can be interpreted to mean that education should be available to all. It can also be interpreted to mean that an individual has a right to be educated according to his talents and ambitions. In the latter instance, equality is protected if the bright and the dull student have equal opportunities to demonstrate their intelligence and then are educated accordingly.[g] Marshall seems to have this in mind when he writes that the Welfare State "must conceive of the basic equality of all as human beings and fellow-citizens in a way which leaves room for the recognition that all are not equally gifted nor capable of rendering equally valuable services to the community, that equal opportunity means an equal chance to reveal differences, some of which are superiorities, and that these differences need for their development different types of education, some of which may legitimately be regarded as higher than others."[62]

It is true and should not go unnoticed that the phrase "equal right to be different" has been manipulated by the privileged in order to protect and pass along these privileges. Yet the phrase points to an important if paradoxical truth, and one which sets upper limits to egalitarianism. Dahrendorf recognizes this paradox when he comments that "within certain limits defined by the quality of citizenship, inequalities of social status, considered as a medium of human development, are a condition of a free society."[63]

It is difficult though possible to do systematic research on this proposition. The possibilities are presented by the fact that movements toward reducing inequalities are initiated in some places and at some times, not in all places and at all times. This indicates that societies differ as regards the areas of life in which the "equal right to be different" holds, which suggests the importance of research on patterns of cultural beliefs about permissible types of inequality. It is everywhere the case that men have a right to demonstrate unequal athletic skills; it is not everywhere accepted that men have the right to demonstrate unequal acquisitive skills.[64]

---

[g]It might be thought that here is a flagrant case of confusing equality of opportunity and equality of condition, but this is not so. A child raised in an uneducated, peasant home does not enter school on an equal footing with the child raised in a highly educated, urban home. But short of penalizing the second child for his fortunes of birth (thereby denying him his equal rights to be different) there is no easy way to impose equality of opportunity.

The three issues reviewed indicate one general approach to studying the extent of inequality tolerable in a society even though citizenship has been universalized and egalitarian ideologies widely pronounced. The strategy has been to ask about the limits on equality and the conditions setting these limits in order to work backwards to answering the basic question about tolerable limits of inequality. The assumption being that values and practices limiting equality reveal some of the conditions allowing inequalities to persist.

It should not do to ignore completely the more direct question: in what ways are inequalities diminished? What bearing does an answer to this question have on the tolerable limits of inequality?

To answer these questions it is useful to distinguish two types of inequalities, one I propose to call the "inequalities of distance" and the other the "inequalities of scope." Inequalities of distance refer to the size of the gap between those best-off and those worse-off, or between any two points along stratification scales. Studies which report the proportion of the national wealth held by the upper 5 percent in contrast to the proportion held by the lower 20 percent or which employ the Geni index of inequality reflect a concern with inequalities of distance. So do political reformers who wish to reduce the ratio between the highest incomes and the lowest incomes.[65] Progressive income taxes are major weapons of those who focus on inequalities of distance.

Inequalities of scope refer to the variety of benefits which are stratified in the society. For instance, if decent health care is so pervasive that the better-off get no more of it than the worse-off, then the scope of inequalities has been reduced. The economists' distinction between money-incomes and real-incomes is useful. When major social services are provided irrespective of ability to make ad hoc payments, the advantage of higher money incomes is confined to limited areas of consumption. The point is made by Nyerere when he urges that inequalities be reduced through "the provision of social services which are available to all, regardless of income; for a man who suddenly has new medical services available to him and his family, or a new house, or a new school or community centre, has had an improvement in his standard of living, just as much as if he had more money in his pocket."[66]

The distinction drawn between "distance" and "scope" indicates the two ways inequalities can be measured: in *how much* better-off the better-off are, and in *how many ways* they are better-off. The less the distance between points along the stratification scales, and the fewer the values of life which are stratified, the more equal the society. It is important to study the mixtures of inequalities which hold in different societies, for we then can ask additional questions.

**4. How much of which types of inequality are tolerated within the limits set by universal citizenship?** Distinguishing the two types of inequality sets two additional research questions, both related to the social policies which promote egalitarianism.

**5. How extensive are the social policies directed at reducing the distance between the top and the bottom strata of society?** Social policies which affect the gradations of wealth in a society are familiar. The distance between the wealthiest and the poorest can be reduced by ceilings on wages, progressive income tax, inheritance taxes, limitations on property holdings, leadership codes, and conflict of interest legislation. Though such policies never completely eliminate inequalities (because of the limits on equality already discussed), they can greatly flatten out the income pyramid. Deliberate policies can also reduce the distance between the least and the most powerful members of society. Decentralization of authority, forms of participatory democracy such as workers' councils and farmer controlled cooperatives, periodic elections and national referenda, are among the more familiar ways of diffusing power broadly throughout the society. Deference hierarchies can also be affected by deliberate social policies, as is indicated by legislation banning titles of nobility or insignias of rank, as well as decisions to eliminate ceremonies and rituals which separate different strata in society, illustrated by purification rituals in India.

As regards policies affecting inequalities of distance, Tanzania has adopted an egalitarian position whereas Kenya has allowed for comparatively greater distance between the better-off and the worse-off, Kenya's policies being partly by design and partly by default. For example, Tanzania has adopted a leadership code which prevents leaders (very broadly defined in the code) from owning shares in companies, from holding directorships in privately owned enterprises, from receiving more than one salary, from owning property for rental purposes, and from being in any way "associated with the practices of capitalism or feudalism."[6][7] Kenya leaders, in contrast, are heavily involved in commercial enterprises, multiple positions, and large land-ownings. (A Kenya parliamentary debate on raising the salary of the speaker concluded that because he had to be in attendance during all sessions he could not tend to his business interests, and therefore merited the raise.) National differences, and they extend to more than leadership codes, suggest the utility of comparing how contrasting policies relate to the inequalities of distance tolerated in societies which have universalized citizenship.

**6. How extensive are the social policies directed at reducing the scope of values which are stratified in the society?** Only the briefest of comments is possible on what is a large and complicated question. To oversimplify, there are two strategies for reducing inequalities of scope. One strategy attempts to guarantee subsistence, security, and basic social services to every citizen on an equal basis, usually through state-directed programs. The other strategy depends on growth in per capita national income and a rising standard of living to bring the costs of social services and consumer goods into reach of all citizens. The latter strategy allows more play to the competitive market-place and to individual acquisitiveness.

There are no pure cases of either strategy, but societies differ substantially in how much emphasis they give to one or the other. What is interesting is that either strategy, if successful, reduces inequalities of scope. That is, it reduces the number of social values—health, education, recreation, housing, consumer products—which are sharply stratified in the society. The better-off still have privileges, but fewer of them.

Though it is early in the development of their economic systems, it appears that Tanzania will put more emphasis on state provided social services and Kenya will put more emphasis on capitalism as a way of raising standards of living. If the economies do develop in different ways, comparisons as regards the consequences for inequalities will be valuable. Moreover, it will be possible to investigate the interplay between the two types of inequality. Tanzania simultaneously is attempting to reduce inequalities of distance and to promote efficient social services on a no fee basis. Kenya is allowing greater inequalities of distance on the assumption that growth in per capita national income will bring about a reduction in the scope of values which only the better-off obtain.

## Conclusion

By way of conclusion I emphasize what the analysis has *not* attempted to suggest. In the first place, I have not said that a social system which harbors universal citizenship and inequalities is necessarily under some sort of strain. Whether social strain is present and what causes it are empirical problems not discussed in this chapter. In the second place, I have not said that citizenship equalities and forms of stratification are compatible in social systems; the compatibility of social phenomena is also an empirical question and one not discussed in this chapter.

What I have said simply repeats a well-known fact: forms of equality and forms of inequality do coexist in the same societies, including Kenya and Tanzania. Analysis of how these phenomena coexist is an inquiry of theoretical significance in its own right, and necessary if we are to account for social structures, social conflict, and social change.

## Appendix

After completing this paper I became aware of a report containing Kenyan data which bear directly on points made in the paper. The report is based on a sample of 4,742 wage-earners in three urban areas, Nairobi, Mombassa, Nakuru, who were interviewed in 1968. It was prepared for the World Bank by Hans Heinrich Thias, with Martin Carnoy as consultant, and appears as *Cost-Benefit Analysis in Education: A Case Study of Kenya* (International Bank for Reconstruction and Development, no. EC-173, November, 1969). I will include here a few of the more relevant findings.

**Education and Income.** The earnings of the better educated are consistently higher than those of the less educated. In the age group 20-24 those who have eleven years of schooling earn on the average 2.14 times what is earned by those with 0-2 years of schooling, for the age group 25-29 it is 2.53 times, for the age group 30-34 it is 3.64 times, and for the age group 35-44 it is 4.10. At each gradation of schooling, there is an increase in earnings. The average earnings (Kenya shillings per month) for the age group 35-44, by years of schooling, is: 0-2 yrs. = 335; 3-5 yrs. = 390; 7 yrs. = 505; 9 yrs. = 898; 11 yrs. = 1,372. (Data taken from Table 5.1).

Although insufficient cases were available to report earnings by age groups of those with more education than eleven years the author notes that "Earnings for Africans with thirteen years of schooling are nearly three times as great as those for Africans with five years of schooling, and 40 percent higher than the average earnings of Africans at the eleven years of schooling level. An African with 15-17 years of schooling makes, in turn, twice as much on the average as an African with thirteen years of schooling." (p. 91)

These differences in earnings are also related to performance on examinations. "Scores on the seven- and eleven-year exams have a marked effect on mean earnings: while average earnings for the "quality" or "pass" group in the seven-year category are 32% higher than earnings for the three to five years of schooling group, a "fail" on the exam results in little earning differences from the lower schooling group." (p. 94)

From data reported in Table 5.1 it is possible to compare respondents who failed the seven-year examination (K.P.E.) and those who passed it but did not enter secondary school. These two groups have completed the same amount of schooling and differ only in performance on an examination at the end of that period. The latter group (depending on age) earns from 30% to 84% more than the former group.

The same general trends appear in the rural sector as well, at least according to a study of the Central Province cited by the report. For instance, the self-employed small landowner with nine-plus years of schooling has an income over three-and-one-half times that of the illiterate farmer, and with each gradation of schooling between these extremes there is an increase in earnings. When the figures are adjusted for acreage and family size, the differences are even more striking. The following indicates gross family income (Kenya shillings per year) for small landowners in the 30 to 40 age group, adjusted for acreage and for family size: head of household is illiterate, average earnings are 489; head of household is literate, average earnings are 789; head of household has 1-3 years of schooling, average earnings are 716; head of household has 4-8 years of schooling, average earnings are 2,086; head of household has nine or more years of schooling, average earnings are 2,874. It can be seen that the household whose head has nine or more years of schooling will gross, on the average, nearly six times as much as the household whose head is illiterate.

**Parental Education and Schooling.** The report also confirms that educational advantages can be passed on from one generation to the next. If his parents are literate a respondent has on the average 60% higher education than if they are illiterate; for females, this figure is 75%. The average father's education of well-educated respondents (12-13 years) was 5.6 years compared to 0.2 years for the fathers of the uneducated respondents (0-2 years of schooling). Differences were sharper for females.

## Notes

1. Such sweeping statements are perhaps out of place in a paper purporting to formulate research questions. Still, such evidence as has accumulated is supportive of the conclusion. For historical and cross-national commentary see Gerhard E. Lenski, *Power and Privilege: A Theory of Social Stratification* (New York: McGraw-Hill, 1966); and the collection of essays reproduced in Edward O. Laumann, Paul M. Siegel, Robert W. Hodge (eds.), *The Logic of Social Hierarchies* (Chicago: Markham Publishing Co., 1970).

2. Illustrative of this viewpoint is Francis X. Sutton's observation, "From a general sociological point of view, the emergence of the modern state rested essentially on the universalization of citizenship and the corresponding attack on privileged statuses that this universalization implied. The demand that all men, however humble, be members of the state could not be separated from concern for their instruction." "Education and the Making of Modern Nations" in James S. Coleman (ed.), *Education and Political Development* (Princeton: Princeton University Press, 1965), p. 57. Reinhard Bendix advances a similar position, "a core element of nation-building is the codification of the rights and duties of all adults who are classified as citizens." From *Nation-Building and Citizenship* (New York: John Wiley & Sons, 1964). This and other quotations are taken from a chapter reproduced in Bendix (ed.), *State and Society: A Reader in Comparative Political Sociology* (Boston: Little, Brown and Co., 1968), p. 233.

3. Bendix, *Nation-Building*, p. 255.

4. "It is probable, therefore, that systems of national education develop as widely as they do, because the demand for elementary education cuts across the spectrum of political beliefs. It is sustained by conservatives who fear the people's inherent unruliness which must be curbed by instruction in the fundamentals of religion and thus instill loyalty to king and country. Liberals argue that the nation-state demands a citizenry educated by organs of the state. And populist spokesmen claim that the masses of the people who help to create the wealth of the country should share in the amenities of civilization." Ibid., p. 247.

5. Max Weber, "Class, Status, Party," in Hans Gerth and C. Wright Mills (eds.), *From Max Weber: Essays in Sociology* (New York: Oxford University

Press, 1946). Although following Weber's conceptualization, I do not use his terminology. Class is avoided in order to save this term for use as suggested by Ralf Dahrendorf in his *Class and Class Conflict in Industrial Societies* (Stanford: Stanford University Press, 1959), that is, to refer to positions vis-a-vis the authority structures of society. Esteem or deference is preferred over status for reasons outlined by Edward Shils in his essay "Deference" which appears in J.A. Jackson (ed.), *Social Stratification* (Cambridge: Cambridge University Press, 1968). Indeed, if I were taking even greater pains about terminology I would drop reference to the word stratification and use only such terms as inequalities and hierarchies for, as will shortly be clear, I have nothing to say about the actual formation of strata in the societies under discussion.

6. W.G. Runciman, "Class, Status and Power?," in Jackson, *Social Stratification*, p. 33.

7. Ibid.

8. Illustrative studies appear in P.C. Lloyd (ed.), *The New Elites of Tropical Africa* (London: Oxford University Press, 1966), and in Coleman, *Education and Political Development*. Coleman, for example, writes, "The relationship between formal education and the formation of the *new* political elite in these countries is so clear-cut, and is documented by so substantial a number of empirical studies, that the point needs no elaboration here," p. 4.

9. See, for instance, Lionel Cliffe (ed.), *One-Party Democracy* (Nairobi: East African Publishing House, 1967).

10. Lloyd, "Introduction" to *The New Elites*, p. 10.

11. The distinction between entry into ruling groups and status within them is elaborated in more detail in Kenneth Prewitt and Heinz Eulau, "Social Bias in Leadership Selection, Political Recruitment and Electoral Context," *Journal of Politics* (Spring, 1971).

12. See particularly Rene Dumont, *False Start in Africa* (London: Sphere Books Ltd., 1966).

13. President Nyerere of Tanzania recognizes and laments this when he observes, "Government and Party themselves tend to judge people according to whether they have 'passed school certificate,' 'have a degree,' etc. If a man has these qualifications we assume he can fill a post; we do not wait to find out about his attitudes, his character, or any other ability except the ability to pass examinations. If a man does not have these qualifications we assume he cannot do a job; we ignore his knowledge and experience." From "Education for Self-Reliance," reprinted in Julius K. Nyerere, *Ujamaa: Essays on Socialism* (Dar es Salaam: Oxford University Press, 1968), p. 57.

14. The literature on this issue is large. One important comparative study is reported in Alex Inkeles and Peter Rossi, "National Comparisons of Occupational Prestige," *American Journal of Sociology*, 61 (1956), pp. 329-339. For a review of earlier studies see T.H. Marshall, "Nature and Determinants of Social Status" reprinted in his *Class, Citizenship, and Social Development* (New York: Doubleday Anchor Edition, 1965), esp. pp. 211-219.

15. Shils, "Deference," p. 107.

16. A Uganda survey of secondary school students shows that they rank medical, legal, and military professionals along with business managers and higher civil servants as the most prestigious occupations, with peasants, domestic servants, and unskilled laborers as the least prestigious. Jonathan Silvey, "The Occupational Attitudes of Secondary School Leavers in Uganda" in Richard Jolly (ed.), *Education in Africa: Research and Action* (Nairobi: East African Publishing House), p. 150. Similar findings have been reported from Rhodesia in J.C. Mitchell, "Aspects of Occupational Prestige in a Plural Society" in Lloyd, *The New Elites*, pp. 260-261; and from Ghana by Philip Foster, *Education and Social Change in Ghana* (Chicago: University of Chicago Press, 1965), p. 269.

17. It should be stressed that the prestige assigned to occupations does not necessarily accord with job preferences, let alone job expectations. For Kenya data see David R. Koff, "Education and Employment: Perspectives of Kenya Primary Pupils"; and for Tanzania data see J.D. Heijnen, "Results of a Job Preference Test Administered to Pupils in Standard VIII Mwanza, Tanzania," both of which are in James R. Sheffield (ed.), *Education, Employment and Rural Development* (Nairobi: East African Publishing House, 1967).

18. Shils, "Deference," p. 107.

19. Ibid., p. 110. The point should not be interpreted as suggesting that schools can transmit whatever values they choose, for, as Arnold Anderson has noted, "the observable variations among individuals or groups in political outlook correspond to no identifiable (or even imaginable) existing patterns of experiences in schools." "Conceptual Framework for Civic Education in Developing Societies," paper delivered at the Seminar on Civic Education and Development, Tufts University, May, 1970, p. 11. Anderson perhaps overstates the point somewhat. Limited evidence from a study in Tanzania indicates that schooling experiences might be systematically related to differences in political and social values; these are reported in Kenneth Prewitt, George Von der Muhll, David Court, "School Experiences and Political Socialization," *Comparative Political Studies*, 3, number 2 (July, 1970), pp. 203-225. Anderson does eventually make the point which is supportive of Shils' observation; "On the other hand, to reiterate a familiar point, there indisputably is a gross correlation between political (or economic) modernity of outlook and the amount and quality of school experience individuals have received." Anderson, "Conceptual Framework," p. 11.

20. Shils, "Deference," p. 110.

21. Nyerere and Kenyatta, as well as lesser political figures, over and over stress the role of education in achieving the broader development goals of the respective societies. It is a theme so pervasive that it is difficult to find a major speech without the customary tribute to the advances made on the educational front. A collection of Kenyatta's speeches appear in his *Suffering Without Bitterness* (Nairobi: East African Publishing House, 1968).

22. The underlying argument is well known as the functionalist interpretation of social stratification. See Kingsley Davis and Wilbert Moore, "Some Princi-

ples of Stratification," *American Sociological Review*, 10 (1945), for a representative statement. I am not here concerned with the accuracy of this theory, or with its deterministic qualities, but rather with what kinds of values come to be held in the society. One comment about the functionalist argument that stratification grows out of the needs of society is in order. The functionalist proposition can be rewritten by replacing the phrase "contribution to the social good" with the phrase "contribution to the ruling class," and perhaps would provide a more accurate account of historical patterns. In part this point is made by Lenski when he writes that *"The distribution of rewards in a society is a function of the distribution of power, not of system needs." Power and Privilege*, p. 63. An even clearer statement of the thesis appears in Ralf Dahrendorf, "On the Origin of Inequality Among Men," reprinted in Laumann, Siegel, Hodge, *The Logic of Social Hierarchies*, pp. 3-30.

23. Again, Nyerere seems to acknowledge, reluctantly, that such beliefs might be widely held in Tanzania and he finds in colonial educational practices the possible cause. See, particularly, "Education for Self-Reliance," pp. 54-56.

24. Kenyatta, speaking to the Festival of Youth, 1966, first alludes to the significance of higher status roles and then quickly adds that farming too is important. "Now we can feel proud that among you are future leaders, doctors, engineers, lawyers, soldiers, policemen and farmers. It is an exciting prospect and I am confident that you will seize every opportunity in the spirit of service to our nation to advance and improve yourselves. Not everybody can reach the top of the profession of his choice. But the service of all is equally important in the life and development of our nation. The farmer who improves the productivity of his land may be making a greater contribution to the national progress than a learned scientist." *Suffering Without Bitterness*, p. 323.

25. Ibid., p. 286.

26. Ibid., p. 326.

27. The most comprehensive statement appears in John W. Meyer, "The Effects of Institutionalization of Colleges in Society," Stanford, mimeographed, 1970, prepared for publication in Kenneth A. Feldman (ed.), *College and Student: A Sourcebook in the Social Psychology of Education*. See also his "The Charter: Conditions of Diffuse Socialization in Schools," W. Richard Scott (ed.), *Social Processes and Social Structure* (New York: Holt, Rinehart and Winston, 1970).

28. Tanganyika is used to indicate that the figures exclude Zanzibar. The data come from Guy Hunter, "Education, Employment and Rural Development: The Problem in East Africa" in Sheffield (ed.), *Education, Employment and Rural Development*, p. 48.

29. Shils notes that "In societies or strata which are highly 'education-conscious,' educational attainment will be more continuously salient as a categorical property than in those which are less 'education-conscious.' " And also, "Education might become more important when a larger proportion of the population

seeks education and possesses different amounts and kinds of education." "Deference," p. 115 and p. 113. Shils here refers to the deference which is accorded to education but his remarks apply equally well to the probability that amount of education will become a salient part of self-identity. Results of a "self-identity" questionnaire administered in Uganda provide strong confirmation of the observation that educational status is an important component of self-identification. Data are reported in Kenneth Prewitt, "Political Perspectives of Opinion Leaders in Uganda," *Social Science Information*, 7 (3), June, 1968, pp. 53-78.

30. T.H. Marshall, "Citizenship and Social Class" in *Class, Citizenship and Social Development*, p. 78.

31. Ibid.

32. Ibid., pp. 78-79.

33. Bendix, *Nation-Building*, p. 249. Arnold Anderson makes a similar point about universalizing education, if in somewhat stronger language, "It is not chance that the 'universal school' of the modern West, now being copied around the world, arose in large measure because ambitious monarchs or thrusting elites wished to extend their charisma or their power over vast areas embracing dozens or hundreds of traditional 'peoples.' " "Conceptual Framework," p. 5.

34. Kenyatta, *Suffering Without Bitterness*, p. 330. As Foster observes, an important function of "education may be precisely one of 'detachment' from the traditional environment." *Education and Social Change*, p. 296. Foster is correct to underscore that this detachment is necessary for economic development programs, but it remains important to ask "development for whom?"

35. Bendix, *Nation-Building*, p. 243. My disagreement holds only if Bendix means formal education, but the context of this sentence indicates that this is indeed what he does intend.

36. Ibid., p. 243 and p. 255.

37. Anderson is a useful corrective to the optimism with which some observers greet civic education programs. See his "Conceptual Framework." Essays about East Africa which cast doubts on the likely successfulness of civic education programs include George Von der Muhll, "Education, Citizenship, and Social Revolution in Tanzania," in Prewitt (ed.), *Education and Political Values: Essays About East Africa* (Nairobi: East African Publishing House, in press); Prewitt and Okello-Oculi, "Political Socialization and Political Education in New Nations" in Roberta Sigel (ed.) *Learning About Politics* (New York: John Wiley & Sons, 1970); Philip Foster, "Education for Self-Reliance: A Critical Evaluation" in Jolly (ed.), *Education in Africa*.

38. The Chief Education Officer of Kenya, Kyale Mwendwa, writes, "Access to education is perhaps the biggest issue in Kenya's domestic politics. Kenyans are avid for more education, both for themselves and their children. If evidence of this is needed one only has to note that there were in 1966 some 20,000 children in unaided secondary schools each costing their parents probably at least £25 a year in fees as well as a share of the cost of erecting such schools."

"Constraint and Strategy in Planning Education," in Sheffield (ed.), *Education, Employment and Rural Development*, p. 277.

39. Kenyatta, *Suffering Without Bitterness*, p. 312; and Nyerere, "Education for Self-Reliance," p. 48.

40. Marshall, "Citizenship and Social Class," p. 89.

41. In his essay "The Origin of Inequality," Dahrendorf writes, "But the idea of a society in which all distinctions of rank between men are abolished transcends what is sociologically possible and has a place only in the sphere of poetic imagination," p. 28. Marshall offers his opinion that the "problem of establishing equal opportunity without abolishing social and economic inequality . . . is inherent in the nature of the Welfare State which must necessarily preserve a measure of economic inequality. This problem, therefore, is a permanent and not a transitory one." "Social Selection in the Welfare State" in *Class, Citizenship, and Social Development*, p. 267. The pragmatic socialist Nyerere writes, "But it would be quite wrong for us to aim at complete equality of income between all workers. Incomes must depend upon work and output too; there must be an incentive for everyone to work a little harder." "After the Arusha Declaration" in *Ujamaa*, p. 169.

42. Marshall, "Citizenship and Social Class," p. 128 and p. 127.

43. Marshall, "Social Selection in the Welfare State," p. 278.

44. See especially chs. 3 and 10 of S.M. Lipset, *The First New Nation* (London: Heinemann, 1963).

45. Such a theme has partly been sounded by T.B. Bottomore, "It may be argued, then, that it is the traditional conception of American society as highly mobile rather than any exceptional degree of mobility at the present time, and the general increase in prosperity (though with a good deal of partially concealed poverty) rather than strong movement towards greater economic equality, which play the main part in weakening class consciousness." *Classes in Modern Society* (New York: Random House Vintage Book, 1968), p. 53.

46. An entirely different perspective from which to critique the opportunity/achievement/mobility trinity is presented in the entertaining work of Michael Young. Carried to its extreme, social arrangements which promote the gifted and the ambitious (IQ + effort = Merit) institutionalize genetic injustice and create a new hereditary elite. See *The Rise of Meritocracy* (London: Thames and Hudson, 1958).

47. Shils, "Deference," p. 111.

48. Ibid., p. 118.

49. Ibid.

50. Kenya data can be found in Mwendwa, "Constraint and Strategy."

51. Nyerere, "Education for Self-Reliance," p. 62.

52. Talcott Parsons, "The School Class as a Social System: Some of Its Functions in American Society" in his *Social Structure and Personality* (New York: The Free Press of Glencoe, 1964). The essay first appeared in *Harvard Educational Review*, 29 (1959).

53. Parsons, "The School Class," p. 145.

54. Marshall, "Social Selection in the Welfare State," p. 266.

55. The outlines of this ideology appear in Nyerere's "Education for Self-Reliance." For very useful commentaries see Philip Foster, "Education for Self-Reliance: A Critical Evaluation"; Von der Muhll, "Education, Citizenship, and Social Revolution in Tanzania"; Lionel Cliff, "Socialist Education in Tanzania," *Mawazo*, 1 (December, 1967), pp. 73-80, reprinted in Prewitt, *Education and Political Values*.

56. Data presently being processed by H.C.A. Somerset documents this; for a preliminary discussion see "Educational Aspirations of Fourth-Form Pupils in Kenya," paper presented at the 1970 Universities of East Africa Social Science Conference, Dar es Salaam, December, 1970.

57. For general discussions see Lloyd, *The New Elites*, pp. 24-25, and Foster, *Education and Social Change*, especially ch. VII.

58. Cliffe, "Socialist Education in Tanzania," p. 76.

59. Pertinent historical data and useful sociological comment is found throughout Lenski, *Power and Privilege*.

60. See above, note 22.

61. Nyerere, "After the Arusha Declaration," pp. 169-70.

62. Marshall, "Social Selection in the Welfare State," p. 266.

63. Dahrendorf, "The Origin of Inequality," p. 30.

64. The essays of T.H. Marshall are particularly relevant. See Part III, "Social Welfare" of *Class, Citizenship and Social Development*, and also *Social Policy* (London: Hutchinson & Co., third edition, 1970).

65. Illustrative of the concern with inequalities of distance is the discussion in Bottomore, *Classes in Modern Society*, pp. 57-59. Allende is illustrative; when he took power in Chile in 1970 one of the first things he did was propose legislation which would limit the highest government salary to twenty times the lowest.

66. Nyerere, "After the Arusha Declaration," p. 169.

67. "The Arusha Declaration," in Nyerere, *Ujamaa* p. 36. The code defines leader as follows: "Members of the TANU National Executive Committee; Ministers: Members of Parliament; senior officials of organizations affiliated to TANU; those appointed or elected under any clause of the TANU Constitution; councillors; and civil servants in the high and middle cadres. (In this context 'leader' means a man, or a man and his wife; a woman, or a woman and her husband.)"

# 8

## Comparative Research on the Relationships Between Political and Educational Institutions

JOHN W. MEYER

There has been a good deal of thinking about the ways in which the political and educational institutions in social systems affect each other. Most of it has been concerned with problems of political and economic development. There have been many arguments about the ways in which the development of modern educational systems might contribute to these kinds of modernization. (See, for example, Harbison and Myers, 1964; and the papers in Coleman, 1965). It is also recognized, of course, that economic development and political modernization lead to educational expansion, but this relationship has been given less consideration in view of the great concern in the social sciences with the sources of political and economic development. In the present proposal we are concerned with research which would continue the investigation of these traditional problems of institutional interrelationships, suggesting some ideas for exploration and some research designs which could effectively utilize more recently available information.

The studies we propose are comparative. It seems clear that many of the ways in which political and educational institutions may affect each other are system-level in character and concern not the details of political influences on the expansion or direction of educational institutions or the effects of particular patterns of educational instruction and interaction on individual students' political ideas, but rather quite general ways in which these institutions operate to create networks of symbolic definition setting cultural conditions or providing cultural materials for each other. To study such problems comparative research is absolutely essential because it is necessary to examine not only the operation of particular organizational forms but the impact on each other of *quite highly institutionalized* political and educational structures which vary primarily from society to society.

We can illustrate the need for comparative research with several specific examples. If, in developing societies, expanded secondary school systems really function politically, not to train a few students to have the attitudes and values appropriate to elite status, but to give everyone in the society a new sense of the basis or legitimacy of a modernizing elite, we cannot discover this by comparing

Michael Hannan and Richard Rubinson, who are collaborating with me on research on several of the problems discussed here, provided helpful comments and suggestions which are incorporated in this paper.

125

the political socialization of graduates of different secondary schools within a society. They may all acquire quite similar characteristics, and we may learn nothing about the way the educational system supports the political structure. We must compare the socialization of students in societies in which the educational system is more highly expanded, and is more closely connected with the political system, with the socialization of similar students in other societies. Or as a second example, if secondary schools or universities affect political socialization when they have the social power to confer upon students entry into political elites, there may be few differences among such schools within a society, but enormous differences between societies depending on the relative development of the institutionalized control by schools of entry into political elites (Weinberg and Walker, 1969). Or as a third example, comparative research may be the only way to show how modernizing political elites tend to expand educational systems as a means of creating and symbolically justifying a new political system and new political goals, rather than as a way of producing new kinds of training or individual socialization. No results at all may appear in studies of specific methods of political control, or comparisons of the effects of specific schools within societies. In short, to discover if political and educational institutions affect each other *at the system level*, rather than through individual socialization or through specific structures of political control, comparative research, with social systems as the units of analysis, is required.

## Two Research Problems

A tradition of rather rationalistic thinking about the effects of educational institutions has led to two mostly tacit assumptions about the ways political and educational institutions affect each other: (a) Education is thought to socialize people to political ideas and norms and train them for political positions (including the social position of citizen). By preparing students for norms and social positions which are not necessarily developed in their societies, schools are even thought to create dissatisfied and sometimes revolutionary elites (see Schumpeter, 1950; Kerr and Dunlop, 1960; and the discussions in Coleman, 1965). (b) Political development or modernization is thought to lead to an emphasis on education as a means of socializing people to new and modern political structures. Modernizing political elites are thought to use educational means to emancipate the citizenry, to create new elites, and to provide kinds of socialization experiences which make possible economic development.

These two assumptions are generalizations which describe how two extremely massive and complex social institutions may affect each other. They are also causal assertions describing relationships among particular variables or measures which describe properties of these institutions—especially their expansion or relative modernization. But the two assumptions contain opposite lines of causal reasoning about the ways political and educational structures affect each other. The first line of reasoning argues that educational institutions affect the development of political ones, and that educational expansion and modernization may play an important role in creating political development. The second line of reasoning argues that developing or expanding political systems may generate educational expansion. The two arguments are by no means inconsistent, and it is conventional to suppose that both may be true—that the institutions of society reinforce each other. But only one of the arguments may be true—or neither of them—and it is of the greatest intellectual and practical importance to distinguish empirically between them. If, for example, it is generally true that developing political systems tend to create expanded educational systems, but that these in turn play an unimportant role in affecting the political system, educational investment may be a very poor strategy for affecting political change.

Either or both of the causal arguments above could account for the empirical observation that countries which are relatively high on measures of political development are also likely to have rather highly developed or expanded educational systems. The first main proposal of this paper is that research is needed which can distinguish the two types of causal effects, developing and using longitudinal data on national societies. Only with such data is it possible to isolate the distinctive effects of political development on educational expansion from the converse effects of educational development on political modernization. No empirical study using presently available information will be able to completely answer such a general question, but the research we propose would at least begin the effort to define and develop the appropriate analyses. This study is concerned with very general relationships between whole institutional sectors of societies. It uses nations as the basic units for analysis. This kind of brute force attempt to approach a complex problem will leave many questions open and many uncertainties in interpreting its results. But research of this character is an absolutely necessary adjunct to other developing lines of research, such as case studies and quantitative studies of the interrelations of organizational structures within societies.

In the long run, however, the prevailing ideas in the literature about the nature of the interrelations of political and educational institutions are too limited. Educational institutions may socialize people to hold substantive political ideas but whether they do this or not they play a powerful role in defining for everyone the types of groups which exist in a modern society. Whether the members of these groups, as isolated individuals, have acquired given political ideas or loyalties, they hold, by virtue of their educational statuses definite and specified places in the social and in particular the political order. Highly developed educational institutions, whether they teach anyone anything or not, may create and define basic constituent parts of society. Similarly, while political institutions may in fact need educational means to train individuals to play their parts in a modern society, they also need school systems to define and justify these parts as elements of the institutional order. A politically modernized state may need secondary schools and universities to justify its elites in modern terms. It may need elementary schools to define large masses of people as *citizens*, and hence as qualified for impersonal participation in the modern state. Beyond the circumstances of individual socialization, that is, schools may provide the kinds of initiation ceremonies which construct, maintain, and justify the elements of the political society (Young, 1965).

These larger socializing functions of schools and school systems greatly need examination. As a second major proposal of this paper we suggest research to investigate them. *Comparative research* is needed on the political impact (conceived more broadly than in terms of simple socialization) of educational institutions. The research must be cross-national but cannot simply employ nations as the sole units of analysis. It must consider the impact of specific types of schools over a wide variety of political and cultural conditions. And it must examine the effects of institutionalization of schools and school systems not only on those attending them but on other parts of the society as well.

## 1. A Longitudinal Cross-National Study of the Interrelationships of Political and Educational Development

No matter what particular measures of political and educational development of nations are employed it is found that the two variables are closely associated. Harbison and Myers (1964) employing a general index of development, show a close association with the indicators of relative educational enrollments. Garms (1967) also shows some clear associations between political variables and national educational expenditures. The literature on educational expenditures generally shows that such variables are more closely associated with economic factors than with distinctively political ones (James, 1963). Garms, however, shows some positive correlations with political variables, even when economic development is held constant. Meyer (1969), in a cross-sectional study also shows a number of associations between indicators of national political development or politicization and relative educational enrollments when economic factors are held constant. In this study it appears that indicators of political development and the expansion of political authority are particularly related to educational enrollments at the primary and university levels.

The interpretation of cross-sectional studies like these is, of course, quite difficult. It is obvious that political development or modernization may be one of the sources of expanded educational systems (see, for instance, Bendix, 1964). There are many reasons why this effect might be thought to occur. Political development leads to demands for educated citizens and more highly trained elites. It produces amplified ideas about the rights of members of society to such resources as education, and is associated with the expansion of economic capacity which can generate both the demand for education and the facilities to meet the demand. Political development also means the shift of loyalties to national political symbols and structures from more local and familistic ones. It may thus lead to the development of educational institutions as devices to create and symbolize more impersonal and national foci of identification. In the same way, educational institutions may be developed to provide more modern and impersonal ways to recruit and legitimate elites. Finally, political development may lead to educational expansion as a way of institutionalizing or symbolizing the values placed on scientific knowledge, individual responsibility, and so on.

But the same finding of an association between political and educational development may result from precisely the opposite effects, too. The possibility that a causal impulse to political modernization is created by developed and expanded educational institutions is one of the main themes of the literature on social and political development (Coleman, 1965). Education can create demands, both in elites and in the citizenry, for political expansion. It can do so by socializing people to the skills, values, and goals of modernization, and also by defining a more modern status structure and by shifting people from traditional statuses into the industrial economy. Institutionalized systems of education can provide a new basis for legitimating modern elites and modern citizenship as core values in many different sectors of a society.

There are thus many causal arguments which suggest that political and educational development affect each other. What is obviously needed here is research which separates the political effects on educational development from educational effects on political development. This is difficult to do partly because isolating such interdependent causal forces requires carefully controlled data over considerable periods of time. Only such data can show how each variable tends to create changes in the other variable over time, and thus begin to isolate the two causal processes.

The simplest beginning would be fairly straightforward: To study political effects on educational development requires measures over time of both variables. It is necessary to compare, among countries of given levels of educational development at one point in time, the rate of subsequent educational expansion of those countries which are classified as more advanced politically with the expansion of those which are less advanced. Thus, considering only those countries with developed educational systems, if those which are more politically modernized expand their educational systems more rapidly over time, we begin to have information which suggests independent political effects on educational development. These data would be, of course, much too simple to make possible any clear conclusions. It would be necessary to hold constant other variables than political ones which might have produced the result. Obviously economic development might have accounted for the apparent impact of political modernization on educational expansion. Economic development at the very least must be held constant (or its effect included in the analysis) in studying the impact of political modernization. But the data we describe, however fraught with problems of interpretation—difficulties in measuring the variables, and the potential operation of spurious factors—would at least begin to eliminate the possibility that the observed effects showed not political impacts on the educational system but educational impacts on the polity.

Similarly, it is possible to begin to isolate the political effects of educational expansion. How do countries which are politically similar but different in their relative educational expansion change politically over time? (Economic factors must be held constant, of course.) Do educationally developed countries show greater increases over time in levels of political development? Do they show changes toward political stability? Even political instability could be a hypothesized consequence at low levels of economic development, however, if an over-expanded educational system is indeed a source of revolutionary political elites (Schumpeter, 1950). Again, in such a venture, all kinds of spurious factors may be operating. Many problems of measurement may beset us but at least in this way we begin to isolate educational effects on political development from the reverse effects.

**Measurement**. Obviously we are not the first to suggest the importance of disentangling the causal relations between institutional structures with quantitative data over substantial periods. The importance of the present proposal lies in the fact that data which characterize over time the political and educational characteristics of countries are beginning to be available. Data on national educational enrollment patterns, however inadequate, go back to 1950 for a substantial number of countries (UNESCO, 1966). It is possible to describe countries by the development, relative to the appropriate population groups, of their primary educational enrollment, secondary educational enrollment and their university enrollment. It is possible to do this separately for male and female students.

Using these enrollment data, it is possible to characterize national educational systems by a number of attributes measuring their relative development or expansion. First, the proportions of the appropriate age groups enrolled in primary and secondary schools, and in universities can be calculated. Second, ratios of the relative development of various sectors of the national educational system can be calculated by showing the ratio of primary school enrollment to the equivalent population age group, the ratio of secondary to primary students, and the ratio of unversity enrollment to secondary school enrollment. These ratios indicate in a rough way the probability that a student at a given level in an educational system will continue to the next level. Thus, countries can be described not only by the proportion of children who enter the educational pyramid at the bottom, but also by the relative extension of the pyramid, or the proportions of those who enter who reach any given step. Third, the educational experience of any given generation or cohort in a society can be described by taking the ratio of the university enrollment to the secondary enrollment about five years earlier, and the ratio of that secondary enrollment figure to the elementary school enrollment in a still earlier period. These ratios would describe the educational possibilities faced by a given generation within a country. Their relationships with later political changes produced in that country as the generation passed through the age cycle could be usefully examined.

Data are also available describing national levels of educational investment (Garms, 1967) so it is possible to characterize at least some nations by their relative expenditures per capita on education over substantial periods of time. These data are complex, since expenditures on education are not always closely associated with actual levels of educational enrollment (Meyer, 1971). This finding may reflect measurement error. Or, educational investments may reflect such economic factors as the relative size of teachers' salaries and the level of *current* investments in school facilities, thus assessing a different set of structural factors, operating over different time periods than educational enrollments.

It would also be possible to examine comparative data on various substantive aspects of national educational systems—their relative emphasis on the significance of technological fields, political ideology, civil service requirements, and so on. However, although these issues have been much discussed in the literature on education, data are not available on a systematic comparative basis.

Measures over time of national political characteristics are difficult to obtain, in part because such concepts as political development or modernization are not formulated or defined clearly, and in part because comparable data for many countries are not readily available. Political development means many different things, and a major research problem would involve sorting out, and studying the consequences of, measures of these various meanings. In part, political development means political expansion—the increase in the resources and number of activities controlled by the political system. This is, of course, closely related to economic development. But in part, development means politicization, or mobilization, which means the expansion of political control *relative* to other institutions, as in the socialist state. Development also is used to refer to the *character* of the political system—the degree to which it incorporates or represents many different social interests, the degree to which it is oriented toward social change and economic modernization, and the degree to which success in it is determined by competence or training rather than more traditional criteria.

Unfortunately, measures of most of the aspects of political development suggested above are unavailable or available for only one point in time, and when available are inadequately measured. For the most part, initial research in this area involves the use of measures which contain many biases and a great deal of error. The effect of these problems on the kind of research we are suggesting is generally to lower the likelihood that positive empirical relationships will appear. But exploratory research of this kind is one of the requisites for the conceptualization and development of more adequately measured variables.

Measures over time of a number of national political characteristics have been developed, however. Cutright (1965) for instance, has developed an index measuring political representation using data which are available for a number of decades. Banks and Textor (1963) have developed measures of a number of political characteristics of countries. These measures are sufficiently stable that they could be employed as independent variables in the analysis of the effects of political characteristics on changing educational structures. Russett, et al. (1964) have also collected a number of political indicators. This work is especially valuable because the same researchers are now publishing a second set of measures of national characteristics, ten years after their first attempt. These data, therefore, could provide measures of political change with which to assess the political impact of relative educational development.

Beyond explicitly political characteristics, it is extremely important to incorporate into the research measures of other aspects of the social organization of countries. All sorts of economic data are available—measures of income, of industrialization, of trade, of energy consumption, and so on. There are also available data on the distribution and characteristics of human populations—their size, urbanization, growth rates, and age distributions. But for many central aspects of social organization, available measures are very inadequate, either because data are missing, because they are full of measurement error, or because they assess only very indirectly crucial organizational characteristics. There are few good data, for instance, on the degree to which such institutions as labor unions, religious organizations, voluntary or welfare-oriented groups, or professional organizations are highly developed in different societies. In fact, to describe the social integration of societies in any general way, we must rely on such indirect measures as telephone or postal messages per capita.

The weakness of the available measures of national social organization, as with political variables, makes the proposed research effort exploratory in character. When measures of uncertain meaning must be used, the interpretation of results becomes ambiguous, and the absence of findings may not reflect an absence of actual corresponding effects, but only the utter inadequacy of the available comparative data. But it would be a major error to postpone research on the interrelationships of political and educational characteristics of countries until some hypothetical time when ideal measures might be available. Research, even at present, may be able to show many suggestive results, and in any case may be able to do a great deal to show us what kinds of concepts, measures, and modes of analysis must be developed in the future.

There is every reason to believe that time-series data on institutional characteristics of countries will become increasingly accessible. And with the availability of modes of multi-variate analysis of sufficient sophistication to analyze data on the limited number of countries which exist in the world, beginning research on these problems would be very fruitful.

## 2. A Series of Comparative Studies
## of the Political Effects of Schools

In all sorts of societies, the political positions, resources, and attitudes of people who differ in education tend to be very different (see, for instance, Almond and Verba, 1963). More educated people are much more likely to hold political offices, to exercise political influence, to perceive themselves as politically efficacious, and to know about and identify with the political system. Cross-sectional studies within countries almost invariably show substantial results along these lines.

Yet the available research on the effects of specific schools on the political attitudes and values of their students shows that they generally have quite limited effects. (See Jacob, 1957, or the excellent summary by Feldman and Newcomb, 1969.) Despite their massive efforts to broadly educate their students, most schools with only infrequent exceptions produce very weak effects on the political identifications and knowledge of their students. How does it happen, then, that the graduates of these same types of schools, when they are investigated as adults in cross-sectional studies, differ so dramatically from other groups in the population?

The answer to this question, we argue, is that there has been too narrow a conceptualization—and thus empirical examination—of the kinds of politically socializing effects schools may have. When the potential effects of schools on the political system are conceived and studied on a broader basis, it will become possible to understand why education turns out to be so closely associated with political ideas and values, and with actual power. We suggest a complex and long-range program of research organized around such an effort.

Most of the available thinking about the political effects in schools has developed around a conventional model of individual socialization. Depending on their internal structure—their patterns of interaction among teachers and students, their "peer cultures" and the organization of their curricula—schools are thought to affect the political attitudes, values, and personality characteristics of their students. They affect larger political structures because these students, as they move out into the larger society, carry with them the attitudes and values created.

However, this is a very limited view of the ways schools socialize members of societies (Meyer, 1965, 1970 and 1971). First of all, a school is likely to greatly affect a graduate whether or not his values or skills are changed in the least. A school can have an effect simply by *defining him as a graduate*. His job prospects change greatly. His opportunities for entry into political and civil service elites are modified. Everyone else defines him as a different person, and he sees himself as having very different rights and possibilities. He is a changed man whether his internal qualities have changed or not.

The fundamental fact *that schools have a social charter to produce a graduate*

*who will be given a certain kind of social definition* has many important consequences for political socialization. In this discussion, we use the term *charter* to
describe the structural position of the school and the social definition which is
attached to its graduates.[a] The institutionalization of a system of schools involves the specification of the ways its graduates are entitled or expected to
enter into the wider society. And the more highly institutionalized the schools,
the clearer is the social charter, or the ideas defining what they produce. The
graduates are understood to possess distinctive qualities and rights. Sometimes
these rights are legally protected, as when certain levels of the civil service or the
practice of certain professions are reserved for graduates of certain schools.

We argue that the effects of schools in politically socializing students are
determined as much by the charter or public definitions of the school as by any
internal curricula or modes of interaction. Students and graduates are likely to
adopt (and others in the social structure are likely to expect them to adopt)
those qualities which are generally seen as attached to their educational statuses.
When schools are chartered to produce political and administrative elites, their
students will take on (and be encouraged to do so by others) the qualities which
go with such elite membership—the appropriate aspirations, roles, and values.
When elementary schools are defined as institutions creating national solidarity,
and are used to channel their students into positions in the modern economic
and political order, their students will tend to think of themselves as citizens of
the nation and to divorce themselves from particular or local identifications. All
these effects will be supported in public opinion, not only the private ideas of
students or graduates themselves.

The institutionalization of a charter for a set of schools affects not only students and graduates, but all the other groups in the political system as well. In
defining the legitimate position and rights of graduates, a changed model of society, and of their own position is created for these other groups—elites and nonelites, graduates and nongraduates. As we will see, this can have a broad set of
consequences for many sectors of the political system.

Once we conceive of educational institutions as not only having internal effects but also consequences by virtue of their *institutionalization* in the political
system a number of research problems become important. Most of these require
comparing the effects of essentially *similar* educational institutions in social
structures in which they are *differently* institutionalized or chartered. Thus, the
basic independent variables of the proposed studies are characteristics of national societies—the ways in which they establish institutionally the political
meanings or charters attached to various schools and types of schools. There are
obviously many different variables involved in the degree to which schools are
politically chartered or have institutionalized political significance. We consider
some of these later.

---

[a]This conception, and a number of the specific points noted below are developed at greater
length in Meyer (1970, and especially 1971).

**Research Design**. We want to suggest the comparison of the effects of schools in different societal settings. But studying the effects of schools is in itself a complicated business (Jacob, 1957; Barton, 1959; and Feldman and Newcomb, 1969). This is particularly true given the intellectual perspective we are suggesting. If schools and school systems have their impact by attaching certain quite general labels to people—labels which have wide currency in the society—then there is no reason why the effects of schools should in any way be restricted to *students during the period of their studenthood.*

The traditional sort of before-and-after studies of students must be expanded in three ways:

1. *In examining the effects of institutionalized school systems on students themselves it is necessary to follow them over a much longer period of time than their actual residency in the school.* If attendance in a given school or type of school has some generally understood consequence for a student's political location in society—whether it confers membership in a particular political elite or simply modern citizenship in the society as a whole—the student, we argue, will tend to espouse this location as a consequence of a whole series of steps in his educational career. This should happen at many points, not simply when the student interacts in the social system of the school itself.

a. An individual encouraged by others to aspire to a given school or type of school will presumably begin to acquire the chartered political attributes attached to that school. The effects of a school, that is, begin with the actor's identification with it as a symbolic element in the social system. Organizational devices, such as preparatory curricula, probably encourage this process.

b. Application to and acceptance by a given school or type of school may change the social status of an individual and lead to his adoption of the political values or aspirations attached to products of such schools. In other words, an individual moves toward membership in a given school he may adopt its chartered qualities and others may encourage him to adopt them before he has any formal or informal interaction in the school structure itself.

c. After the student has completed his school experience, a whole series of postgraduate effects on his political ideas are possible and likely. As he experiences the special treatment others give school graduates in the political system his ideas and aspirations are likely to be changed. In the more extreme instance, as he comes to occupy the political offices or jobs to which his education tends to entitle him, his conceptions of the political system and his own role in it must inevitably be affected. In other words, one of the ways in which schools may affect their students is not through a direct impact on their values or attitudes, but by leading them into distinctive roles. These roles, then, by well known social-psychological processes, may lead their incumbents to have definite attitudes or values. It is traditional in the world of education to hope that a school may have some distinctive impact on its students such that they become mighty and successful. We are arguing that schools may have impact on their students by being allowed to *confer* on them probable success and might.

2. *In studying the political effects of schools it is necessary to cover a broader range of variables than simply the values and attitudes of students.* If schools create political effects by attaching roles to students which they are legitimately chartered to confer, it is crucial to study not only school effects on the values of students, but the actual types of social positions into which the students are allocated. Thus we need to investigate how schools increase the political interest of their students, but also the degree to which these students are actually channelled into political organizations. It is necessary to study not only students' attitudes and identification with the national government but also the actual likelihood that students will be located in government offices. In studying elementary school effects in developing societies it is important to see both whether graduates have acquired a patina of national identification and also whether they actually tend to control the local political organization of the society. More important than the examination of the impact of schools on the psychological self-esteem or sense of political efficacy of the graduates is the study of the *actual* esteem and efficacy which these graduates are chartered to acquire. If we discover that schools astonishingly increase the sense of political responsibility, efficacy and self-esteem of their graduates, it is much more likely that this results from the fact that graduates of the schools are entering into a social elite which is, in fact, authenticating respect, esteem and political efficacy, than that it results from some dynamic internal attributes of the school (Meyer, 1965).

Thus it is important to study how schools affect the allocation of students into actual positions in the social structure, not only how they affect abstract ideas or values. It is also important to see how the wider range of social rights allotted the students and graduates are developed in their own awareness and intentions, e.g., how students' plans for occupational and especially political careers are constructed and modified by the types of school which they attend. In all such research, of course, to study the distinctive impact of schools, background and ability factors must be held constant. We want to compare those who do attend given types of schools with similar individuals who do not. But the importance of such comparisons run beyond the need to simply have a control group against which to assess the impact of schools on their students. For, it is a basic part of our argument that schools have impact on those who do not attend them as well as upon those who do.

3. *It is necessary to examine the political effects of schools on other groups in the society as well as on students.* The most obvious application of this observation is to the study of school nonattenders. If schools have political effects because a variety of political positions or memberships are, in effect, reserved to their graduates, then the process of becoming a *nonattender* or a *nongraduate*,

whether by elimination or positive intention, is a process by which actors in effect are separated from these memberships. Thus in societies in which schools are highly politically significant, or chartered, those who attend should be expected to undergo a process of politicization or involvement in the political system *and those who do not attend should end up as detached from the political system*—especially from elite positions in it. The only way we can tell this, of course, is by comparing socialization in such societies with that in societies in which schools are less closely connected with the political system. In these latter societies the differences between graduates and nongraduates in political involvement should be reduced and the apparent effects produced by the schools should also be reduced.

In the same way the attenders must be followed beyond their educational career, it is also necessary to study nonattenders. The processes by which an individual is allotted the qualities of a nongraduate can presumably take as long, and as many steps as those which prepare the graduate.

Beyond specific comparisons of graduates and nongraduates it is crucial to examine the impact of the development and political institutionalization of schools on many different sectors of the society at large. The development and chartering of a system of schools as the basic source of political citizens or elites may affect the political conceptions of all sorts of people—graduates or nongraduates, elites or nonelites. The redefinition of the bases of ordinary political membership from localistic and familistic identifications to those built around nationwide and universalistic systems of elementary schools may produce important shifts in the political conceptions held by all sorts of actors, whatever their own educational and political experience (Bendix, 1964). And people of all sorts may be inclined to see elites defined in educational terms as more *legitimate*, better justified and explained, and more oriented to modernization than elites recruited or defined in other terms. This may be true, even though the elites are in fact the same people as would have been defined by a more traditional system, and even if they actually have no more competence or commitment to modernization when defined in educational terms.

The effects we are discussing here may occur through the intermediate social organization and communications system of societies. The development of new and education-based definitions of citizens and elites is probably transmitted to the wider society through the structures of local economic and community organization, labor unions, religious organizations, mass media, and so on. It is therefore extremely important to study how the specific elites involved in these institutions are affected in their political ideas and activity, and in their own recruitment and organization, by the educational changes we are considering. It seems most likely that the conceptions of ordinary people are at least partly affected by changes in these intermediate organizations.

These ideas suggest some of the enormously complicated ways in which educational institutionalization may affect political structures. It is our intention to encourage research on a much wider range of problems of political socialization than have been discussed traditionally. By doing this, we hope to account in a more adequate way for the complex, but substantial, relationships between educational institutions and political ones.

**The Independent Variable**. The basic studies we propose investigate the effects of political socialization of greater and lesser political institutionalization of the educational system. Obviously there are many difficulties in defining or measuring this variable as an attribute of national societies or of specific educational organizations and systems within societies. In practice, it is necessary to develop a number of measures and to investigate empirically their interrelationships. At this point it is useful to suggest some of the dimensions which might be employed in conceptualizing and measuring the degree to which educational structures are politically chartered (see the more extended discussion in Meyer and Rubinson, 1972):

1. The extent to which the educational system or its various parts are the direct responsibility of the national state.
2. The extent to which graduates at any given level are in government service, and the degree to which positions in the government service are reserved for such graduates.
3. The degree to which the political party apparatus is managed by graduates; and the degree to which positions in the political elites are reserved for such graduates.
4. The degree to which elite political and governmental positions are conceived in public opinion to be the appropriate property of specific educational elites. Obviously, public conceptions of the activities of graduates may be different than the activities themselves.
5. The degree to which the social status or position of student is seen as a distinct social position. This factor is presumably a consequence of other aspects of the institutionalization of educational systems, but also plays an important causal role. That is, the greater the degree to which an educational system is politically chartered to produce future elites, the more likely the creation of a distinctive conception of students as a group of people with special political and social interests and status. The degree to which the social status of the student is conceptualized as distinctive and the degree to which it is seen as political in content are extremely important factors in political socialization and require a great deal of investigation (Meyer and Rubinson, 1972).
6. The degree to which educational backgrounds or status are used in explaining or justifying political status. Knowledge, competence and intellectual authority—qualities which are constructed and defined by the educational system, will be used more frequently to explain and justify the authority of political elites as educational systems are more chartered to produce them.

7. The degree to which political ideas are explicitly used to explain and justify the investment in educational institutions. The more commonly educational institutions are created to have political consequences in training citizens or elites, the more likely they will be to have such consequences.
8. The size relative to the appropriate population groups of educational enrollments in particular sectors of the educational system: Presumably, simply increasing the proportions of the population who are processed by a nationalized elementary system may increase the extent to which this system tacitly begins to define membership in the society. In this way it comes into closer correspondence in its cultural meaning with ideas of citizenship.

We have suggested above attributes which might indicate the degree to which educational institutions are chartered to produce political products. Since these attributes probably reflect many different social processes, a major research task is to investigate the interrelationships across countries of such characteristics as these.

**Some Specific Hypotheses to Be Investigated**. In order to make clear the value of comparing the effects of schools in systems where they are differentially institutionalized, we can suggest a number of rather specific hypotheses. In the studies suggested below it is, of course, necessary to hold constant many characteristics of countries beyond the one in which we are primarily interested—the political chartering of educational institutions. In particular it is necessary to hold constant measures of the general levels of economic and political development so as to isolate the particular effects of educational organizations.

1. The more politically institutionalized or chartered a given school or school system, the more students in it will come to identify with the political system and perceive themselves as politically efficacious. They will also be more likely to see the political system itself as legitimate. They may be more likely to identify with the values and goals of national political development and to perceive the political system itself as leading in this direction. This attitude may occur, in part, because political recruitment from the educational system is itself seen as indicative of modernization.

    Students in systems which are more politically chartered may also identify more with their social status as students and see this status as having distinctive political interest and greater political authority than students in other kinds of systems. This follows from our argument that one feature of the political chartering of educational systems is the greater institutionalization of the social status of *student* (Meyer and Rubinson, 1972).
2. In societies in which educational institutions are more politically chartered, even nonstudents and adults who are not members of elites may come to perceive the political system as more legitimate and a modernizing force. They may, however, see themselves, if anything, as less efficacious than in other

types of systems, since political rights and authority justified on educational terms may exclude them.

Effects on identification with the political system are less clear. It may be that nonstudents in such social systems, even though they perceive the political elites as supported by legitimate educational institutions, would be less likely themselves to identify with the political structure because of their relative exclusion.

3. In systems in which educational institutions are more chartered politically, modernizing elite members, whether or not they themselves have attended the appropriate schools, should tend to acquire qualities similar to those of students in such systems. We expect that they would identify more with the political system, see it as more legitimate, perceive themselves as more efficacious, and identify more with the values and goals associated with political development. This should follow if educational institutions in such societies in fact contribute broadly to the support and legitimacy of political institutions. This added structural support should add to the confidence of elite members in general, whether or not they have attended the appropriate schools.

Of course, highly chartered educational systems may cause the breakdown of the political community itself. Students and elites may constitute a revolutionary force in the political system by virtue of the confidence in their own legitimate authority which may extend considerably beyond the established boundaries and established positions of the political structure (Schumpeter, 1950; Goldrich, 1965; Arnove, 1967; and Coleman, 1965). It is clear that in colonial societies these groups—educationally chartered elites—were fundamental sources of political revolution. This may also be true in other developing societies.

Traditional elites in societies in which educational institutions are increasingly chartered as sources of political membership and authority would not be expected to show these same effects. Such elites may be quite likely to become alienated from political systems which cut off their access to power and the definition of their positions as containing essential political authority. Such elites may react against a political system simply because of the way authority is being redefined and reallocated in terms of educational qualifications, even though the actual benefits of education may come primarily to them.

## Overview

The studies proposed above all attempt to analyze the effects of educational structures on the orientations and actions of actors in the political system. Longitudinal studies of both students and nonstudents are needed which cover more phases of the educational cycle than are usually considered (including educational effects which occur before and after a given schooling period), and consider a much broader range of political consequences than simply the attitudes or values of individuals. In particular it is necessary to focus on the actual placement which students and nonstudents receive in the social and political order, and on the consequences which this placement may have for political orientations and activities. Such placements reflect the social charter of schools—the status which is defined and socially established for their products or graduates. These social charters may greatly affect the ways in which both students and nonstudents acquire—and are encouraged by others to acquire—political orientations.

The social charters which define the political significance or status of graduates of various types of schools also may directly affect other elements of the political system, quite apart from their contribution to the socialization process. These processes need to be examined with comparative, cross-sectional studies of the effects of the political institutionalization or chartering of educational systems on the political behavior of many different groups—political elites, leaders of and participants in all sorts of intermediate organizational structures, and ordinary citizens.

## Conclusions

The lines of research suggested in this paper all consist of attempts to define more clearly and to expand our conception of the ways educational systems effect political institutions—in particular, political modernization or development. Traditional lines of thinking in this field have tended to focus on relatively limited numbers of effects—the ways educational systems lead students to adopt new norms, and the ways they may contribute more highly trained individuals to the modern economy and political system.

In the first of our proposals we suggest a way to begin to distinguish educational effects on the political system from political effects on education. The longitudinal analysis of interrelationships of political and educational characteristics of national societies is a first major step in this direction. The second major proposal suggests a series of studies designed to outline a broader range of sets of educational effects on political behavioral organization. An examination is needed of the effects of schools both on students and on nonstudents. A wide range of political effects should be examined, including those on political attitudes and values and those on the actual status—political and occupational—of individuals in the social structure. We also suggest studies of the effects of the political chartering of schools—their use to define new social conceptions of political elites and of political citizens—on a wide variety of elite and non-elite groups in social systems.

All of these studies are attempts to employ comparative research to transcend more individualistic conceptions of the ways the educational system functions in societies.

## References

Almond, Gabriel A., and Verba, Sidney. *The Civic Culture*. Princeton, New Jersey: Princeton University Press, 1963.

Arnove, Robert F. *The Impact of University Social Structure on Student Alienation: A Venezuelan Study*. Stanford, California: Stanford International Development Education Center, 1970.

Banks, Arthur, and Textor, Robert. *A Cross-Polity Survey*. Cambridge, Massachusetts: M.I.T. Press, 1963.

Barton, Allen. *Studying the Effects of College Education*. New Haven, Connecticut: The Edward W. Hazen Foundation, 1959.

Bendix, Reinhard. *Nation-Building and Citizenship*. New York: John Wiley, 1964.

Coleman, James S. (ed.). *Education and Political Development*. Princeton, New Jersey: Princeton University Press, 1965.

Cutright, Phillips. "Political Structure, Economic Development, and National Social Security Programs." *The American Journal of Sociology* 70 (March, 1965).

Feldman, Kenneth A., and Newcomb, Theodore. *The Impact of College on Students*. San Francisco, California: Jossey-Bass, 1969.

Garms, Walter Irving, Jr. "Multiple Correlates of Educational Expenditures by Nations," unpublished doctoral dissertation, Stanford University, Stanford, California, 1967. Shorter version published in *Comparative Education Review* 12 (Oct., 1968), pp. 281-299.

Goldrich, Daniel. *Sons of the Establishment*. Chicago, Illinois: Rand McNally, 1966.

Harbison, Frederick, and Myers, Charles. *Education, Manpower, and Economic Growth*. New York: McGraw-Hill, 1964.

Jacob, Philip E. *Changing Values in College*. New York: Harper & Row, 1957.

James, Thomas. *Wealth, Expenditures, and Decision-Making for Education*. Stanford, California: Stanford University Press, 1963.

Kerr, Clark, et al. *Industrialism and Industrial Man*. Cambridge, Massachusetts: Harvard University Press, 1960.

Meyer, John W. "Working Paper on Some Non-Value Effects of Colleges," Bureau of Applied Social Research, Columbia University, New York, New York, 1965.

——. "Economic and Political Effects on National Educational Enrollment Patterns," *Comparative Education Review* (February, 1971), pp. 28-43.

———. "The Charter: Conditions of Diffuse Socialization in Schools," in W. Richard Scott (ed), *Social Processes and Social Structures*. New York: Holt, Rinehart and Winston, 1970.

———. "The Effects of the Institutionalization of Colleges in Society," in Kenneth Feldman (ed.), *College and Student; A Sourcebook in The Social Psychology of Education*. New York: Pergamon Press, 1971.

Meyer, John W., and Rubinson, Richard. "Structural Determinants of Student Political Activity: A Comparative Interpretation," *Sociology of Education*, Spring 1972, (forthcoming).

Russett, Bruce, et al. *World Handbook of Political and Social Indicators*. New Haven, Connecticut: Yale University Press, 1964.

Schumpeter, Joseph A. *Capitalism, Socialism and Democracy*. (3rd. ed.) Chapter 13, "Growing Hostility." New York: Harper & Row, 1950.

UNESCO, Statistical Yearbook. Louvain: UNESCO, 1966.

Weinberg, Ian, and Walker, Kenneth. "Student Politics and Political Systems." *The American Journal of Sociology* 75 (July, 1969).

Young, Frank. *Initiation Ceremonies* Indianapolis: Bobbs Merrill, 1965.

**Part 3: The Governance of Public Education: Power, Roles, and Decision Making**

# Introduction to Part 3

The papers in this section focus on who controls our schools and the policy implications of changes in the influentials. Harmon Zeigler asserts little is actually known about the distribution of influence among various potential and actual participants in the educational decision-making process. He contends:

Our first task is not more theory. Our job is to compile a list of participants in governing the schools and assess the influence of each. I suggest we consider the activities of the following participants: (1) administrators, (2) school boards, (3) teachers, (4) interest groups, (5) students.

He outlines a number of key questions for researching each of the participants.

Professor Peterson suggests three decision-making models through which these various actors make policy—the organizational process model, the political bargaining model, and the rational decision-maker model. He stresses each model presents only one facet of the totality of the situation and only by interrelating the three models does the full picture emerge.

Professors Lipsky, Iannaccone, and Elazar concentrate on specific actors or models for decision-making in public education. Building on his prior work on street level bureaucrats, Lipsky proposes a study of teacher/client interactions including: (1) incentive systems in which teachers work and (2) recruitment and maintenance of employees within the school systems. One objective would be to provide a critical link in our understanding of the relationship between student achievement and intervening variable of client encounter with the system.

Professor Elazar would combine the systems and policy-making process to explore community control. Among other things he proposes to tackle the unsettled issue of what is "the community" and the implications of the federalist system for community self-government.

Professor Iannaccone believes priority should be on the local education agency, particularly the growing gap between policy studies and planning versus implementation and administration. His experience with preparing school administrators leaves him troubled about the development of outside networks of a "new intellectual proletariat" without responsibility for the operation of local school systems. He does not defend the establishment but proposes researching the "gap between planning and action," and the consequent lack of change within the local educational agencies.

Professor Crecine asserts we should be interested in political variables only if they turn out to be important determinants of educational outcomes. A logically prior decision is to determine which set of outcomes one is attempting to explain, predict, etc. Only after we have some insight into educational production functions can we determine the most relevant political variables. Professor

Crecine then analyzes prior studies on resource allocation decisions by local educational agencies in this framework.

**Models of Decision Making**

PAUL E. PETERSON and THOMAS WILLIAMS

The charge to write a simulated research proposal can be a stimulating opportunity. Assuming unlimited resources, one can propose to study in depth and with the necessary *verstehen* a large enough sample of cases so that a definitive account of the topic under investigation could conceivably be written. Whether or not the proposed undertaking could be realized, the attempt would still provide standards against which actual investigations could be compared; moreover, simple concentration on a utopian proposal, unconstrained by usual considerations of foundation or governmental expectations, available skills, and the competing demands on the proposal writer's own time and energy, may entice one's imagination into perhaps fanciful but in the end more rewarding realms than those which one pursues in more practical moments. Many proposals discussed at this conference will surely reveal the virtues of an opportunity for such wide-ranging reflection. But there may also be some merit for at least one participant to reflect instead on a soon to be completed study that he hopes will contribute "something" to the field. It is true the study may be too limited by resource and other constraints to contribute more to the field than other research projects that might be devised. On the other hand, the discussion will be based on some experience with the "real world" of educational politics and a prolonged effort to make some sense of one aspect of it.

The study of the decision-making of the Chicago school board, which Thomas Williams and I hope to complete in the not too distant future, has all the defects of the case-study approach that have been identified in the bibliographic essay for this volume written by Wirt. Although it may have the virtue of permitting a closer look at the internal processes of big city school systems, enabling the analyst to examine urban school board decision-making both in terms of the structure of its own organization and in the context of its political environment, one certainly cannot offer a case study as a major contribution to the data base on educational politics. Our methodological approach was also undistinguished by any novelties worth discussing here. A certain amount of statistical data was analyzed by methods which we hope were not more sophisticated than were appropriate for the data. But the bulk of the information was gathered through interviews with participants in the policy-making process, through the examination of school records, and through close attention to newspaper reports.

Yet contributions to the study of educational politics can be theoretical as

149

well as methodological or sheer increments in the size of the data bank. Although theorizing was not specifically mentioned in the charge to conference participants, one can argue, on the basis of the data presented in the background papers, that continuing theoretical contributions are badly needed in this emergent field, if it is a field, of educational politics. With the discovery that Easton's systems analysis, however insightful and provocative many of its details clearly are, may be too general a theory to help with the specific theoretical problems of a special arena of policy-making, students of educational politics may begin to cast a broader net in order to develop useful analytical insights.

Any attempt to theorize about educational politics must begin by noting what is distinctive to the field. Only if it can be shown that educational politics are distinctive in some fundamental respect from politics in other policy areas can one speak of a particular theory of educational politics. We doubt that any such claim can be sustained. But it may be worthwhile to consider the theoretical implications of the one effort that has been made to identify a unique characteristic of the politics of education: the claim that educators are particularly guilty of declaring politics to be an illegitimate intrusion into their professional enterprise. Perhaps the polemics of this debate can be transformed into analytical tools that will provide a beginning towards middle range theorizing about the urban educational policy-making process.

## Political Scientists, Educationists, and Three Models of Decision-Making

Conflict between school boards and their administrative staffs over educational policy has been an endemic theme in the politics of education. The growth of large educational systems in rapidly growing American cities, the increasing diversity and complexity of services provided by schools, the professionalization of educational administrators, and the general reform movement in urban politics all reduced the control that lay boards of education exerted over school policy. Shrewd politicians, who awarded contracts and positions of responsibility on the basis of kinship, friendship, and partisan regularity, gave way in many cities to more honest and efficient direction of educational policy by professional administrators. It was generally conceded that the proper relationship between the school board and administrator was for the board to determine policy and for the superintendent to administer that policy. But it became increasingly prevalent for superintendents to offer their professional advice to school boards on policy items. As a consequence, the distinction between policy and administration, which was never clearly delineated theoretically, has also become hopelessly obscured in practice. Today, in many urban cities contradictory criticisms of the school system are offered simultaneously. On the one hand, it has been argued that the board is an ignorant, innocuous legitimator of decisions made by an autonomous administrative staff. On the other hand, it is said that the board is politically motivated and interferes in matters which more properly belong in the administrative sphere, where decisions could be made according to educational principles.

The study of the politics of education in fact began with an interesting, though ultimately muddled, debate over the proper relationship between the professional educators and politicians, as represented by school boards, public officials, and interest groups. Urban reformers thought education should be separated from the "dirty world" of "machine politics" by bringing its direction under the control of professionals. Their slogan "Keep politics out of education" was particularly effective because education has for centuries been seen as a distinctive activity, which was not to be directed by the same people as those who determined sanitation, street, and police policies. School boards have since the nineteenth century operated with considerable independence from other municipal institutions. More recently, political scientists, seeking to defend politicians from the disrepute into which they had fallen, argued that it was impossible to keep education out of politics. Educational decisions in modern societies are public decisions, they claimed; as long as the compulsory power of the state is used to enforce educational policy on the citizenry (through taxation, compulsory attendance, and regulation of the schools), educational decisions are political decisions.[1] Though the argument sounds convincing, it is merely a tautological observation. Political scientists have simply defined as "political" those activities which are related to the "authoritative allocation of values for a society."[2] Although the definition may be analytically useful, it does not by itself prove, as the early studies of the politics of education implied, that power had shifted too far in the direction of the professional administrators. Political scientists seemed to believe that once the public character of educational policy had been noted, it was obvious that professionals should play an advisory and administrative role only, that policy should be left to the determination of a lay board chosen according to rules that had some democratic legitimacy. We might agree with such a normative position, although it remains to be shown whether lay or professional control produces the wisest pattern of educational policy. Yet normative conclusions cannot be drawn from tautological observations.

Even though this debate has produced no definitive normative guidelines, it has suggested to us an analytical strategy. The debate in fact points to two competing models of decision-making. The first, which we shall call the organizational processes model, is the analytical counterpart to the normative position of traditional educators, who argued that schools should be kept safely within the hands of professional administrators. The organizational processes model says that large school systems can be coordinated only through the activities of a large, complex, formal organization. Urban school boards, therefore, are extremely dependent upon that organization for information, for policy recommendations, and for policy implementation. Consequently, the policies that the board pursues will be determined by certain characteristics of the organization upon which the board depends. Organizational interests, the "shared values" of its membership, and its code of standard operating procedures all limit the alternatives available to decision-makers. Together they shape the character of educational policy. This analytical perspective shares with the traditional educationist the assumption that the professional educational experts are crucial for determining educational policy. But it does not necessarily perceive the expert as the diviner of educational truth and wisdom; instead, it understands the expert as being limited in his search for the truth by his interests, values, and routine pattern of operations.

The political bargaining model is a second, competing analytical framework that can be drawn from the debate we have reviewed. It is the analytical analog to the argument of political scientists and certain avant garde educationists that the school board and elected public officials have the right, as democratically selected public leaders, to determine the character of the public's educational programs. The political bargaining model says that educational policy is the outcome of a political contest among the disparate interests, groups, organizations, and segments of opinion within the political community. Each actor (or group of actors) in the political game advances his (or their) preferences with more or less conviction, greater or lesser ability, on a wider or narrower range of topics. The relationships among actors are structured in such a way that some actors have more influence over the outcome than others. The power relations among the actors and the skill and perseverance of each of them will influence the outcome of the bargaining game. The model shares with the political scientist a concern for the way in which the school board members, as representatives of the general public, influence school policy. But it does not see the board as the expressor of the public interest; rather, it sees members of the board as one of many participants in a political contest so structured as to favor some participants over others.

Note, however, that the argument as reformulated no longer focuses on power relations between two concrete, empirical structures—the school board and the administrative staff—but deals instead with the adequacy of two distinct analytical models. While it is true that the organizational processes model seems most adequate for understanding the administrative staff's contribution to policy, structures external to the school system have organizational characteristics as well. PTAs, political parties, citizen's committees, teachers unions, neighborhood organizations and civil rights groups are organizations whose contributions to educational policy might well be interpreted from the perspective of the organizational processes model. Even more surely, the political bargaining model does not apply simply to the external environment of a school system. The bargaining which occurs within the administrative staff may be extensive and bitterly contested. Conflicts between staff and line, between central office and field administrators, among administrators in socially and geographically distinct areas, and between the "old guard" and the "young Turks" are often the major preoccupation of organizational "insiders." If the organizational processes model identifies the common interests and values of bureaucrats, the bargaining model explores the power struggle among them. Moreover, it draws no sharp boundary line between an organization and its environment. Different segments within an organization may develop different contacts with power centers external to the organization, which are useful and can sometimes even be determinative for the internal organizational struggle.

If the debate between political scientists and traditional educationists points directly towards two distinct models of educational decision-making, the debate itself implicitly rejects still a third model of decision-making. Both sides to the debate begin by rejecting the premise that administrators function in such a way as to help boards of education achieve their goals in the most efficient manner possible. They agree that policy decisions are not based on rational consideration of the best method for achieving the agreed goals of the board of education; both sides implicitly agree that the staff does not assist the board by identifying and implementing the most desirable methods available for achieving these goals. Otherwise there would be no conflict between school board and administrative staff, and the entire debate would be meaningless. The point of departure for the debate, then, is a common rejection of a rational decision-making model.

An extreme formulation of a rational decision-making model would be offered only by a naive simpleton. In fact rational decision-making models have frequently been constructed as "straw-men" to be knocked down by hard-headed empiricists. Yet the model, properly reformulated, may not be totally irrelevant for understanding school board decision-making.

Each of the three models—rational decision-maker, organizational processes, and political bargaining—offers a distinctive way of understanding the decision-making of the school board. It should be clear from the beginning, however, that we believe that *each model presents only one fact of the totality of the situation*. Although the analogy may not be exact, it can be said that each model is like one snapshot of a three-dimensional event. Only by interrelating the three models does the full picture emerge. In the remainder of this paper we shall develop more fully each of these analytical approaches.[3]

*Model I: The Board as a Rational
Decision-Maker*

In order to revive the rational decision-maker from his present status as a "straw-man," it is necessary to avoid both the Scylla of too exact a definition of rationality and the Charybdis of such a loose notion of rationality that the concept is meaningless. It may be possible to steer safety through such a dangerous course by regarding rational decision-making as a middle range rather than a "covering all" theoretical model.

The debunkers of rationality models demand that the actor have rationalized both the goals he seeks and the means he chooses to pursue them. Accordingly, it is argued that the rational actor must identify the exact interrelationship among man's values which will realize the Good and Perfect Universe. If it is conceded that this is not necessary, it is said the actor must have a value system which is consistent, coherent, and gives precise guidelines for action in practical situations. Attacks on rationality models focus on the difficulty, in fact the virtual impossibility, of maximizing all values that are important to actors and to the imprecision with which actors have established principles for selecting among values in conflict. Board members want a school system to pursue universalistic policies, to respond to local needs and problems, to minimize costs, to hire well-qualified teachers, to win and maintain public support for the schools, to instruct the children according to sound educational principles, and to assure a rapid flow of information throughout the system. All of these and other goals are part of what board members mean by serving the public's interest in good education. Yet these values may in many cases compete with one another, and no clear hierarchy of values exists for board members, which enables them to choose among conflicting values. The very plurality of values makes rational decision-making very nearly impossible.

All of this may be conceded without denying that a more limited conception of rationality may still provide a useful basis for analyzing board decision-making. If it is difficult to speak of rational value systems, one can speak of the rationality of the instruments which the decision-maker selects to achieve the goals that he seeks to maximize. Instrumental rationality does not assume that actors have a consistent hierarchy of values; it only assumes that a rational actor selects from the alternatives available to him the one which is most suited for achieving whatever goals (rational or not) the actor has in mind. The actor is *instrumentally* rational, for he selects the most efficient means to reach the desired ends. One can speak of a school board, then, as being instrumentally rational, even though its members do not hold to a consistent value system. In any given policy situation, certain goals can be identified which board members are seeking to maximize. In developing a policy affecting the racial distribution of pupils in a school, for example, the board may be seeking to stabilize the white community. In organizing its administrative staff, it may seek to maximize staff efficiency without jeopardizing the staff's autonomy from outside pressures. In determining teacher salaries, it may wish to pay no more than is essential for attracting adequately qualified teachers to the system. Even though one or more of these goals may not be rationally selected (in the sense of fitting consistently within the board members' value systems), the board may be acting in an instrumentally rational fashion so as to maximize these particular goals.

Even with this more modest instrumental conception of rationality, it has been persuasively argued that any political actor (to say nothing of a board of education) can scarcely decide among alternatives rationally. The analogy of a chess game illustrates the difficulty of acting rationally in a complex situation even when the goal of the actor is clearly defined.[4] Selecting the best of all possible alternative moves in a chess game is a task which exceeds the capacities of the most sophisticated of contemporary computers, to say nothing of the limited capacity of the human brain. Moreover, even if such information could theoretically be obtained, the costs of collecting additional information may exceed the benefits to be gained through adopting a more efficient strategy rather than a less efficient one.

These limitations on even instrumental rationality have induced certain scholars to offer an alternative, more subjective, definition of rationality, which avoids the Scyllian rock that destroys *any* actor's claim to rationality only to be sucked into the Charybdian whirlpool that reassures *every* actor that he is acting rationally, thereby reducing rationality models to meaningless tautologies. Utility theories in economics, and, more recently, in political science provide instructive examples of the advantages and problems involved in a completely subjective definition of rationality. An individual acts rationally, utility theory assumes, whenever he adopts a strategy which *he believes* has the greatest possibility of maximizing the values which *he believes* to be relevant to his situation. Note the contrast with the still objective, though instrumental, conception of rationality offered in the preceding paragraph. There it was assumed that once an actor's relevant values and goals were known, his behavior could be judged by an outside observer as being more or less rational, depending on the efficiency with which the acts were realizing his goals and values. From the perspective of the subjectivist, however, a man may be acting rationally even when to an outside observer the actor appears to be destroying his own cherished goals; if the actor himself does not perceive the error of his ways, the actor is presumed to be acting in a subjectively rational fashion.

The subjective notion of rationality has been offered as a solution to a difficult problem for microeconomists. Theories of the firm have assumed that the firm acts rationally in an objective sense so as to maximize profits.[5] Empirical studies of the market behavior of individual firms, however, indicate that at least in some cases firms clearly were not maximizing profits, thereby calling into question certain of the basic assumptions of microeconomic theory. Utility theory has been offered as a response to this difficulty. Firms maximize their utilities, the theory goes; while profit maximization may be among the utilities that firms seek to maximize, it cannot be said that it is in all cases the only utility of the firm. The point is clearly valid. Yet the theory which says that firms seek to maximize utilities cannot be verified, since accurate information about the utilities of individual firms cannot be obtained. If at any point market behavior is inconsistent with utility preferences, as measured by the instrument of some observer, it can only be said that the instrument did not accurately measure the utilities of the firm accurately.

An analogous debate between objectivists and subjectivists has occurred recently in a body of literature which is seeking to develop a theory of micropolitics. In an early seminal work, Anthony Downs argued that political leaders in democratic polities seek to maximize their winning coalition in elections; all their political activities are oriented rationally towards this end.[6] Mistakes and errors are due simply to the lack of information available to the political actor. This theory faces the same difficulties that the profit maximizing theory in microeconomics confronted: observable behavior is at times rather obviously inconsistent with the basic assumption of the theory. Certain politicians, for example, pursue such extremist goals that they can scarcely be oriented primarily towards maximizing a winning coalition. Frolich, et al., recently refined the theory by suggesting that political entrepreneurs are interested in maximizing utilities, not winning coalitions.[7] Only in certain cases are the two identical. Some political actors receive greater utilities by remaining in permanent opposition than they would receive if they gained office. But, again, this reformulation of micropolitical theory cannot be disproven; as Kelley has pointed out, by definition "an actor will always choose . . . outcomes with highest utility."[8] It is impossible to identify behavior which is not rational, for in no case can you prove that the individual is not maximizing his utilities.[a]

The circularity of the argument for this concept of rationality reveals it to be a Charybdian whirlpool. In order to avoid its strong but ultimately disastrous currents, let us steer back towards a more objective definition which, with all of its difficulties, has the potential for providing the basis for a middle range, if not a "covering all," theory of political action. Insisting on an objective definition of rationality, it must be emphasized, does not mean insisting that goals and values are rationally determined. Behavior is instrumentally rational whenever the means selected are appropriate for the goals being pursued, no matter how these goals were established. More exactly, "action is rational insofar as it pursues ends possible within the conditions of the situation, and by the means which, among those available to the actor, are intrinsically best adapted to the end for reasons understandable and verifiable by positive empirical science."[9]

Parsons' critique of this positivist position points out that inasmuch as "there is nothing in the theory dealing with the relations of the ends to each other, but only with the character of the means-end relationship," the theory assumes "that there are no significant relations (among ends), that is, that ends are random in the statistical sense."[10] But as Parsons himself admits, the criticism car-

---

[a]Actually, the theory argues that actors consider both the utility of outcomes and the probability that they will occur in choosing among alternatives. The relevant probabilities are those that actors assign to outcomes. Even if the actual probability of an outcome occurring were .9, the actor would be acting rationally if he acted as if the probability were .1—only provided that he believed the probability were .1. This definition of rationality provides the theorist with double the requisite insurance. Not only does the identification of behavioral choices with utility maximization insure (by definition) rational action but the assumption that actors choose on the basis of their own perceptions of the probabilities that particular outcomes will occur (rather than according to probabilities that an objective observer might assign) reinsures that the actor will always act rationally.

ries weight only if the theory "is held to be literally descriptive of concrete reality" rather than being "consciously 'abstract,'" which is our intention here.[11] For certain analytical purposes it may be assumed that the school board is seeking to maximize the probabilities that white communities are stabilized, or that the board is interested in obtaining the best teachers at the lowest possible salary. Microeconomists make a similar assumption when they assume that firms are interested in maximizing profits. Anthony Downs' assumption about the behavior of politicians was also a simplification for certain analytical purposes. It is true that the rationality of means cannot be separated from the rationality of ends insofar as one is attempting to describe concrete reality, but this in no way denies the usefulness of developing abstract models based on such an assumption.

The analytical character of the model is particularly evident when the analyst claims that he is offering no more than a middle range theory, which is the case here. Attacks on assumptions that firms maximize profits and politicians maximize votes are most persuasive when they criticize any pretensions that these assumptions can lead to the development of general or "covering all" theory. Empirical data simply does not warrant such a claim. Our argument would be open to similar criticism if we were to argue that all school decision-making was based on the board's commitment to a particular policy goal. If it is simply claimed, as we do here, that what is offered is only a middle range theory which helps explain certain aspects of board decision-making, the force of the critical attack is considerably blunted. It is conceded that boards at times may not use generally available information in order to identify the most instrumentally rational strategy. Nonetheless, it is not unreasonable to assume that boards do seek to devise the strategy which seems to be the most efficient for achieving their goals and that they do seek to gather information that will help them choose among various strategies. A commonly agreed upon goal will powerfully constrain a board's discussions, as each alternative is examined carefully to see whether it will further that goal.

Such an assumption of objectively rational action is increasingly helpful for analyzing board behavior the more clearly and definitely the goal can be specified. Profit maximization and vote maximization are reasonably (but not perfectly) defined goals. "White stabilization" and "lowest salaries for the best teachers" are more clearly defined goals than is "quality education for all children." By assuming that the board is maximizing a clearly defined goal, the analyst minimizes the danger of slipping into a subjectivis-concept of rationality. The more vaguely the goal is defined (maximizing utilities is the best illustration), the more one is in danger of speaking tautologically when one says that boards seek to devise the strategy which *seems* to be the most efficient. But the more clearly defined the goal, the more it will become clear when a board is not devising the strategy which *seems* to be the most efficient for achieving that goal.

The rational decision-making model thus becomes appropriate for analyzing the decision-making of a collectivity of actors, such as a school board. It is often claimed that only individuals can be rational, not boards, firms, or institutions. In a sense this is true. But if it can be assumed that the individual decision-makers for the institution (the members of the school board) have a common conception of institutional goals, then it is possible to consider objectively whether their decisions implement these institutional goals.[b] The rational decision-making model helps to show the limits within which these debates occur and indicates the basis for the decision: certain arguments in the discussion indicate one strategy is instrumentally the most rational.[12]

## Model II: The School Board as Head of a Formal Organization

If Model I regards the board as a rational decision-making entity, Model II identifies a set of constraints on the information of the decision-maker, which limit the number of options the board considers and biases the board's perceptions as to which of the still available options is most rational. This set of constraints stem from the fact that boards gather information, consider alternative policies, and must eventually implement policy by means of a large, complex, formal organization. The organization enormously increases the amount of information that can be collected for decision-makers, provides an opportunity for the board to receive recommendations from professionally trained individuals sufficiently experienced so they can anticipate the consequences of alternative options, and increases the board's capability of implementing its policy decisions. An organization that approximates the "ideal-typical" bureaucracy that Weber described is a proficient instrument for enlarging the scope of instrumentally rational action. Yet no organization has a bureaucratic structure which is a perfect instrument for the policy-maker. However essential organizations may be, organizational characteristics establish their own set of constraints on the alternatives open to decision-makers. These constraints are a function of the organization's standard operating procedures, organizational interests, and the shared values of its members.

**Organizational routines.** An administrative staff communicates to its board through channels which are structured by certain formal guidelines and informal norms and expectations. These channels of communication are likely to be structured in such a way as to facilitate the rapid conduct of routine affairs. In Allison's words: "Organizations perform their higher functions, such as attending to

---

[b]In fact the assumption remains useful even if only the smallest number of individual members of the decision-making group necessary to commit the institution to a policy (usually, a majority) hold a common conception of the institution's goals.

problem areas, monitoring information, and preparing relevant response for like-ly contingencies, by doing 'lower' tasks, for example preparing budgets, pro-ducing reports, and developing hardware."[13] These operating procedures, once established and standardized, place constraints on the problem-solving activities of an organization. They narrow the options that are actively considered. They bias the evaluation of options in directions consistent with organizational struc-tures and routines. They limit the range of policies that the organization is capable of implementing. Consequently, organizational behavior is prone to "error" in crisis situations, those times when almost by definition the routines of the organization will be inappropriate for dealing with problems the system faces. Rather than selecting the most rational alternative, the organization is like-ly to suggest one which more closely conforms to the standard operating pro-cedures.

**Organizational interests.** The structure which evolves in order to perform routine functions efficiently also gives rise to a variety of roles within the organi-zation. These roles, as do any set of social roles, have certain interests. The con-cept of role interests has been challenged on the grounds that social roles do not have interests, only individuals do. This may be true of the "real" world. Social roles are analytical constructs that do not exist in the "real" world, and there-fore they cannot have any "real" interests. However, role interest as an analyti-cal concept can have great utility, as is evident in the frequency with which it is used. Organizational interests, class interests, union interests, judicial interests: all of these and similar phrases are commonly used and accepted. In every case, the reference is not to any particular individual but to the role which the individ-ual is performing. Indeed, it is easier to settle on a definition of role interest than to conclude what is in the interest of an individual. One school of thought argues that individual interests cannot be known apart from the preferences of the in-dividual; another school of thought argues that individual interests cannot be reduced to simply what the individual wants.[14] An individual may not be aware of his own interests, the argument runs. Yet it is difficult for any outside ob-server to take into account the relevant information necessary in order to deter-mine what is in the interest of, i.e., what is "good for" a particular individual. The problem is more easily resolved when speaking of social roles.[15] Those things that enhance the desirability of performing a particular role are in the interest of that role. Policies which improve the life chances of incumbents of specific roles by increasing the wealth, power and/or prestige of role incumbents serve these role interests.

Since organizations are complex sets of role relationships, organizational in-terests are those things which enhance the desirability of performing roles within the organization. Policies which are in the interest of an organization are policies which increase salaries of organizational members, increase the number of posi-tions within the organization (for this improves the promotion opportunities of incumbents of existing roles), recruit higher-ranking personnel from lower ranking positions within the organization (for this also improves promotion opportunities), increase organizational autonomy from outside pressures (for by increasing the number of options available to role incumbents, it increases their power), and improve general working conditions.

Organizational interests limit the instrumental rationality of the actions of decision-makers dependent upon the organization for information, policy recommendations, and implementation. Goal displacement theories emphasize the extent to which organizational maintenance needs interfere with the maximization of the ostensible goals of the organization. In order to secure substantial private donations, hospitals may emphasize glamorous public relations gimmicks at the expense of patient care. Unions may concede demands for pay increases and improved working conditions in exchange for employer recognition of union legitimacy and "check-off" privileges.[16] Schools may emphasize flashy music programs and art shows for parents and interested citizens, even when school personnel realize that basic educational goals suffer in the process. In short, organizational interests have been known to place limits on the instrumentally rational character of policy formation.

**Shared values of organizational members**. If organizations are reluctant to act contrary to their interests, neither do they eagerly promote alternatives inconsistent with the values of the members of the organization. Members may come to hold values which are sufficiently distinctive and sufficiently relevant for decision-making that they independently influence the processes of informing, recommending, and implementing. This occurs particularly when organizational members belong to a single profession, as is the case with educational administrators. Members of a profession tend to be recruited through similar channels, to have a similar educational background, to endure similar "periods of testing," to perceive in similar ways the heroes who pioneered in the field, to orient themselves towards similar career goals, to read and hear of "progress" in the profession from similar sources, to relate to colleagues in a similar fashion, to develop common images about clients and other outsiders who are relevant to the work of the profession, to understand professional problems in a similar way, and to evaluate the importance of particular professional endeavors similarly. In short, the "sharedness" of the values of organizational members can only increase when it is an organization of professionals. Educational policy-making will be less than fully rational to the extent that the images and myths of the educational profession are inappropriate for the problems with which they are dealing.

Organizational routines, organizational interests, and the "shared values" of organizational members have more than a random relationship to one another. The share values of organizational members are usually consistent with their role interests. In fact professional values may provide effective reinforcement of and justification for structurally determined bureaucratic role interests. Standard operating procedures, too, are likely to be consistent with both organizational interests and professional values; moreover, they in turn may become valued objects themselves. Procedures that may be purely instrumental at the time of their inception may become sacred and revered patterns of operation as time passes.

Since organizational interests, shared values, and operating procedures dovetail together to bias the decision-making process, the contribution that each of these factors makes independently may be difficult to decipher. In a school system based on the concept of the neighborhood school, organizational structures, interests, values and operating procedures may work together to perpetuate that system. Efforts to change that system may well be frustrated by the challenge they pose to interests, values and routine patterns of operation. In such a case it is difficult if not impossible to determine to what extent interests, values or routine procedures bias the administrative staff's orientation towards proposed changes. Yet it is more important to demonstrate the way in which the decision-making is affected by the cumulative and interactive impact of all these factors than to specify the independent contribution of any one of them. Such is the analytical purpose of the organizational processes model of decision-making.

The organizational processes model modifies the rational decision-making model previously presented. It identifies a set of constraints on decision-makers that depend upon large, formal organizations for information, policy recommendation, and policy implementation. These set of constraints, it is hypothesized, will tend to bias decision-making away from the rational maximization of board goals so that the decisions are more consistent with organizational interests, values and operating procedures. But the organizational model is similar to the rational decision-making model in that it assumes the school board to be a unitary actor, even though subject to a set of uniform constraints imposed by an organization. School boards, however, consist of a number of discrete individuals, each of whom has his own interests, values, perceptions, and goals. Although the assumption of a unitary actor may be useful for certain analytical purposes, a comprehensive analysis of decision-making cannot depend completely upon this simplifying assumption. The political bargaining model to which we now turn permits an exploration of the divisions and conflicts within the school board which until now has been assumed to be a unitary actor.

*Model III: The School Board as an Arena*
*for Political Bargaining*

Models which assume that school boards are unified actors ignore the internal struggles for influence over school policy among board members themselves. But school boards usually consist of five or more members each with his own interests, beliefs, perceptions and capabilities. They have different conceptions of the goals that the school board should maximize. They have different views of the way in which these goals could best be maximized. And they have differing sources of information coming from the school administrative staff and other sources. It is therefore essential to introduce a model which sees the decisions of the board as something other than maximizing common goals in an instrumentally rational fashion or as the product of the selective biases of the administrative staff. This model, which may be called the political bargaining model, conceptualizes the board as an arena within which various actors pursue differing ends with differential resources and with varying capabilities of resource mobilization. Decisions that are reached are the outcomes of the bargaining among the various actors.

The political bargaining model has been widely utilized for analyzing domestic policy-making in the United States. Case studies in urban politics and the legislative process have used the model extensively. Allison's particular achievement was to point out its utility for understanding foreign policy-making within the executive branch of the government. In so doing, however, Allison obscured the range of policy-making processes that can be subsumed under the political bargaining model. Allison observed that each actor has certain "stakes for which games are played."[17] This includes "each player's conception of the national interest, specific programs to which he is committed, the welfare of his friends, and his personal interests."[18] This inclusive listing of the stakes of political bargainers overlooks the fact that as the stakes vary, the character of bargaining games change dramatically. Rather than simply characterizing all such activities as bargaining games, it may prove helpful to distinguish at least three distinctive types of political bargaining which are distinguished by the varying assumptions made concerning the "stakes" of the decision-makers.

**Democratic bargaining**. The democratic decision-maker is the political leader who implements policies preferred by the majority of the population. He enacts majority preferences for the very self-interested reason that he is seeking to maximize his votes in the forthcoming election. In fact it is the ambitions of politicians which a number of analysts have identified as the key to the possibility in a large complex industrial society of a democratic polity where leaders are responsive to the will of the majority.[19] The democracy of a New England town meeting at which each citizen speaks his mind and the majority decides is impossible in all but the smallest and most homogeneous of communities. Yet the political leadership can implement what the majority prefer (or would prefer if they gave the matter their consideration) so long as the politicians are subject to popular control in free, competitive elections. The politician, ambitious to remain in office, will anticipate what the public wants and pursue the appropriate policies so that he will be rewarded with reelection.

Groups who wish to influence the decisions of democratic politicians must then shape public opinion in accord with their preferences and convince political leaders that the goals they favor coincide with the preferences of the majority. They will try to obtain the maximum amount of favorable publicity for their cause; they will supply evidence to show that their position is backed by large numbers of voters. The decision-maker, in turn, will wait for the development of coalitions that will aggregate group demands until a majority position has emerged; they will search for compromises which are supported by a majority.

Of course, democratic bargaining will not be found unless decision-makers are subject to the control of the electorate. Although theories of democratic bargaining usually treat free elections as a dichotomous variable which are either present or absent, the reality is more complex. School members vary in their dependence on the voting electorate even within a formally democratic polity. Some are appointed rather than elected, and terms of office vary in length. The comparatively obscure position that individual board members often play in the total political scene further limits their accountability to the voters. For these and other reasons, the democratic bargaining model must be supplemented by other models of the political process.

**Pluralist bargaining**. The pluralist decision-maker is the political leader who responds sympathetically to the legitimate interests of all groups participating in the political process.[20] The pluralist politician is not interested solely in reelection, and therefore he does not hinge his decisions simply on what the majority wants. Rather, he feels that there are a variety of groups in the city with an interest in the character of the school system, and that each group may appropriately seek to protect or enhance its interests. Although the pluralist is not cynically interested in reelection, he is realistic about the need for cooperation among a wide range of interests in order to keep a complex system as a viable functioning entity. The pluralist politician will search for ways of satisfying—at least minimally—the various competing interests that have a claim to be heard. The pluralist waits patiently in order to give all points of view an opportunity to express himself, takes into account the intensity with which various interests feel about the issue, and mediates a reasonable compromise.

In a pluralist bargaining situation groups focus their attention on the decision-makers. They seek to gather expert testimony that will show the impact of the policy on society as a whole, and, particularly, on their special interest. They will seek to convey this information to the decision-maker through both public and private channels, but the private channel may be used to convey the most critical information. Groups who have private as well as public access to the decision-makers are those that are regarded as having more legitimate stake in the outcome than groups given only public access, and their influence on the outcome is likely to be greater.

In contrast to the democratic bargaining game, in which decision-makers implement the preferences of the majority, the pluralist bargaining game may well be biased so as to prefer certain groups and interests over others, even when the latter are a numerically larger body of people.[21] Only groups which have been admitted to the institutionalized bargaining order are likely to carry much weight in the process.[22] These groups may be nothing other than the "power elite," "power structure," or "ruling class," as the economic, social, and/or cultural elite have been called by sociologists. In some cities the business community may be the only interest with legitimate covert access to decision-makers. But this is not necessarily the bias of all urban political systems in the United States. The institutionalized bargaining order may include organized labor, and it may include certain professional interests in particular policy areas. In fact in larger, more complex cities the institutionalized bargaining order is likely to change with the functional areas of urban policy. The bargaining order with respect to educational policy will usually include teachers, PTAs, educational reform groups, religious groups (reflecting the religious composition of the community), civic (re: business) leaders, and, in a union city, organized labor. In some cities ethnic and racial groups have recently been admitted to the institutionalized order, provided that they call for harmonious cooperative, and integrative relationships among nationality and racial groupings. In order to discover the particular bias of any specific institutionalized bargaining order, a detailed investigation of the policy-making process is required.

**Ideological bargaining.** The political ideologue reaches decisions that are in accord with his own well-elaborated system of beliefs. The decision-maker has a well-developed conception of the public interest, and he relies on this ideology to guide his decisions on controversial issues. His ideology may be consistent with the interests of the social groups of which he is a member. His ideology may be consistent with his political ambitions. He will nonetheless sacrifice the interests of his social group or his political ambitions on an ideological alter. The ideologue is therefore generally unpersuaded by group pressures, noisy demonstrations, lengthy public hearings, detailed private communiques. His political position is only likely to be shaken if (1) expert testimony indicates that the goal he is pursuing will not be achieved by the means that he had been intending to employ, or (2) individuals or groups with a known ideological preference that is similar to his have taken a contrary position on the issues at hand. The ideologue is not interested in compromise for its own sake; he will only compromise if forced to do so by the political power of the opposition. The ideologue sees the issues as conflicts over principles rather than as competition among various interests. Convinced of the correctness of his position, the ideologue is not likely to stray from it if he is simply subjected to the traditional tactics and strategies of group politics. Rather, he will become angry with the "pressure" being placed upon him, and will feel it is his duty to stand up against these pressures.

The consistency of the belief system of ideologues produces reasonably consistent actions by individual ideological bargainers over time and across a range of issues. Ideological actors will see a variety of problems from a consistent perspective, they will see interrelationships among the various policy questions with which they must deal, and they will attempt to establish a consistent orientation with respect to most of them. In contrast, the pluralist politician will pursue conflicting ends as he moves from one position to another simply in order to distribute benefits to all groups within the institutionalized order. The democratic politician will be only as consistent as his electorate, a population which is not known for its stability or consistency on most political matters.

Consequently, a crucial group strategy will be to place ideologically allied actors in strategically placed positions. Groups seek to elect or to have appointed favorably predisposed ideologues to authoritative positions where they can promote policies of interest to the group. In fact groups prefer ideological to pluralist decision-makers whenever the decision-maker is ideologically convinced that the position of the group is right, for the ideological decision-maker will try without being pressured to protect the group's interest rather than simply responding to mobilized group influence. On the other hand, if the decision-maker is ideologically opposed to group's position, the group is at a severe disadvantage. Whereas in the democratic bargaining process groups could win victories simply by demonstrating that they *could* defeat decision-makers, in ideological opponents (i.e., remove them from office) in order to win policy victories.

Decisional outcomes in an ideological bargaining game will be determined by the ideologically dominant perspective among those in authoritative positions; an ideologically cohesive majority can administer regular and repeated defeats to the minority. Change can occur quickly, but this is most likely to happen when decision-makers change.

**Three types of bargaining models**. These three types of political bargaining models range along a dimension that makes varying assumptions about the degree to which decision-makers act according to explicit principles. The democratic politician is a purely self-interested, ambitious politician who is entirely unprincipled in his behavior. The pluralist politician is guided by only the most general principle that decisions must not threaten the vital interests of any member of the institutionalized bargaining order. Within that framework the decision-maker is permitted considerable latitude. The political ideologue, on the other hand, has a set of programatically relevant principles that give more or less explicit guidelines on particular policy issues, which the ideologue regards binding upon him. The ideologue may be willing to compromise these principles, if this is necessary in order to get the necessary political support. But the acceptance of less than a "whole loaf" is done only when it is politically expedient and never on the grounds that compromise is a good in itself. The political ideologue is the polar opposite of the democratic politician along a continuum of principled versus unprincipled action.

These are analytic models, it must be repeated. It is difficult, if not impossible, to comprehend and interpret the motives of political actors. Did a board member act for reasons of political ambition, out of a desire for compromise, or out of a conviction that his decision was the only option that was in accord with his principles? Any attempt to suggest the "real" reasons for the decision are inevitably doomed to fail. On the other hand, some assumptions about the bases of political action are more useful than others. Some assumptions can explain a wide range of actions over an extended period of time. They are more consistent with the totality of available data on decision-making. They may even have predictive value. Although these assumptions cannot be shown to correspond with the "real" reasons for the decisions, they are nonetheless extremely useful for understanding, interpreting and even predicting political action.

Political bargaining models differ from the rational decision-making model in that they do not assume constant rationality on the part of political actors. Bargainers may or may not be maximizing their goals in the most instrumentally rational fashion. In fact the outcome of bargaining games will not simply be a function of the distribution of political resources among actors but also a function of their effectiveness (i.e., rationality) in bargaining situations. Political bargaining models also suggest that policies of a group of decision-makers may not be instrumentally rational implementation of specific policy goals because (1) no majority of actors agree on policy goals and therefore compromises must be reached which no one would fully endorse; (2) the majority may have agreed policy goals but the political ambitions or the desire for compromise among one or more members of the majority may inhibit the realization of those policy goals; or (3) members of a majority may differ in their assessment of the proper means of implementing the policy goal and in the bargaining process compromise on a solution which is not only *not* the most efficient but even is recognized by all concerned that it is not the best alternative. Thus, the political bargaining model, as does the organizational processes model, points to a set of constraints on actors which limits the utility of the rational decision-making model.

Nonetheless, there is a point where the distinction between political bargaining models and rational decision-making models disappears. If the requisite number of decision-makers (for enacting authoritative policies) consists of political ideologues who have an agreed set of policy goals and agree on the most rational strategy for implementing these goals, the result of the bargaining among them will be identical to the result predicted by the rational decision-making model. The rational decision-making model thus becomes a specific case of a particular political bargaining model. But this special case assumes an agreement on goals and means which, if it existed, would hardly call for processes that could be called bargaining. Then it is more useful to assume the decision-making body as a rational decision-maker than as a group of political bargainers.

## Conclusions

The policy-making process is complex; any single model of decision-making will either be so general as to be tautological or, in being more specific, provide only a partial explanation for the decision. Drawing on the insights that Allison has brought together, we have in this paper sought to develop three major different models of decision-making—the rational, the organizational, and the political bargaining. We have found it necessary to further explicate the political bargaining model by developing three subtypes of bargaining processes. In our analysis of Chicago school politics we hope to develop further the interrelationships among these models and show the way in which they can be usefully applied to the study of urban educational politics.

## Notes

1. A pioneering article on the politics of education articulated this viewpoint. See Thomas H. Eliot, "Toward an Understanding of Public School Politics," *American Political Science Review* 53 (December, 1959), 1032-51. See also Roscoe C. Martin, *Government and the Suburban School* (Syracuse, New York: Syracuse University Press, 1962), pp. 69-75.

2. This widely used definition of the political system is taken from David Easton, *The Political System* (New York: Alfred Knopf, 1963).

3. The approach developed in this paper has quite obviously been influenced by Graham Allison, "Conceptual Models and the Cuban Missile Crisis," *American Political Science Review* 63 (September, 1969), 689-718.

4. The example is taken from Julian Feldman and Herschel E. Kanter, "Organizational Decision-Making," in James G. March (ed.), *Handbook of Organizations*, (Chicago: Rand McNally & Co., 1965), pp. 615-617.

5. Profit-maximizing and utility theories, as used by economists are discussed in Ibid., pp. 629-636.

6. Anthony Downs, *An Economic Theory of Democracy* (New York: Harper & Brothers, 1957).

7. Norman Frolich, Joseph Oppenheimer, and Oran R. Young, *A Theory of Leadership* (Manuscript, 1969).

8. E.W. Kelley, "Utility Theory and Political Coalitions: Problems of Operationalization," in Sven Groennings, E.W. Kelley, and Michael Leiserson (eds.), *The Study of Coalition Behavior* (New York: Holt, Rinehart and Winston, 1970), p. 473.

9. Talcott Parsons, *The Structure of Social Action* (New York: Free Press, 1968), p. 58.

10. Ibid., p. 59.

11. Ibid.

12. The concepts of systems analysis are an example of this rational approach.

13. Allison, 700.

14. The whole problem is most adequately discussed in Richard Flathman, *The Public Interest* (New York: John Wiley & Sons, 1964). See also Hanna Pitkin, *The Concept of Representation* (Berkeley: University of California Press, 1967), Ch. VII-IX.

15. For more on this problem, see Paul E. Peterson, "Forms of Representation: Participation of the Poor in the Community Action Program," *American Political Science Review* 64 (June, 1970).

16. Union recognition, not pay increases, was the key issue in the first major New York City school teacher's strike in November, 1960. See Stephen Cole, *The Unionization of Teachers* (New York: Praeger, 1969), pp. 170-172.

17. Allison, 710.

18. Ibid.

19. In addition to Downs work, cited earlier, this perspective has been set forth in Joseph A. Schumpeter, *Capitalism, Socialism and Democracy* (New York: Holt, Rinehart & Winston, 1960); V.O. Key *The Responsible Electorate* (Cambridge, Mass.: Harvard University Press, 1966); and Robert Dahl, *Who Governs?* (New Haven: Yale University Press, 1961). See also Joseph Schlesinger, *Ambition and Politics* (Chicago: Rand, McNally & Co., 1966). Empirical data showing that many local politicians do not appear to be ambitious and a discussion of the problems this raises for political representation in local communities can be found in Kenneth Prewitt and Heinz Eulau, "Political Matrix and Political Representation: Prolegomenon to a New Departure from an Old Problem," *American Political Science Review* 63 (June, 1969), 427-441.

20. An early, pluralist classic is Robert A. Dahl and Charles E. Lindblom's, *Politics, Economics, and Welfare* (New York: Harper & Row, 1953). See, especially, Ch. XII. See also Charles E. Lindblom, "The Science of Muddling Through," *Public Administration Review* 19 (1959), 79-88. The model is applied to urban politics in Norton E. Long, "The Local Community as an Ecology of Games," *American Journal of Sociology* 64 (November, 1958), 251-261, which is reprinted in Edward Banfield (ed.), *Urban Government* (New York: Free Press, 1969), pp. 465-479. The definitive study of New York City politics, a city for which the pluralist bargaining model seems peculiarly appropriate, is written from this viewpoint. See Wallace Sayre and Herbert Kaufman, *Governing New York City* (New York: W.W. Norton, 1965).

21. As Schattschneider has put it, in the interest group utopia, "the heavenly chorus sings with a strong upper accent." E.E. Schattschneider, *The Semisovereign People* (New York: Holt, Rinehart and Winston, 1960), p. 35. The bias of the pluralist bargaining system is also discussed in Peter Bachrach and Morton S. Baratz, "Two Faces of Power," *American Political Science Review* 56 (December, 1962), 947-62.

22. The institutionalized bargaining order consists of those vested interests which are generally recognized by policy-makers as legitimate participants in the policy-making process whose vital interests need to be considered in reaching decisions. For a fuller discussion, see J. David Greenstone and Paul E. Peterson, *Politics and Participation* (Russell Sage Foundation, forthcoming).

# 10 Who Governs American Education: Research Strategies

HARMON L. ZEIGLER, JR.

In proposing a topic for research, I will violate several traditions which have appeared with startling persistence in the youthful field of the politics of education. First, I do *not* propose to study political socialization. Second, I do *not* propose to use systems theory as a basis for gathering information.

Concerning political socialization, I am not impressed with the arguments of Hess and Torney that the school is the major agent of socialization. The jury is still out on the question, and I suspect that the most feasible way to seek an answer is through longitudinal research.

Concerning systems theory, there is little point in reviewing the numerous essays by political scientists and educationists trying to fit existing research into this mold. I am in agreement with those who argue that systems theory is, in essence, a useful device in raising appropriate questions, e.g., in ordering our hunches. Professor Wirt's bibliographic essay at the end of this volume expresses this viewpoint well.

Instead of building a research problem out of systems theory, I propose to ask a question asked frequently by many who have no recourse to systems theory. As phrased some years ago by Gross, the question is simply: who runs our schools? Lest this question appear too mundane, let me suggest that, as of now, there is no clear answer to this question. I believe that little is actually known about the relative distribution of influence among the various potential and actual participants in the educational decision-making process.

The list of such participants is not necessarily simple to develop. If one were studying, say, the Congress, enough previous research on this *single* institution exists so as to give one a pretty good starting point. However, there are approximately 19,000 school districts; and relatively little is known about them. When one considers the singular functions of school systems, the salience of education to parents and children, and the tremendous investment of financial resources, there is little reason to doubt the political significance of school systems. Unfortunately, one searches in vain for systematic studies of school districts of the sort characterizing other political institutions in the United States. To be sure the surge of political socialization studies and the flurry of reports dealing with teacher militancy and racial desegregation have brought to the fore the essentially political character of schools. There are, also, occasional case studies which treat various aspects of the schools from the point of view of the political process. But only a handful of studies can be described as having approached the public schools as political institutions. Even fewer have considered the attack in terms of how and to what end schools are governed.

Given the paucity of evidence, our first task is *not* more theory. Our job is to compile a list of participants in the governing of schools and assess the influence of each. While making no pretense at inclusiveness, I suggest that we consider the activities of the following participants: (1) administrators, (2) school boards, (3) teachers, (4) interest groups, (5) students. I recognize that this list is based upon the assumption that the basic locus of control is *local*, hence the exclusion of state departments of education and the various federal agencies with an interest in education. I am excluding state and national participants solely because the sheer magnitude of the task of assessing local influentials is staggering. I also recognize that, in even preparing a list, certain assumptions about the governing process appear to be made. For instance, does not the presentation of a list assume that influence is distributed among those various agents *irrespective of the nature of the struggle for influence*? I do not think that it does. That is, I anticipate that the ranking of the participants would vary from issue to issue and from one type of district to another. However, in spite of this "pluralistic" assumption, I still think it likely that for *most* districts and on *most* issues, the ranking will remain fairly stable.

To illustrate, Crain argued that, with respect to decisions about integration, the school board was able to seize the initiative and operate the schools in a manner that was displeasing to the superintendent. However, since Crain was interested in only a single issue, it is possible that—had he studied the other conflicts—the superintendent would have proven to be dominant. Thus, in the districts studied by Crain, it is likely that the single issue of integration was a small portion of the decisions made and that, in an overall assessment, the role of the board was substantially less than his research would lead us to conclude.

Let us consider the list of participants, in some detail, having dealt with these troublesome questions.

**1. The school board and the superintendent.** There are approximately 121,000 board members with the formal responsibility of running the schools. Although I cannot be certain, I suspect that there are more board members than, say, city council members; yet we know virtually nothing (other than the usual information, e.g., they are disproportionately representative of the middle and upper-middle classes) about them. Compared to other units of government, school boards are a dark continent.

I think we should explore school board behavior because school boards are a symbol of one of the prevailing mythologies of American education: local control of the decision-making process by laymen. Why the American system of education has its foundations in such an ideology is the subject of a variety of explanations, most of which make reference to the cultural traditions of an emergent society or, if the writer is of a particularly bitter frame of mind, to the anti-intellectualism and distrust of "experts" which is—so the assumption was—part and parcel of the exuberent and youthful democratic traditions of the country. Contrast America with England, for example, where school boards were abolished precisely because it was decided that laymen had no business meddling in the affairs of professionals. While similar proposals are occasionally made in this country, there is clearly no social support for such radical tinkering with the mechanisms of "participatory democracy."

In spite of the persistence of such an ideology, the researchable question is: how can such laymen compete with experts. What resources can they muster and how do they use these resources? The ideology of lay control does not have the benefit of a reasonably articulate set of defenders while the educational system itself has been producing a corps of professional managers whose ideology—while hardly consensual—is more carefully promulgated than is that of the proponents of lay control. School superintendents, subject to a relatively uniform (in contrast to board members) occupational recruitment pattern, possess an occupational ideology which is somewhat at variance with the traditional mythology as described above. This ideology centers on expert autonomy for the superintendent and a fiduciary role for the board. Such an ideology is hardly unique to school superintendents and no doubt is shared by the various professions which, taken collectively, comprise the revolutionary cadre of the "managerial revolution."

The available evidence suggests that superintendents take a dimmer view of the supervisory responsibilities of boards of education than do board members themselves. Assuming, therefore, that superintendents and boards have competing ideologies, who wins and why?

It is perhaps natural for a superintendent—whether the prototype of the Lasswellian power hungry politico or not—to find it annoying to have a half-dozen or so relatively uninformed laymen bustling around in matters believed to be purely administrative. Superintendents might make the old, absurd, but remarkably persistent distinction between policy and administration. If such a distinction is being made, it may well have very little to do with the actual division of responsibilities between board and superintendent. While empirical studies of board-superintendent relations are rather sparse, the thrust of available evidence suggests that, desires and aspirations to the contrary, school boards do relatively little supervising and a great deal of delegating responsibility. But certainly this is not always the case. A great deal depends on the issue, the community, etc. On the one hand we have arguments that school boards perform the function of legitimating the policies of the school system to the community, rather than representing the various segments of the community to the school administrators. On the other hand, there are certainly some boards which, if nothing else, nip at the heels of superintendents. There are, in other words, contexts within which the superintendent is placed under strong constraint by the board.

What are these conditions? One possible avenue of inquiry is the relation between board-superintendent conflict and general community conflict. It is well known that superintendents—in addition to their expert role—also espouse an ideology of education being above politics. Whatever nonsense is contained in this ideology, there is, from the point of view of the superintendent, probably a great deal of common sense in isolating the educational from the general political system. When community conflict reaches the board level, does the tendency to supervise the superintendent increase?

Another way of looking at the same problem is to think of routinized versus nonroutinized decisions. Given the greater technical resources of the superintendent, his relative expertise in matters of management, and his commitment to his career, it is perhaps to be expected that board members will avoid challenges to professional authority if the issue can be phrased in such a manner as to make professional authority a negotiable resource. Perhaps Crain's study of integration can best be understood as a category of decision for which there was no professional authority.

Perhaps, then, the strategy of the "successful" superintendent is to avoid phrasing issues in terms which tap the emotions of diverse and competing segments of the public. If this is done, then the competition between a full-time professional and less committed participants is likely to be highly uneven. The unequal distribution of resources between professionals and laymen helps to understand the cooptation of board members, a pervasive theme in the literature of organizations. The ability of managers to master the complex flow of information, to rely upon the capabilities of a staff, and to devote a major portion of their time to a problem are resources unmatched by comparable ones on the part of board members. Unlike many elected public officials, school board members typically do not speak for a clearly defined functional or geographical constituency. Unless an issue is clearly beyond the professional competence of the superintendent, as was apparently the case with desegregation, board members appear to be at a disadvantage. It is probable, therefore, that school boards are somewhat more acquiescent than are other public bodies in their relations with administrative officers.

To reduce the problems described above to workable proportions, we might focus upon the existence of opponents to the superintendent. The questions are:

1. On how many boards does a substantial proportion of the members frequently oppose the superintendent?
2. In what kinds of communities does opposition develop? In addition to the usual ecological variables, I have in mind ascertaining something about the level of support for education, gathered from surveys and from the outputs of the community (frequency of defeat for bond or tax levies, for example).
3. What kinds of *formal* structures of decision-making foster opposition to the superintendent? The formal structures in which decisions are made have been

the focus of widespread concern on the part of various reformers in both local government and educational administration. Indeed, most of the energy on the part of reformers was directed toward various institutional modifications on the assumption that "desirable" behavioral consequences would flow logically and naturally from these modifications. In municipal reform, the nonpartisan ballot and city-wide elections, for example, were instituted because such forms would keep "politics" out of local decision-making. If there is no Democratic or Republican way to collect the garbage it is even more true, according to the rationale of reformers, that there is no Democratic or Republican way to educate children. Accordingly, school boards are constructed so as to minimize partisan conflict. Nevertheless, there is enough variation to enable us to examine the relation of opposition to the superintendent with (a) whether elections to the board are partisan or nonpartisan, (b) whether elections are district or at large, (c) whether school related elections are held simultaneously with other elections, (d) the frequency of elections, and (e) the legal term of office. All of these variables can be linked theoretically to the exacerbation or softening of conflict that has been presumed to encourage certain sorts of pressures. For instance, we would hypothesize that district elections would create more constituency pressure and hence provide a base of resources for opposition to the superintendent.

4. What is the internal control of succession to the board? Are board members subject to electoral opposition? Are incumbents regularly returned to office? These variables give us some idea of the "openness" of the system. The more open the system, the greater the conflict between board and superintendent.

5. How are board members recruited? The recruitment of board members might be linked with their behavior toward the superintendent. It may be that the reasons for seeking the job and the manner in which a person is recruited are of equal influence to the occupational socialization of the job itself. Recruitment should be a good predictor of socialization which, in turn, should help us understand the way a person looks at the world. Of course, such a clear model is not necessarily empirically true. For instance, there is apparently little relationship between the role orientations of legislators and city councilmen and their patterns of recruitment. In our case the possibility of a linkage may be high because it may be possible to discover that opponents and supporters of the superintendent had different reference groups prior to their becoming school board members, or that opposition to the superintendent was a part of a potential board member's intellectual baggage before he joined the board. Basically, my concern over recruitment centers upon whether or not opponents and supporters are recruited by agents from within the "educational establishment" or by agents from within the general political system, such as by groups whose interest extends to matters other than education. It may also be that opposition is more likely to take place when board members are "self-starters" without any organizational ties to the community.

6. What are the resources of board members. Essentially, resources are weapons in an exchange, assuming that both parties to the exchange are contesting the authority of the other. Those who deal in exchange theory propose two categories of resources: (a) detachable, and (b) nondetachable. A detachable resource is one that is transferable, e.g., not linked to a unique individual while the opposite is true of nondetachable resources. For instance, organizational membership is detachable but socioeconomic status is not. With regard to detachable resources, a further distinction can be made. Resources can also be internal or external. External resources, which are brought by the board member to the interaction with the superintendent, might be the control of a bloc of votes, or the representation of an identifiable constituency. Internal resources might be typified by technical knowledge which, as we have suggested, is a resource monopolized by the superintendent.

In a sense, the competition between the board and the superintendent might be viewed as one of external versus internal resources, with the board, because of its legal status, having greater access to external resources and the superintendent, because of his training and the requirements of his job, gaining easier access to internal resources.

Resources of board members which may influence level of opposition to the superintendent are: length of tenure, socioeconomic status, organizational membership, and interaction with community groups.

7. What are the values of opponents and supporters? Is the superintendent the defender of the status quo, as Crain has suggested, or are boards more likely to play this role?

**2. Teachers and students.** Although teacher militancy has become an increasingly important topic of research among educationists and political scientists, there are many unanswered questions relating to their role in the governing of schools. For the sake of feasibility, I propose to limit the research on teachers and students to their rising expectations for participation in decision-making. American school systems have traditionally been organized along fairly hierarchical lines, with teachers and students occupying a position near the bottom. In spite of the surge of militancy, the available evidence suggests that these underdog groups remain without much power in their competition with school boards and superintendents. There is also evidence, however, that the actual role of teachers and students and their aspirations are at variance. What appears to be happening in education is a small reproduction of what is happening in the larger society: groups with an inferior influence position are seeking to expand their power.

The difference between these groups and school boards is that there is very little ideological support for an expanded role in the decision-making process. Teachers like to think of themselves as "professionals" but it is difficult to agree with this self-concept. Among other attributes, professionals are supposed to have some degree of autonomy in exercising their special competence. Yet teachers cannot exercise much independent authority even within the classroom to which they are assigned. There is among teachers an "employee" orientation which requires a basic loyalty to the "boss" (the superintendent and the school board). Yet it is apparent that, even if the employee orientation is dominant, some teachers hold a genuinely professional view, which impels them to seek to expand their power at the expense of administrators and lay authorities.

If teachers have traditionally adopted a subservient position, this is even a more accurate description of the role of students. If those who have traditionally held power have resisted the demands of teachers, they have done so even more vehemently with regard to the demands of students. Further, when student demands are voiced, teachers frequently find themselves defending the status quo.

In essence, we have the opportunity to study the conflict between a growing professionalism on the part of teachers and growing dissatisfaction on the part of students and the authoritarian structure of the school bureaucracy. The researchable questions are:

1. What is the extent of militant professionalism among teachers? Estimates now range from between 10 and 40 percent, depending upon the measure used.
2. What proportion of students are seriously interested in taking a more active role?
3. What kinds of school board members and superintendents are likely to respond with favor on demands from below?
4. How much support from external sources, e.g., the public, can teachers and students expect? Tentative evidence indicates that there is substantial public support for a greater voice for teachers, but considerably less among school board members and superintendents. Presumably, the public is much less tolerant of students; certainly boards and superintendents have taken a dim view of student power.

**3. Interest Groups**. Another threat to the status quo comes in the form of various segments of the public. Some evidence of a decline in public support can be seen in the rise in the proportion of local bond issues rejected. While the "taxpayers revolt" might be a fruitful topic of research, we are better off examining the role of *intermediaries* between citizens and officials, e.g., special interest groups. As early as 1958 Gross asserted that interest groups were occasionally successful in exerting pressure to split the board and weaken financial support. On the other hand, Crain has argued that interest groups were of little consequence in influencing the course of integration decisions. The problem here, as elsewhere, is that studies have usually been issue specific, with no effort being made to develop a general notion of the role of interest groups in school governance. The appropriate task is one of uncovering the influential groups in educational decision-making and assessing the overall impact of group activity upon the decision-making process. The questions are:

1. What is the inventory of groups whose activities come to the attention of decision-makers? Is the pressure predominantly from the "right" or the "left"?
2. What is the intensity of group activity? It is probably true that some boards operate in an environment relatively free of group activity, while others are besieged by interest groups. We need to know the factors associated with variations in group activity. Some possible clues are: the complexity of the community (group demands should be more intense in complex social environments); the level of stress within the community (interest group activity should become more intense as stress increases); the extent to which the structure of board decision-making is "political" (interest group activity should be more intense in more political structures).
3. What are the consequences of group activity? If we view interest groups as bargaining agents in the allocation of public resources, then we need to know what difference they make in the way school districts conduct their business. We raised the question earlier of whether or not interest groups thrive in an atmosphere of heightened tension. Does it therefore follow that group activity might contribute to heightened tension which accompanies a decline in public confidence? Imagine, for example, a school district suffering a decline in public support. Assuming that interest groups will probably become active in this district, does their activity translate the loss of confidence into observable phenomena? What is needed is some measure of the consequences of group activity which would tap the dimensions of "issue arousal" and "issue disposal." I am thinking, for example, of the relation, if any relation exists between interest group activity and, say, financial defeats or superintendent turnover.

### The Strategy of Research

The strategy of research can be understood as consisting of two parts: macro-analysis and micro-analysis. The theoretical justification for reliance upon two levels of analysis stems from my desire to generalize about the American educational system while at the same time providing detailed information about the vagaries of the decision-making process. Given this set of requirements, the strategy is one of broadly based survey research and detailed case analysis, based upon the generalizations of the survey research, to provide follow-up information.

Neither survey research nor case analysis is solely adequate for the task, since each method has inherent weaknesses. The weaknesses of survey research are that its findings are based upon reports of behavior rather than observations of behavior: it is difficult to describe the decisional process in any detail based upon these reports. The weakness of the case method is that, in order to generalize, we must commit the fallacy of reasoning by analogy. That is to say, because two units are structurally, functionally, or behaviorally homologous, i.e., there is real or near identity between them, it does not follow that we can treat them as analogies and assume that statements about one are as good as statements about the other. This is why the case approach has had remarkably low theoretical yield.

The strategy thus consists of two distinct phases. In the first phase, the survey, we need to select a relatively large number of school districts. In these districts, interviews would be taken with superintendents, school board members, teachers, students, and the general public. Of course, I recognize the extraordinary problems and expense in conducting such a survey, but the utility of gaining comparative data from a variety of groups is sufficient stimulus to press on with the job. In this phase, the analysis should be primarily at the nonindividual level. Although the information is necessarily based upon individual responses, the data should not be analyzed primarily in the traditional fashion of tabular presentation of individual responses. Although the individuals *in* a group and the group as a whole make decisions simultaneously, in the real world of decision-making; it is the group as a whole and not the individual members which is the effective decision-maker. It follows that we want to make statements about the group as a whole rather than the behavior of its component parts. This is particularly true in my case since I want to compare the behavior of many groups. Of course it is impossible to observe the behavior of the group without observing the behavior of the individuals in the group. As Eulau suggests, the solution is to bring all the unit's properties to the same level of analysis.

To illustrate, interviews with the entire population of teachers, much less citizens, of a district is obviously impossible. However, it is quite feasible to interview all the members of a school board. To take the example of opposition to the superintendent, boards can be classified simply according to the proportions of opponents. Or to take the example of interest group activity, we should be able to develop a measure of group intensity for each district. If the data can be expressed at this level, then causal modeling, or at least multiple regression, should be employed.

In this first phase, we will also need to make some decisions about the kinds of districts to be selected for more detailed analysis. Some possible alternatives are: (1) classifying districts according to the level of tension and selecting districts which typify each level of tension; (2) classifying districts according to the extent of conflict between board and superintendent; (3) classifying districts according to whether influence is largely in the hands of the superintendent, the board or both.

## References

Robert Crain. *The Politics of School Desegregation*. Chicago: Aldine, 1968.
Heinz Eulau. *Micro-Macro Political Analysis*. Chicago: Aldine, 1969.

Neal Gross. *Who Runs Our Schools*. New York: John Wiley, 1958.

Robert Hess and Judith Torney. *The Development of Political Attitudes in Children*. Chicago: Aldine, 1967.

M. Kent Jennings and Harmon Ziegler. "Interest Representation in School Governance." Paper prepared for 1970 meeting of the American Political Science Association, Los Angeles, California.

Michael Kirst. *The Politics of Education at the Federal, State, Local Levels*. Berkeley: McCutchan, 1969.

Alan Rosenthal. *Pedagogues and Power*. Syracuse: Syracuse University Press, 1969.

Alan Rosenthal. *Governing Education*. Garden City: Doubleday, 1969.

Harmon Ziegler. *The Political World of the High School Teacher*. Eugene: Center for Advanced Study of Educational Administration, 1966.

Harmon Ziegler and M. Kent Jennings. "Response Styles and Politics: The Case of School Boards." Paper prepared for the annual meeting of the American Educational Research Association, March, 1970, Minneapolis, Minn.

# 11

## School Decentralization in the Context of Community Control: Some Neglected Considerations

DANIEL J. ELAZAR

### The Problem

The demand for community control of the schools is usually understood as a demand by blacks and other racial or quasi-racial minorities for greater control over the institutions within their inner-city "ghettos."[1] In fact, it is, in one form or another, a well-nigh universal demand in the United States today, one that transcends the immediate interests of inner-city residents, important as they are. Indeed, the demand for community control is not a new demand but simply a restatement of one as American as mother's proverbial apple pie.[2] It has simply been brought back into the public eye by the militancy of blacks, Puerto Ricans, and Chinese in the country's great central cities in their search for a right common to most Americans but which they have never been able to exercise.

The demand for decentralization of big city school systems, which includes the demand for control over the personnel responsible for the schools within them, is the most widely recognized element in the quest for community control, but is not the only aspect of that quest. Suburban residents' desire to maintain relatively small independent school districts is of the same order. But because the suburban school systems were constituted in that way from the first, their demand does not involve a militant campaign for the attainment of the objective. Still suburbanites must wage more subdued campaigns to maintain their version of community control. Their situation generally goes unrecognized for what it is and, worse than that, is usually attacked for what it is not. One additional dimension has now been added to the suburban interest in community control. It was in the suburbs that the notion that education was somehow "not political" reached its peak. With the erosion of that idea, one finds growing demands in the suburbs for moderating the professional educators' control over the schools and injecting greater citizen participation at least in the shaping of educational policy. This, too, is part of the demand for community control, one that is no different in its essentials, from that of the inner-city minorities.[3]

Finally, the demand for community control of the schools still flickers in the "peripheral" areas of the United States, in those small town and rural communities which have borne the brunt of the consolidation movement of the past generation and were the first to lose control at the immediate community level for the sake of principles of administrative and organizational efficiency wide-

179

spread in educational circles beginning a generation ago. While the reduction in the number of school districts from a high of approximately 125,000 some thirty years ago to the present 19,000 or so has virtually eliminated the question in its original form for many communities, the reshaping of the communities themselves in light of technological changes connected with the metropolitan frontier has no doubt revived it in the new, consolidated districts. In these districts there is the added problem of how to maintain community control while at the same time maintaining a sufficiently comprehensive educational program manned by personnel of sufficiently high caliber.

All three situations described above reflect different but equally meaningful dimensions of the quest for community control. In all three, two other problems remain crucial factors in the quest: school finance and racial segregation. Virtually no school system today is immune from budgetary problems while the demand for equalization of fiscal resources, whether on a metropolitan, statewide, or national level, has become an insistent one. Regardless of the level of political interest in community control, the fiscal problems must be solved if it is to be considered a viable arrangement. At the same time, political decisions can be taken that will adequately deal with the fiscal issues within a context that provides for community control, if such should be the will of those who shape the political decisions involved.[4]

Racial segregation as an issue is intimately tied to the entire question of community control, especially since the whites' argument for segregated schools generally has been couched in those terms. There are even strong hints of it in the black militants' present demands for the same in their areas. By its very existence as an issue, it raises questions about the limits and possibilities of the demand within a national society such as that of the United States.[5]

The question that is placed before those concerned with education and politics is precisely that, to determine the possibilities, limits, and likely consequences of community control of the schools or its alternatives. This is essentially a political question. That is to say there are no extra-political considerations that will automatically determine how the decisions on community control should go. Rather, by taking particular political decisions it will be possible to shape the other factors in the way in which we want them to be shaped, either to enhance or limit the possibilities for real and realistic community control.

**The Perspective**

While we are concerned here with the demand for community control of schools, we must begin any inquiry into the meaning and likely consequences of that demand and its satisfaction or frustration by understanding that it is part of a larger demand for community self-government.[6] Again, just as the suburban experience is especially useful in defining the meaning of this demand in the case of the schools, so is it useful in defining the demand for community self-government generally.

The political meaning of the development of suburbs lies in just that area. People sought *suburbanization* for essentially private purposes, revolving around better living conditions. The same people sought *suburbs* with independent local governments of their own for essentially public ones, namely the ability to maintain those conditions by joining with like-minded neighbors to perserve those life styles which they sought in suburbanization. They soon discovered that control of three great functions was necessary to provide a solid foundation for meaningful local self-government: (a) control of zoning to maintain the physical and social character of their surroundings; (b) control of the police to protect their property as they wished it protected and to maintain the public aspects of their common value system; and (c) control of their schools to develop an educational program for their children that met their perceived needs and pocketbooks. It has become evident over and over again that suburbanites will fight as hard as necessary to retain control over three broad functions as long as they see them threatened by "outsiders" who would change them in such a way as to alter the life styles of their communities.[7] The suburbanites' instincts were quite correct in all this. Despite the thrust toward centralization in American society, control over these three functions does maintain the kind of local control which they desire, in most cases.[8]

The functions that suburbanites will fight to retain as "close to home" as possible are essentially the same as those presently being demanded by blacks in the great cities who wish the same rights as their suburban countrymen for their neighborhoods (most of which are not really neighborhoods at all but congeries of neighborhoods with populations as great as those of the more substantial suburbs, if not of large cities). They, too, justify those demands on the grounds that it is necessary for them to control their destiny in these public matters in order to be able to achieve their private and public goals. Given the premises from which they began, they are indeed correct. The same reasons lie behind the efforts of peripheral communities outside of metropolitan America to maintain their institutions of self-government.

The struggle over community control is necessarily conducted within the context of the American political system and is accordingly bound by that system. Thus, it is not a struggle for the recreation of the sovereign *polis* (except perhaps in the minds of the most extreme militants) but for the achievement of maximum local control over vital public functions in a properly-scaled locality. Most Americans of whatever race, creed or ethnic origin, share common values and goals as Americans. What they seek are variations on the "American way of life," not completely separate ways. Thus they strive for the kind of local control that makes the maintenance of those variations possible, not local separatism. Moreover, they strive for that control within the context of a meaningfully-sized place, the definition of which has changed periodically throughout American history.

The most pronounced characteristic of the American system, from this perspective, is its federal character and the precise nature of that federalism. In the first place, the very existence of federalism offers the possibilities of legitimately achieving a very substantial degree of community self-government within the system. Indeed, one might say that the existence of federalism creates the conditions and stimulates the demand for community self-government. Regarding the second, the highly intertwined system of cooperative relationships linking governments on all three planes—federal, state, and local—in common action to perform functions and deliver services shapes the limits and the possibilities for community self-government. Both of these aspects will be further treated below.[9]

## The Schools and the Civil Community

Understanding of the problem of community control must begin with the exploration of two questions: how is the community to be delineated and what is the place of the schools within it. In the United States, communities are essentially artificial (meaning consciously man-made) creations purposely founded and organized in the course of the country's development by people with immediate common interests, often of the most narrow economic character or for the most limited social purposes. With some rare exceptions, they have not been organic entities embracing all of life and linking the same families over generations, nor were they ever conceived to be. Rather, their residents are linked by the need to commonly pursue certain interests that thereby take on a political or civil character. Hence they are best understood as *civil communities*, people living in a common territory bound together for political or civil purposes. The maintenance of common political goals provides the basis for community and the existence of institutions designed to pursue those goals provides its framework.[10]

Given the nature of the American political system, which tends to encourage what is often called "fragmentation" of government on the local plane, responsibility for the maintenance of those goals is usually entrusted to many different institutions which can be grouped in "sets." Taken together, they create the institutional "bundle" that gives shape to a particular civil community, defines its limits and character, and serves its needs. The sets are:

1. the formally established local governments serving a particular locality, such as the municipal governments, the county, the school districts, and the like;
2. the local agencies of the state and federal governments insofar as they are adjuncts of the local community existing primarily to serve it, such as the local branches of the state employment office and the post office;
3. the public nongovernmental bodies serving local governmental or quasi-governmental purposes, such as the chamber of commerce and the community welfare council;

4. the political parties or factions functioning within the civil community to organize political competition;
5. the system of interest groups functioning in the local political area to represent the various local interests; and
6. the body of written constitutional material and unwritten tradition serving as a framework within which sanctioned political action must take place and as a check against unsanctioned political behavior.

The foregoing governmental, public nongovernmental quasi-governmental institutions are linked with each other and with the local citizenry through a congeries of "games," (the "education game" is a major one) any of which will involve some or all of them. These "games" in turn create "complexes" which represent the institutionalized relationships between the governmental and nongovernmental, public and private participants. These "games" and the "complexes" which participate in and manage them reflect the political dynamics of community in each locality.[11]

In a very real sense a civil community consists of the sum of the politically relevant "complexes" and "games" which function in a given locality and which are tied together in a single bundle of governmental activities and services. This bundle of governmental activities and services is manipulated in the locality to serve the local political values system. There is no standard set of political jurisdictions that can be used to delineate the individual civil community. Each civil community must be delineated in its own terms. In any particular, the territorial basis of the civil community may consist of a city or township, an entire county or other regional political entity, a school district, a regional planning district, or the like.

The schools and the "games" which surround them are subsumed under one or more of the foregoing categories. The public schools are among the local governments while the parochial and perhaps even the private schools can be counted among the public nongovernmental institutions.

Not every entity with its own local government is, willy-nilly, a civil community. Some entities are too small, some are too large, and some are too fragmented. In the case of the first (a category that embraces quite a few suburbs and some of the country's peripheral cities or towns), their governmental and other institutions may simply mask the fact that they are really no more than neighborhoods, capable of political expression but not really capable of self-government, even in the limited sense used here.

In the case of the second, (a category which embraces every city of over 500,000 population in the United States and some smaller ones), the mere fact of a common government does not create community. In fact, those cities are generally less fragmented governmentally than their smaller sisters but are more likely to be congeries of subcommunities that have few if any common civic goals of a *local* character and which have conflicting *local* interests. Nominally local governments, the governments of these cities are in fact neither local nor supralocal. More often than not, they impede true local government without being able to provide the kind of general government provided by the states or the federal government.

The third category consists of localities otherwise capable of functioning as civil communities whose residents are for some reason unable to pull together sufficiently to do so. Unable to successfully pursue any common ends, they remain without form politically regardless of the character of their formal structures.

The question of community control is directly related to the problem of civil community. Thus it may be that, in any particular locality there are good convergences among all the appropriate elements or sets in existing civil communities, that there are better convergences in potential civil communities than in actual political jurisdictions, or that, particularly in the case of the biggest cities, local government exists but not civil community.

The conclusions to be derived from determining what happens to be the case in particular localities must necessarily assist us in dealing with the problem of community control of the schools within real or potential civil communities. What are the likely or possible effects of community control on the schools and on the community itself? Will the schools' educational program be substantially changed? In what ways? To what effect? Will community control of the schools serve as a rallying point for the community? Assist in the development of its self-image as a community? Change its composition or character by encouraging particular kinds of immigration or out migration? These are only a few of the questions that must be raised.

### Educational Options and Community Control

The sheer complexity of American society today places the foregoing questions in a radically different context than they were in the days of the "community school" debate a generation ago. Then it was generally assumed that schools would be serving homogeneous territorial communities and, properly run, would find no particular difficulty in serving the great bulk of the educational needs of the great bulk of the community's members. Whether that view was correct or not even then (it entirely ignored the existence of parochial schools and minority groups, for example), it is not now. Today part of the study of the possibilities, limits, and consequences of community control of the schools must be a study of the provision of options, both within the civil community as defined and in determining the definition of the community.

One choice of options that immediately presents itself for investigation is that of the neighborhood versus the regional or specialized school. The neighborhood school principle is based on the view of the civil community as a relatively homogeneous whole that can be effectively subdivided into smaller units that are equally or even more homogeneous internally, for even closer relationships as well as for sheer convenience of the citizenry and their children. The idea is, in essence, that children will go to public school within the same geo-social framework in which they live and play. This leads to a number of questions. What is a neighborhood for school purposes? To what extent are regional schools something other than devices to achieve the breakdown of certain kinds of neighborhoods or communities? To what extent is schooling a means of creating or maintaining neighborhoods? All these are questions that must be explored.

More recently, a new view of the civil community has begun to emerge which sees its primary components as social or cultural groups that function in place of or within neighborhoods rather than homogeneous neighborhoods as such.[12] Heterogeneity in such communities either cuts across all potential neighborhood lines or is manifested in "symbiotic" rather than homogeneous neighborhoods where two or more such groups live together for reasons of mutual advantage. This emerging view is manifested in a second set of options which consider nonpublic as well as public schools as parts of the civil community's overall educational system. The nonpublic sector used to consist exclusively of parochial schools and a few upper class "academies." Today not only has the variety of parochial schools increased to include more Jewish and Protestant schools as well as Catholic, but "private" schools catering to a widening variety of middle class interests have begun to emerge as well.

The study of the role of the nonpublic schools in the overall framework of the local community has been substantially neglected. Today such neglect is no longer possible, particularly as Americans begin to seriously consider options such as the issuance of educational scrip to every family so that each may choose the kind of schooling it wants for its children, that would drastically change or even eliminate the present system of public education as we know it.

Clearly, such factors as the size of a particular civil community or the composition of its citizenry would influence the impact of such changes and the changes themselves would clearly affect the character of the community. In very large cities, for example, the proliferation of "freedom of choice" schools not built on any neighborhood principle might very likely exacerbate the already fragmented character of the community while in small and medium size civil communities, the very lack of distinctive neighborhoods and the availability of other opportunities for intergroup contact might lead to very different consequences. All the options involving nonpublic education—e.g., religious (or parochial) day-schools, private day schools for special purposes or interests, and shared time programs that combine public and nonpublic education-should be examined in this context.

In this connection, the contents of the educational program in the public schools should also be examined as a third option. Under the system of territorial democracy practiced in the United States until well into the twentieth century, local school systems (which were usually quite small) determined their own educational programs including the religious, cultural, and social values they attempted to transmit as representing the "American way of life." The major thrust of the twentieth century, at least until recently, was away from such local decision-making and toward the imposition of common national standards of what could or could not be taught. The rise of black and other militants with their demands for an education that would strengthen their peoples' search for a common identity, has opened the possibility for a new version of the older approach toward the use of the school as a medium for transmitting different versions of the "American way of life" rather than any single one. Consequently, even the maintenance of public schools as we know them may bring local curricular changes of a very distinctive character for neighborhoods, for whole civil communities, or for "neighborhoods" on their way to becoming civil communities.

Determinations as to the use of any or all of these options must be treated as major *political* questions, not simply as educational ones, since it is at precisely this point that education and politics meet. Viewed from this perspective, education is, indeed, the handmaiden of politics in the highest sense.

## The Mobilization of Educational Resources[13]

We have already pointed out that the question of community control can only be considered in the context of the American political system as a federal one in which the political units are bound together in cooperative relationships. Consequently, a significant aspect of the study of the question must involve inquiry into the roles to be played by the extra-local governments in any system of locally-controlled education. In other words, we must ask what can a community actually control and what it can not, politically, administratively and economically? Under what conditions can it exercise control? What resources must be made available to it? By whom? Under what conditions? Are there any extra-local units, forces or actions that will particularly advance or deter community control? Why?

Studies of intergovernmental relations have repeatedly confirmed that, while participation in the provision of resources for given programs virtually guarantees the donor a role in shaping those programs, it does not by any means guarantee a level of influence commensurate with the resources provided. Thus most states have rarely exercised control over education commensurate with the amount of money they provide their school districts. Conversely, some states exercise more control than contributions might call for. In essence, the provision of resources and the exercise of influence represent separate political decisions which are related only when the decision-makers wish to relate them. Consequently, they may be treated as separate decisions, potentially related, when they are considered in the context of support or opposition to community control in one form or another.

While the roles of all the extra-local governments or authorities in the United States—state, federal, and regional—are potentially significant in determining the outcome of the community control issue, the role of the states will in all likelihood be the most significant. The states begin by having authoritative custody over the organization of education within their boundaries, the development of educational standards and requirements, and the determination of the mode and character of financing educational systems. More than that, they have final authority over the legitimation of the civil communities themselves. In both connections they are bound to affect the school systems within their boundaries. Theoretically, at least, they have the ability to make true community control possible by creating the legal framework for it and by "backstopping" their communities with technical assistance, financial resources, and proper standard-setting so that community control becomes feasible. On the other hand, the existence of conditions or interests supporting the status quo with power in the state house could render the possibilities for achieving real community control remote.[14]

The federal role in education has been growing again in recent years, not only in the provision of support for certain educational endeavors but in the stimulation of educational innovation. An activist federal government can operate so as to lend its support to the movement for community control or work against it. Today federal influence operates in both directions, supporting black ghetto efforts on one hand and seeking the metropolitanization of local educational systems on the other, encouraging local innovation in educational techniques and restricting local policy-making on religious questions. The very existence of any clear-cut federal policy is doubtful. Indeed, given our knowledge of the complexities of policy-making and administration on the federal plane, we may conclude that it is unlikely that any coherent policy will ever emerge from Washington. (We may even reflect on whether such a policy should emerge.)

The relationship between federal aid and the educational establishment must be viewed from this perspective as well. The various federal programs can be examined individually in terms of their effects on the community control issue. Since "community control" works both ways and is often used as an argument to maintain racial segregation, federal policies should be examined in this regard as well.

Finally, the growing—if still small—influence of regional arrangements on the educational scene also has its bearing on the community control issue. Regional arrangements are presently of two kinds: There are interstate arrangements such as Education Commission of the States which serves over forty states primarily in a research and advisory capacity and others such as the Appalachian Regional Commission which provides both funds and a forum for political "tradeoffs" among the member states for educational purposes related to regional economic development. The first has yet to demonstrate any direct impact on the community control issue, but is important for its efforts to reintroduce the country's political leadership into the educational picture. The second has already had an effect on the peripheral communities in its region, strengthening the educational systems of those it considers promising from an economic perspective and weakening others by denying them additional resources for growth. There are also intrastate regional relationships, usually but not exclusively in metropolitan areas. To date, these, too, are essentially coordinating or research relationships but areawide structures to create a new fiscal base for financing education in the region by available funds are under serious discussion in many quarters. They, too, can be supportive of or detrimental to the community control principle, depending upon the goals set for them politically and the way these goals are implemented.

In the end, the question of community control of schools will remain tied to the larger system of community control in general. We Americans will have to choose what path we wish to follow in an age in which centralization is not only taken for granted but is considered right and proper among those who are fearful that the diffusion of power will interfere with the achievement of goals which they espouse. The residents of the "inner city," no more than 20 percent of our population, have done all Americans a service by reviving the issue of community control as a meaningful one, but their success or failure in the pursuit of that goal will also hinge upon the success or failure of the other 80 percent in the pursuit of similar goals. Local self-government is a fundamental aspect of the American dream. Whether it will remain a realistic one depends less on the "objective" factors usually cited to justify continued centralization than on the political decisions of American citizens desirous of shaping the world in which they live.

### Notes

1. See, for example, Milton Kotler, *Neighborhood Government* (Indianapolis: Bobbs-Merrill); Donna Shilah, *Neighborhood Governance: Proposals and Issues* (New York: Institute of Human Relations, 1971); and Marilyn Gittell, "Saving City Schools" in *National Civic Review* (January, 1968).

2. Alan Altschuler makes this point, in part, in *Community Control* (New York: Pegasus, 1970). See also Daniel J. Elazar, "Community Self-Government and the Crisis of American Politics" in *Ethics* (January, 1971).

3. Thomas H. Eliot dismisses this in "Toward an Understanding of Public School Politics," *American Political Science Review* (December, 1959).

4. Advisory Commission on Intergovernmental Relations, *State Aid to Local Government* (Chapter III), and *Fiscal Balance in the American Federal System*.

5. See, for example, Charles Abrams, *Forbidden Neighbors* (New York: Harper and Row, 1965).

6. Alvin Tottler (ed.), *The Schoolhouse in the City* (New York: Praeger, 1968), contains a number of essays relevant to this point.

7. Elazar, op. cit.

8. See Morton Grodzins, *The American System* (Chicago: Rand McNally, 1966), particularly Part Two.

9. Grodzins, ibid.; Daniel J. Elazar, "Local Government in Intergovernmental Perspective" in *Illinois Local Government* (Urbana: University of Illinois, 1963).

10. Roland Warren describes the character of the American community in *The Community in America* (Chicago: Rand McNally, 1963).

11. Norton Long sets forth a similar idea in "The Local Community as an Ecology of Games" in *American Journal of Sociology* (November, 1968).

12. See, for example, Nathan Glazer and Daniel Patrick Moynihan, *Beyond the Melting Pot* (Cambridge, Mass.: MIT Press and Harvard University Press, 1963) and Raymond E. Wolfinger, "The Development and Persistence of Ethnic Voting," *American Political Science Review* (December, 1965).

13. See Thomas N. Dye, *Politics, Economics, and the Public* (Chicago: Rand McNally, 1966), Chapter IV, "Educational Policy"; and Philip Meranto, *The Politics of Federal Aid to Education* (Syracuse: Syracuse University Press, 1967).

14. See, for example, Robert H. Salisbury, "State Politics and Education" in Hubert Jacobs and Kenneth N. Vines (eds.), *Politics in the American States* (Boston: Little, Brown, 1965); and Paul Mort, Walter Reusser, and John Polley, *Public School Finance* (New York: McGraw-Hill, 1960).

## Bibliography

Abrams, Charles. *Forbidden Neighbors.* New York: Harper and Row, 1965.

Advisory Commission on Intergovernmental Relations. *State Aid to Local Government*, Chapter III.

Advisory Commission on Intergovernmental Relations. *Fiscal Balance in the American Federal System.*

Altschuler, Alan. *Community Control.* New York: Pegasus, 1970.

Dye, Thomas N. *Politics, Economics, and the Public.* Chicago: Rand McNally, 1966, Chapter IV.

Elazar, Daniel J. "Community Self-Government and the Crisis of American Politics." *Ethics*, January, 1971.

Elazar, Daniel J. "Local Government in Intergovernmental Perspective." *Illinois Local Government*, Urbana: University of Illinois, 1963.

Eliot, Thomas H. "Toward an Understanding of Public School Politics." *American Political Science Review*, December, 1959.

Gittell, Marilyn. "Saving City Schools." *National Civic Review*, January, 1971.

Glazer, Nathan, and Moynihan, Daniel Patrick. *Beyond the Melting Pot*. Cambridge, Mass.: MIT Press and Harvard University Press, 1963.

Grodzins, Morton. *The American System*. Chicago: Rand McNally, 1966.

Kotler, Milton. *Neighborhood Government.*

Long, Norton. "The Local Community as an Ecology of Games." *American Journal of Sociology*, November, 1968.

Meranto, Philip. *The Politics of Federal Aid to Education*. Syracuse: Syracuse University Press, 1967.

Mort, Paul; Reusser, Walter; and John Polley. *Public School Finance*. New York: McGraw Hill, 1960.

Salisbury, Robert H. "State Politics and Education." Hubert Jacobs and Kenneth N. Vines (eds.), *Politics in the American States*, Boston: Little, Brown, 1965.

Shilah, Donna. *Neighborhood Governance: Proposals and Issues*. New York: Institute of Human Relations, 1971.

Tottler, Alvin (ed.) *The Schoolhouse in the City*. New York: Praeger, 1968.

Warren, Roland. *The Community in America*. Chicago: Rand McNally, 1963.

Wolfinger, Raymond E. "The Development and Persistence of Ethnic Voting." *American Political Science Review*, December, 1965.

# 12 Increasing Irresponsibility in Education: A Growing Gap Between Policy Planning and Operational Groups

LAURENCE IANNACCONE

The question of direction of research priorities in the politics of education may be answered in either of two directions. One direction pays primary attention to cumulative contributions to the field of knowledge. Questions of social need determine the other direction, as might be expected from a field defined more to include all the phenomena about a social need rather than as a discipline. The social action side of us is satisfied by this direction of research, while the scholar side of us by the other.[1]

The theory oriented, social action driven professor in the politics of education is faced by a conflict of choice between these. Our society, however, confronts a different and more serious conflict. Most of this paper will be addressed to what I view as a significant and growing problem for those of us who are serious about the social action of changing schools by the application of intelligence to policy-making: *the problem of a growing gap between policy-making and implementation.*

## The Local District

Before I turn to this problem, I wish to touch briefly upon the other aspect, understanding the politics of education. Were I to pursue this orientation, I would seek *to increase our grasp of the politics of education in the local school district.*

Thomas Eliot's statement, "the political pattern is different," in each local district constitutes a nearly irresistible challenge to the theoretician in me.[2] We have made some dent in sorting out the politics of education in states.[3] We also know much more, though it is little enough, than what we did a few years ago about the federal politics of education.[4] While the center of legal power in education lies in the state, the long tradition of keeping state education departments weak has put the action in the local educational agency (LEA).[a]

Were I to take seriously the understanding of LEA politics in America, I would take the following approaches:

1. I would distinguish urban districts from other LEAs because of the persistence of politically oriented educational interest groups which are institution-

---

[a]In Massachusetts, for example, it is clear that the S.E.A. has automatically reallocated its discretion over federal programs to the LEA's as these reflect the states localism and its organized educational interests.

191

alized in the large cities and which are distinct from state educational interest groups linked to the macro-political universe of the state capitol.

2. I would examine the nonurban LEAs in terms of an adaptation of Howard Becker's typology of sacred and secular societies.[5] Some fruitful, theoretically guided research exists along these lines and suggests that this typology can supply a useful framework for lifting the thousands of LEAs from the random universe suggested by Eliot to a meaningful one.[6]

The urban-nonurban categorization and the sacred-secular continuum have already formed the basis for some empirical testing of hypotheses within the larger and more abstract theoretical framework of dynamic tension existing between a continuously changing societal dimension and an intermittently changing governmental dimension.[7] And useful insight has resulted from this.

Work along these lines has only begun. The task of theoretically categorizing local school governments for political research is necessary. One must avoid the extremes of generalizing from single district case studies or of statistically merging fundamentally dissimilar local governmental units (the classic problem of counting cantelopes and basketballs as the same sort of round objects). Similarly, concepts such as Becker's which help distinguish social time or developmental stages in LEAs, especially of the urban type, are needed to avoid the mistake of equating the politics of one period in a given district's life from another. Theodore Lowi's work on New York City suggests one fruitful direction along these lines for a large city.[8]

## A New Intellectual Proletariat

But enough on this aspect of contributing to the body of knowledge surrounding the politics of education. Let me now turn to the main thrust of this paper, the politics of education as viewed by a social action orientation. As I turn to this, I note that:

1. There is a growing gap between policy-making and planning studies, and implementation and administration. The seriousness of this issue may be highlighted by Henry Kissenger's statement: "Where to draw the line between excessive commitment to the bureaucracy and paralyzing aloofness depends upon so many intangibles of circumstance and personality that it is difficult to generalize." He points out that the intellectual, in order to contribute to policy, ". . . must steer between the Scylla of letting bureaucracy prescribe what is relevant or useful and the Charybdis of defining these criteria too abstractly."[9]

A course as dangerous as this can hardly be steered carelessly. A growing gap between policy-making and implementation suggests an increase in social distance between those engaged in the two activities.

2. Edgar Litt's work in Massachusetts' politics suggests that this gap (whether growing or not) is more than a game played by university-based intellectuals.[10] It may be rooted in the social fact of a growing intellectual, technical, managerial class as a significant element in American politics in opposition to the yeomen and labor classes. Thus, the gap of which I speak may be a manifestation of a deeper and politically more significant cleavage in American social life.

3. The problem becomes the more serious as the bureaucrat increasingly becomes thought of by the intellectual as *a mere bureaucrat*. The point is made by Adam Yarmolinsky. He says:

> When I speak of the government bureaucrats ... I speak of the individual who has the action, because the primary responsibility of the bureaucrat is not to figure out the best way to do something but to get it done. ... It is their very commitment to getting things done that makes them resist new and perhaps better ways of doing things. The effect of bureaucrats in the system is to encourage attention to the business at hand. It is, also, frequently a useful antidote to sloppy thinking. But it emphatically does not encourage the production of new ideas, or suspension of judgment until new ideas can sink in.[11]

Yarmolinsky restates the fundamental problem this way: "How improve the climate for new ideas in government?" His solutions or proposed solutions need not concern us here, since I am merely concerned at this point in emphasizing the nature of the problem.

Attitudes of disdain, if not contempt, of the policy-maker for the bureaucrat and vice versa are doubly dangerous if rooted in social or political class differences.

4. With this in mind, let me turn directly to education. If Keppel's dictum that education is too important to be left to educational administrators or to school men means that others, and specifically the intellectuals outside of education, also have a role to play, it is one thing; but if it means instead that policy-making in education is too important to let school men be seriously involved in it, and that only others should be making policies, then it means something quite different. More and more, it seems to me, the perception is developing within the educational bureaucracy and among the zealot disciples or whiz kids of the Keppel-Howe era that the dictum means that only others should be making policies. If this trend continues, the gap between policy-making and those who have the action will inevitably increase. And it seems to me that this process is already underway.

For example, the perception held by New York City school people that Bundy's staff and Lindsay's team felt disdain for those who had the action in the city schools exacerbated the political conflict which reached into the legislature. That perception was established at the beginning of Bundy's work by his decision to leave the city bureaucracy out of his committee and staff, except for the token representation of Alfred Giardino.


Thomas Cronin, in "The Presidency and Education," points out that: "It has been fashionable to call for the creation of new structures staffed by policy scientists who would integrate research efforts and priority setting throughout federal domestic programs."[12] This has resulted in what he calls "outside networks," by which he means ". . . those individuals, groups or advisory institutions who contribute to White House intelligence and decision-making processes, but who are not generally employed by either the White House or the federal government."[13] By people not generally employed in the federal establishment, he means individuals who do not have the action—and this specifically pinpoints the gap with which I am concerned.

Ironically, this reference reminds me of an event some fifteen years ago in New York State where a leader of a key educational organization stated at a meeting: "We are against the idea and my research division is going to research that question and will give our reasons."

In connection with the outside networks, Thomas Cronin and Sanford Greenberg state that one form of needed research is ". . . comparative studies, empirical examinations of alternative advisory network roles, and the varied outcome and effect of these roles."[14] I concur with their judgment. But I would also suggest that this needs to be done within a context larger than merely the examination of the outside networks in federal educational policy-making and even state educational policy-making. I will deal further with this larger context shortly. For now, let me point out that we are not merely observing the development of an outside network, or new intellectual proletariat which is *in* but not *of* education, *safely based outside* of the public schools, and without the responsibility for action. We are, in addition, seeing the development of a new power structure in education.

The gap is further extenuated *beyond the outside network problem* by the rising demand for accountability, by the crude application of program planning-budgeting systems in education, and more immediately by performance contracting. The latter raises the entire issue of accountability and measurement and, it seems to me, transforms the issue into the question Plato raised a long time ago with his guardians. Who guards the guardians?

The research venture is itself a political factor when the subject of study is a public service area—its operations, its ideological developments, and above all, its effectiveness. Ironically, in passing, I note the stance taken by one of the critics of the establishment, David Cohen of Harvard, who like Keppel feels education is too important to be left to the educator. Now that the Keppel program has been in existence for some time, he says: "You can't research outcome per se or learning outcomes in order to judge program effectiveness when you deal with social programs."[15]

I hope no one misunderstands me here as spending my time defending an establishment which I have long attacked. But I think there is a very real problem before us. Indeed, struggles between the intelligentsia and operators within educationists ranks preceded the development of conflicts between the policymakers and operators. Hence, the problems posed by this gap are deeply rooted ones. Some attention to these roots may be warranted. It may clarify why I consider the present growing gap a serious element in the politics of education.

## An Historical View

Public education as we have known it has long been sick in the United States. The cumulative effects of the Depression and World War II are among the chief recent causes of its illness. The invisible scar of the depression stands all too visible in the operation of the New York City Board of Education. The hiatus of World War II for the public schools left the task of building physical plants to the late forties, and the post-war explosive suburban growth led to the rapid development of new school districts with no chance for careful thought about schools. The cycle of the Lonesome Train in Levittown became the characteristic pattern—a cycle which runs from rural districts to guilded showplace to target for John Birchers in one generation.[16]

The illness of the public schools resisted the remedies of the physicians who undertook its treatment prior to sputnik. These physicians were the critics of education. Some were members of the education professions; others were long standing friends, such as James B. Conant; and still others, such as Admiral Rickover, were self-appointed experts. Their focus was on the intellectual or anti-intellectual strength of school programs. In many ways, the resistance tells us a great deal about the nature of the educational establishment, particularly in the big cities where to this day the invisible scar of the depression is seen in those central office personnel who see their role as that of defending the system against the corrupt politicians of city hall.[17] Then the treatment of the ailing system appeared to gain momentum as a consequence of post-sputnik criticism. The patient apparently responded to the NDEA effort with the development, even though on a small scale, of the cooperative research program in Washington.

With the sixties and the passage of ESEA, the schools started to move in a new direction; the growing racial problem took precedence over improved quality of education. Another group of critical intellectuals was added to the ranks of the schoolmen's opponents. This group, less concerned than the earlier critics with a school's accomplishment of its intellectual tasks, was primarily interested in the schools as a central agency in carrying out the egalitarian thrust of this century. The social activists, seeking to use the school as an instrument for solving American social problems, have moved in a new direction towards restructuring school governance and/or its economic base. This direction can now be seen coming to fruition in the combination of proposals for a voucher system which seeks to break up the monopoly of education. This could produce a political coalition of segregation academies in the south, the Birchers, particularly in the southwest, the parochial school interests, and the liberals. I wonder, at this point, whether these actors may be viewed better not as physicians but as morticians called in to bury a dying patient.

So long as the criticisms of education were concerned with increasing the efficiency and effectiveness of schools for learning skills and intellectual content, the critics had the support of much of the public, even though they opposed the establishment. But when the criticism shifted to the system's failure to fulfil its social role on the racial issue in American society, the public, including many former critics, either moved back to supporting the status quo in schools or distinguished themselves from the new critics, the social action types. Thus, in part, a polarization of the critics of the schools has taken place with the John Birch group on the right and the Ford Foundation on the left. The two extremes may find in the voucher program a political basis for working together, resulting finally in a class school system. The resultant form of public education is likely to carry our socioeconomic class structure into the classroom operation by distinguishing one school from the other along class and race lines as never before. Ironically, I might add, the job of integration, of reducing inequality, of bringing people together in a single institution, poorly though it was done, seemed to work better as long as the focus of attack on the school was on the quality of its education rather than on the schools as firstly instruments of social policy and only secondarily as instruments concerned with the task of reading, writing, and learning.

As it may appear, what I have been briefly sketching out can be viewed as three periods in the recent history of American educational policy-making, the last two of which display an increasing gap between policy-making and school operation. The first period was controlled by the bureaucrats inside the educational establishment. The second period displayed the activity of others, outside of the establishment, ranging from critics like Bester through to Conant. It saw the growing influence of researchers and theoreticians with backgrounds in such areas as educational psychology. They were primarily interested in the enhancement of learning per se, without great regard for social problems. Viewed in terms of organizational reference groups and linkages, the first group can now be found at the national level, in the American Association of School Administrators which meets in Atlantic City each year, whereas the second group is associated with the American Educational Research Association. The third group, which is becoming increasingly influential in educational policy-making, are people who are essentially concerned with social action. They do not see the school as a place where they expect to spend their life working. They are only generally concerned with the teaching-learning process in the schools. They are much more concerned with the school as an instrument of social policy. They are needed. They have many valuable roles to play, roles ranging from reform school board members to educational researchers. But just as I do not believe religious groups should be allowed to use the schools to teach their dogmas, so I do not believe in turning a school, such as the King-Tim in Roxbury, over to groups such as black paramilitarists to further their dogma.

**Some Hypotheses**

Let me now move beyond this brief and probably biased historical and sociological description to suggest some hypotheses concerning what has been and is happening. My central hypothesis, already stated, is that in much of American politics there is a growing gap between the individuals who have the action and groups composing an outside network of policy-making. This gap is generally rooted in the differences between the political cultures of the upper class (the more educated, the professionals, the technical, managerial groups) and the political cultures of the yeomen, the urban workers, and the southwestern new rich. This gap has been growing in education at least since World War II. Sociologically, the gap divides the intellectual critic further and further from the operating school man. It appears that as this gap grows, the schools change less and less.

Three sub-hypotheses may be offered concerning the origin of this gap. They tend to be explanatory rather than testable.

1. The gap is due to fragmentation in the politics of education. A growing pluralism within education is characterized by different schools of "scribblers." Just as the school men scribblers identified by Stephen Bailey[18] and others such as Paul Mort at one stage functioned to articulate social need into a program of action for schools in various states, so new, often anti-school men, social action types are functioning to provide articulation of what is needed in schools in our day. The hypothesis suggests that the fragmentation in educational politics that is happening nationally is similar to, if not the same, as that occurring on a state level. This can be seen in the breakdown of monolithic educational interest structures so closed that they are no longer capable of adjusting to the needs of a changing society. Implicit in this fragmentation-stage hypothesis is the identification of the stage and the current policy-making operations split as one element in a recurrent, sequential cycle in the politics of education.[19]
2. What we are witnessing is the first stage of a revolution in education. And the desertion of the intellectuals, which Crane Brinton notes as the first stage of

revolution, emphasizes the failure of the old system and indicates that we are on the threshold of a real revolt in education and the end of that old system.[20] The direction of the future may be seen in the beginning political alliance among the northeastern liberals, led in part by the Ford Foundation, and by some of the people at Harvard and other universities, including the Wisconsin economists; the southern segregationists with their academies; the private school interests, at both the higher and lower school levels; and the Birchers. Our experience is that not infrequently legislation results from political opponents agreeing on solutions while continuing to disagree on such matters as the nature of the problems to be solved and the values to be maximized. I suspect that the adage "Politics makes strange bedfellows," would better reflect our experience if we reversed its order to read: "Strange bedfellows make politics—at least such as produce legislation."

3. A third hypothesis may be stated in more psychological terms. The gap we are now experiencing is the result of a frustration of the intellectuals, specifically the failure of John Gardner and others to change the educational operation. The shift in emphasis toward social concerns may be a kind of sublimation, similar to that expressed by Lionel Rubinoff in his book, *The Pornography of Power*. It is a characteristic result of frustration and substitutes a change in words after the experience of failure to change deeds.[21]

In sum, what I have so far attempted has been to identify the problem of a growing gap between policy studies and implementation, reflecting the cleavage between intellectuals and bureaucrats in education. I have also offered three possible explanations or hypotheses concerning the nature of this gap. These hypotheses are rather global and may not be directly testable. However, this gap and its nature may be better understood by studying policy commissions and their work, but above all their *workers*. In other words, I propose an examination of a class of sociopolitical mechanisms, and their functions will provide a useful purchase on answering some of the questions that are raised by the statements I have made above, and by my concern for the possibly growing gap between policy-making and action. You will note the methodological assumption, I am sure, that an examination of such mechanisms and their functions can help answer the kind of questions that are raised by the explanatory frameworks, such as I proposed earlier.

I propose that evaluation in the form not only of assessment, accountability responses, or something as specific as program planning and budgeting, but also of such things as surveys and studies in general of public institutions are *in and of themselves* political mechanisms. I do not mean by this what David Cohen refers to in an article in the AERA journal, that the findings of research and of evaluation have political relevance and, therefore, constitute an element in subsequent political struggles.[22] Instead, I mean that the mere act of study, of doing a survey, of doing research, of evaluation, in and of itself, is a social weapon, a tool in political struggles. For example, the attempt by any organization to do a self-study at a point in time when critics are beginning to mount criticism against it is rather clearly a mechanism of defense in the political struggle for existence by the organization.

## Four Dimensions: Categories for Study

This example suggests one dimension along which we can attempt to understand the political function of studies—the simple notion of "in" versus "out." Examining who calls for and initiates a study in terms of his or their being in or out of office may be useful. I note, for example, that individuals demanding a study when they are "out" not infrequently let that study die after they have moved into office.[23] This dimension coupled with the three categories of persons I mentioned earlier (the established school men, the education researchers, or the social activists) suggests a 2 x 3 table of in-out positions and by the orientations of the persons initiating and conducting studies (see table 12-1).

Studies of these sorts may have the function of either "cooling out" or "cooling off" political conflicts around education. A study takes time. The time it takes may allow for the intensity of conflict to be reduced and for tempers to cool. If the time is used to decrease tension and to facilitate collaborative efforts to change the operation of schools, this is cooling off. On the other hand, if this

Table 12-1.
In-Out Positions

| Types of Participants | Who Initiates | | Who Conducts | | Career Effects + or - |
|---|---|---|---|---|---|
| | In control of schools | Out of control of schools | In control of schools | Out of control of schools | |
| School Men | | | | | |
| Research Types | | | | | |
| Social Action | | | | | |

time-out has as its major function merely the filling of time while tempers cool, with no intention that the study will result in changes, then the study merely "cools out" the critics.[b]

Finally let me suggest a fourth dimension derived partly from the sublimation hypothesis. Partly it reflects Michel's iron law of oligarchy and the sociologists understanding of the means-ends reversal phenomenon. One should examine the people who do a study also in terms of another aspect of all political mechanisms involving people: What effects does doing the study have upon their careers? We know something of the network of influence developed by school men who conducted surveys in the early part of this century. We should be interested in asking whether similar networks are developing in our day.

These four dimensions combined together suggest a crude taxonomy which could be used as a basis for studying policy studies, and also, lead us to a moral question to which I will return at the close of this paper.

Let me for the moment give examples of studies where those who are out attack the ins. These studies range on a continuum from the attack of would-be officials to unseat an incumbent to the less immediately self-interested exposers of muckrakers and finally to the social critics attempting to produce change in some dimension of the public service. The history of education is filled with such studies, some of which have been very effective.[24] Joseph Rice's work at the turn of the century is singled out by many as a significant landmark in changing schools. The Coleman report may be less significant, but I would tend to classify it here too.[25] The opposite category of studies, in which the ins attempt to defend themselves against the outs, fills the dissertation and survey files of schools of education all over the country. Raymond Callahan's book on *Education and the Cult of Efficiency* deals at some length with such studies.[26]

Turning now to studies of the cooling off or cooling out variety, I see Mark Shinnerer's report on New York City's schools (which he called a study of studies) as a disgusted reaction to years of studies designed to take the heat off and nothing more.[27] In contrast, there is the Hope Commission and its work on education in Ontario. Here one finds a long, extensive study which disappointed many people because much of what the study pointed to was not done afterwards. Yet, if one examines carefully not only the makeup of the commission itself but also the kinds of ongoing negotiations and changes in provincial education that went on during the study, one may conclude that the process itself involved political manipulations and negotiations which resolved many of the political issues that the commission was designed to study.[28] In such cases the study commission becomes a mechanism of government which provides an arena for accommodating interests as well as ideas. Cooling off with action deserves special attention from the student of educational politics in our day. In connection with this form of study, let me add one observation. The Flexner report

---

[b] I am thinking here of the difference between what is intended by cooling off periods in labor negotiation legislation, for example, in contrast to the confidence man's work of reducing his victims outcrys when he is bilked so that the victim will not go to the police, cooling him out.

on medicine seems to have done a most effective job in transforming that field. But if Flexner had done a more bone-cutting, sharper, incisive job with his survey of medicine, the probabilities are that his report would never have been accepted by the medical profession since it would have called for more change than they felt they could possibly handle.

The ten-year history of studies on the decentralization issue in New York City provides examples of each of the categories above except the last. Enough has been written of the efforts of the system to study itself to defend the status quo in the early sixties and to cool out the situation without action in the mid-sixties. Lindsay's picking up the spring legislative mandate of 1967 and giving it a thrust which the legislative leaders never expected is an instance of an "out" trying to use a study to get "in." Much of what the Ford Foundation has done clearly fits the sublimation hypothesis and footnotes the intelligentsia's contempt for the bureaucrats. The proposals of 110 Livingston Street, supported by the Council of Supervisory Associations and the United Federation of Teachers, illustrate the fruit of self-study to provide a defense against demands for change. The efforts of the New York State Board of Regents, though late and very incomplete, came close to the cooling-off-while-negotiating type of study.

The following categories comprise a possible taxonomy for looking at surveys and studies:

I. Problem Definitions
    1. Cleavage between Political Cultures
    2. Intellectuals and Bureaucrats
    3. Policy Studies and Operations

II. Explanatory Hypotheses
    1. Fragmentation State in a Recurrent Politics of Education Pattern
    2. Early Stage in a Revolution in Education
    3. Sublimation of Frustrated Intellectual Hopes

III. Taxonomy for Studying Studies
    1. Participant Types: Schoolmen/Researchers/Social Activists
    2. Nature of Participation: Initiating/Conducting
    3. Locus in Relation to Office: In/Out
    4. Career Effects: Positive/Negative

IV. Operational Categories for Use in III
    1. Initiating Source
    2. The Resources and Their Origins
    3. The Selection of Personnel
    4. The Characteristics of Personnel
    5. The Characteristics of Groups Supporting
    6. The Characteristics of Groups Opposing
    7. The Verbal Outcomes of the Report
    8. The Action Outcomes of the Report
    9. The Career Outcomes of the Report

## A Look Ahead

Research along the lines I have suggested will confront a moral problem which concerns me greatly, the irresponsibility of change agents. Dr. Stephen Bailey (Syracuse University) and I used to disagree over whether there was any real power in the educational establishment. I think part of the time we were talking past one another. Part of the time I was talking about its power to maintain its autonomy versus what, I think, Stephen was talking about, its influence over governmental affairs. I think that the educational bureaucrat's power is of a kind that slaves have dumb-looking, looking even dumber than they really are—the kind of power that reduces change efforts into what the Italians refer to as making a hole in water. This is what I see in the attempts to change elementary and secondary education: making a hole in water. The process of the last decade concerns me because in it I see the following results:

1. An increase is appearing in the gap between planning and action. This, I think, is reflected in what is beginning to happen to training programs—the training of day-to-day operators is completely divorced from the production of bright planners who never intend to and never will occupy day-to-day action roles in running schools.
2. This can lead to the esoteric research of esoteric social action.
3. Much of the talk of policy ignores the action at the building level in the LEA and not much change ever goes on there.
4. The best people may not move into the action of working in schools but will probably satisfy their career needs and delude themselves about making a difference by engaging in studies of planning and policy-making unrelated to operation at any point.
5. Many school administrators may actually be welcoming this gap between planning and action.

My central thesis is simply that there is a growing gap between the people who engage in educational policy-making for elementary and secondary schools and the people who work in the schools. I am deeply concerned that the nature of this gap be studied with a view towards closing it. An historical view of developments since World War II may help to clarify this gap. Studies should, I believe, focus upon the political functions of surveys, evaluations, investigations and commissions. In addition, attention should be given to the people who do such studies and their political role as well as career mobility. Finally, I am disturbed by the possibility that the continuance of this trend will produce a major increase in irresponsibility. If this gap widens, one probable outcome is that policy-makers without the responsibility for running schools will become satisfied with making recommendations while school men will be satisfied to let them do so. In this way the public interest will appear to be met by recommendations while schools slowly deteriorate a little at a time but largely go on as before, giving way easily like water before major thrusts for change but seeking their old level as these retract. If this happens, the policy-makers will be as responsible as the operators for it.


## Notes

1. The distinction is discussed by Harold D. Lasswell, "The Policy Orientation" in Daniel Lerner and Harold Lasswell (eds.), *The Policy Sciences* (Stanford, Calif.: Stanford University Press, 1951).

2. Thomas H. Eliot in Nicholas A. Masters, Robert H. Salisbury, and Thomas H. Eliot (eds.), *State Politics and the Public Schools* New York: (Alfred A. Knoff, 1964), p. v.

3. See for example, Stephen K. Bailey et al., *Schoolmen and Politics* (Syracuse University Press, 1962); and L. Iannaccone, *Politics in Education* (New York: The Centre for Applied Research in Education, Inc. 1967).

4. Philip Meranto, *The Politics of Federal Aid to Education in 1965* (Syracuse University Press, 1967); and Stephen K. Bailey and Edith K. Mosher, *ESEA The Office of Education Administrators a Law* (Syracuse University Press, 1968).

5. Howard Becker, *Systematic Sociology* (New York: John Wiley & Sons, 1932).

6. Laurence Iannaccone and Frank W. Lutz, *Politics, Power and Policy: The Governing of Local School Districts* (Columbus, Ohio: C.E. Merrill, 1970).

7. Ibid.

8. Theodore Lowi, *At the Pleasure of the Mayor: Patronage and Power In New York City, 1898-1958* (New York: The Free Press of Glencoe, 1964).

9. Henry A. Kissinger, "The Policy-maker and the Intellectual" in Thomas E. Cronin and Sanford D. Greenberg, *The Presidential Advisory System* (New York: Harper and Row, 1969), p. 165.

10. Edgar Litt, *The Political Cultures of Massachusetts* (Cambridge: M.I.T. Press, 1965).

11. Adam Yarmolinsky, "Ideas into Program," in Cronin and Greenberg, pp. 92-93.

12. Thomas E. Cronin, "The Presidency and Education," in Cronin and Greenberg, p. 228.

13. Ibid., p. 89.

14. Ibid., p. 90.

15. David Cohen, in *Review of Educational Research*, April, 1970, vol. 40, no. 2, pp. 213-239.

16. Joseph F. Maloney, *The Lonesome Train in Levittown* (Indianapolis: Bobbs-Merril, 1958), I.C.P., Case Series 39.

17. James M. Haught, "An Exploratory Study of the Central Office Staff and Public School Decision-making," (Unpublished Dissertation, Syracuse University, 1970).

18. Bailey, op. cit.

19. L. Iannaccone, *Politics in Education*, Chapters 4 and 5 discuss this at State and LEA Levels.

20. Crane Brinton, *The Anatomy of Revolution* (New York: Vintage Books, 1957).

21. Lionel Rubinoff, *The Pornography of Power* (New York: Ballantine Books, 1969).

22. David Cohen, op. cit., pp. 223-24.

23. See above p. 200 and note 16.

24. See, for example, Ramond E. Callahan, *Education and the Cult of Efficiency* (University of Chicago Press, 1962).

25. James S. Coleman, et al. *Equality of Educational Opportunity* (Washington, D.C.: U.S. Department of Health, Education and Welfare, 1966).

26. Callahan, op. cit.

27. Mark A. Schinnerer, *A Report to the New York City Education Department* (New York, 1961).

28. Report of the Royal Commission on Education in Ontario, (Toronto, 1950).

# 13 Toward a Theory of Street-Level Bureaucracy

MICHAEL LIPSKY

An import focus for research on the politics of education is the study of the interactions between teachers and their "clients," both parents and students. This perspective is supported by the convergence of a number of separate developments in both political science and the study of education.

1. For some time social scientists have advocated greater research on governmental services at the point of consumption. To understand the relationship between government and citizens it has been suggested that research focus on aspects of government services where government "meets" people. While legislative policies may generally determine the allocation of resources for education, the ways in which public employees provide services paid for by those funds may play considerably larger roles in determining the quality of services and citizen regard for the government providing them.[1]
2. Recent research on educational policy has specifically suggested that the nature of teacher-student interactions is important in determining student achievement levels. Rosenthal's research concerning the relationship between teacher expectation of students and student achievement supports the contention that teacher attitudes toward students influences student achievement levels independent of teachers' training, congruence of teacher-pupil backgrounds, and student socioeconomic profiles. Recent interest in introducing performance standards in educational innovation is based on similar reasoning. Hypothetically, manipulation of tangible incentives to teachers and students in the school setting will result in changes in attitudes and measurably improved performance.[2]
3. Teacher-client relations today are severely strained in many urban settings. Debates over school decentralization illustrate this point. Many if not most of the reasons offered by supporters of school decentralization proposals focus on alleged difficulties in teacher-client relations. It is said that teachers for the most part are insensitive and incapable of responding to the needs and strengths of minority group students. Decentralization proponents consider the trade union interests of teachers antithetical to the promotion of administrators from backgrounds similar to those of the students. It is charged that civil service protection of white personnel continues to receive support in educational politics at the expense of minority student development.

205

These problems are exacerbated in school systems where children continue to perform below national standards, regardless of the extent to which schools bear primary responsibility for performance levels. Anger and frustration directed toward schools are likely to continue as piecemeal educational reforms and additional resources are directed toward schools whose students fail to display significant improvement.[3]

4. To the extent that interest in decentralization continues, publics attentive to educational policy will show increasing concern with factors affecting success at relatively low levels of the educational system hierarchy. Just as individuals active in educational politics have recently appeared more interested in affecting decision-making at the individual school level (often out of despair over their ability to affect system-wide decision-making),[4] so they are also interested in the determinants of individual school success, perhaps (and to some extent regrettably) at the expense of interest in systemwide success determinants.

If it is the case that the teacher-client interaction is an increasingly appropriate topic of concern, how best to approach such study? A central issue in this connection is the *conceptualization* of teacher-client interactions. Should one approach teacher-student interactions as unique? Or, to understand teacher-student interactions better, should they be compared to interactions of other actors in relating to clients?

The answer to these questions has important implications for developing theory. If teacher-student interactions are unique, then theory must be built by focusing exclusively on the behavior of people in these roles. But if these interactions may be compared with others outside of the educational realm, then a new world of comparative approaches may open up. We may then concentrate on identifying *similarities* between the behavior of teachers and that of other actors. And, having established similarities, we may continue by identifying critical *differences* between teachers *as types of actors*, and others whose behavior we have studied. The payoffs here might be quite high, since we will have placed teacher behavior in a range of other behaviors, and then isolated differences which we have some reasons to think might be significant.

In some recent work I have tried to explore the possibilities suggested above. I have conceived of teachers as one of many "street-level bureaucrats" in urban political affairs, and have tried to identify significant ways in which people in such roles behave toward their clients in specific situations.[5] In this paper I will sketch the potential for research in educational politics which might follow from this theoretical perspective.

A street-level bureaucrat is defined as a public employee who deals with non-voluntary clients, and whose work is characterized by three conditions. (1) He is called upon to interact constantly with citizens in the regular course of his job; (2) He enjoys relatively wide latitude in job performance; and (3) The potential impact on citizens with whom he deals is fairly extensive. These work circumstances apply to a fairly wide range of jobs in the public service. The work of teachers, police patrolmen, welfare investigators, and even in some case, lower court judges, is characterized by these conditions.

The analysis is intended to apply to situations in which street-level bureaucrats experience certain work-related stresses. These stresses arise because: available resources for job performance are inadequate; work proceeds in circumstances where clear physical and/or psychological threat exists, or where the bureaucrat's authority is regularly challenged; and expectations about job performance are ambiguous and/or contradictory, including an unattainable, idealized dimension. I am not suggesting that every street-level bureaucrat works under these conditions all of the time. I am suggesting that these conditions are sufficiently applicable to make this analysis useful.

Teachers, like other street-level bureaucrats, frequently confront the job-related stresses suggested here. Large classes, inadequate materials and curricular assistance, overburdening clerical functions, lack of adequate ancillary personnel to assist with students requiring special attention, lockstep lesson plans prohibiting development of new techniques, and so on, often characterize teacher work environments.

Increasingly, teachers working in inner-city schools must confront the threat of physical violence. Perhaps more importantly, they frequently *think* they must confront it. This results when isolated episodes of violence focus generalized fears in highly charged atmospheres, or when teachers whose backgrounds differ from their students feel that they are unequipped to discipline pupils.

Teachers also are often confronted with ambiguous or unclear role expectations. Generally we seek to discover the source of role expectations among peer groups, the reference publics of individual actors, and public expectations generally.[6] Significantly, teachers, like other street-level bureaucrats, often receive conflicting signals concerning expectations of performance. Principals expect and try to demand conformity to certain orientations, fellow teachers encourage conflicting perspectives, while the general climate toward public education, expressed through a variety of means, requires still other kinds of performance. Parents and students, who in some areas are increasingly vigorous in articulating expectations about the public schools, provide still other demands on teachers' conceptualization of the job.

Importantly, these role expectations change more quickly than personnel. Thus individuals socialized into teacher roles at the beginning of their careers come to dominate the educational system and perform according to these early-acquired norms. Meanwhile, community expectations of teacher performance may be changing rapidly—certainly more quickly than street-level bureaucrats are prepared to accommodate.

The potential rewards in conceptualizing street-level bureaucratic behavior in this way come from attempting to understand the mechanisms developed by individuals playing these roles to accommodate the stresses indicated above, and generally managing work-related pressures. Bureaucrats generally will attempt to handle work-related pressures by developing routines, simplifications, and other coping mechanisms or strategies. By routines I refer to the establishment of habitual or regularized patterns of task performance. By simplifications I refer to those symbolic constructs in terms of which individuals order their perceptions so as to make the perceived environment easier to manage. It is these mechanisms which significantly structure the street-level bureaucrat-client interaction, and largely account for the general contours of client treatment.

For example, inadequate resources forces bureaucrats to treat cases in terms of simplifications and routines, even though ideally each case should be reviewed and treated on its merits. Thus criteria based on factors other than demonstrated learning ability affect teachers' treatment of students when there are too many students to deal with on a case-by-case basis, or when other stresses intrude.

Institutionally, the tracking system functions to provide routines for placing students in groupings which guarantee teachers relatively homogeneous classroom situations. Unfortunately, in the real world, teachers, like others, tend to make decisions about pupils on bases other than objective criteria. When race, quality of dress, or accent contribute to the simplifications in terms of which teachers (and ultimately, school systems) track students, the social consequences of this bureaucratic coping mechanism become pernicious.[7]

Teachers also routinize in order to minimize threat. Indeed, elementary school teachers are literally urged to "routinize as much as possible" in order to succeed.[8] The imposition of symbols of authority, and teachers' heavy emphasis on the importance of maintaining authority positions, may also be understood by their need to develop routines to secure them from threats of disruption and to insure an atmosphere in which "teaching" can take place.[9] Like policemen who behave roughly toward people perceived as "potential assailants,"[10] teachers may act sternly toward potential "troublemakers" out of a desire to anticipate and deal with difficulties before they get out of hand.

Teachers, like other street-level bureaucrats, may attempt to fulfill role expectations, despite limited resources or the ambiguity of expectations, by redefining their role, or their clientele. Thus they may satisfy themselves that it is appropriate to display interest in *some* children who are considered bright, and not others, when *all* cannot receive special and individualized attention. Thus teachers' perceptions that some students are primitive, racially inferior, or "culturally deprived" may arise not only because they are consistent with views held in society generally.[11] In this case such attitudes also function to facilitate fulfillment of role expectations by placing responsibility on the clients of service. From this perspective, tracking arrangements also are supportive of these needs, since with such mechanisms school *systems* become responsible for student progress and direction, thus freeing teachers from making all but marginal decisions about student placement and ranking.

Of particular interest in the analysis of street-level bureaucracy is the relationship between simplifications and stereotyping. While all bureaucrats may develop simplifications at various times to process work, what is critical are the bases on which simplifications are made. Stereotypes are one form of simplification. But stereotypes are objectionable not because they are a form of simplification, but because they are developed along criteria which prejudice the chances of stereotyped individuals to be judged objectively.

The illustrations of teacher reactions to job-related stresses can be paralleled by observations of police behavior, and other street-level bureaucracies. By focusing on teacher behavior as bureaucratic, and by examining teacher behavior in the context of the behavior of other public employees who relate to non-voluntary clienteles in similar ways, we should be able to offer insights into educational reform proposals based on this analysis of teacher behavior. Such proposals often include changes in recruitment practices and requirements, teacher training, and increased employment of personnel with fashionable specialties. They do not focus on the work environment of teachers, and the ways in which such environments might be reshaped along more useful lines.

It is not proposed that all street-level bureaucracies are shaped in identical fashion. The bureaucracies mentioned here obviously differ from one another in significant ways. Moreover, the "street-level" perspective is only useful for a limited range of issues. Thus, David Rogers' study of top-level decision-making in the New York City school systems does not contradict this perspective so much as it provides a different perspective for a different set of questions. Similarly, James Q. Wilson's study of police administration would be an important place to begin the study of policemen as street-level bureaucrats, since he has cogently identified critical questions for middle-level police administration.[1][2]

The notion of street-level bureaucracy, if it attracts any interest in the study of the politics of education, will do so because it provides a conceptual framework within which to approach the study of teacher behavior. It provides not so much a specific research agenda as a means for organizing research questions.

Research should concentrate on the mechanisms by which different kinds of teachers come to develop role expectations. To some extent these expectations are linked to the general socialization of people who select themselves for the teaching profession. But other areas also affect expectation development. Schools of education, peer groups, "veteran" teachers, and community mores generally, impact teacher understandings of role expectations. And the ways these various "sectors" affect teacher role expectations have broad implications for educational reform. If teacher job expectations are perceived to be important areas in which to introduce change, does it make more sense to change teacher training or to alter the scope of the community to which school personnel have reference? Or does the recruitment of different kinds of people for teaching positions make greater sense for educational reform? These questions, by no means new to educational professionals, are linked together by the focus on research on teacher role expectations.

At what point are teachers capable of teaching students on individual bases, and under what circumstances must they "process" students in terms of possibly injurious and dysfunctional simplifications? Concentration on the ways in which teacher attitudes function to shield them from responsibility for the product of their efforts has a place in these proposed studies.

We need to know much more about the nature of teacher-client interactions. Just as social scientists investigating police behavior have engaged in observing, classifying and analyzing police-citizen encounters,[13] so it would be useful to have similar research on the nature of teacher-client interactions. Just as Reiss provided data on questions of police brutality and of biases of race and class imputed to policemen, so we might provide insights into the impact of teacher behavior on student attitudes and motivation, in addition to illuminating such specific considerations as the affect of teacher career expectations on different kinds of students.

Research on guidance counselor interactions with students might investigate counselors' expectations of and advice to students in terms of their socioeconomic backgrounds, language capability, and general demeanor. Interviews with teachers and students following counseling sessions might illuminate the exchanges observed. Interviews with the participants, in addition to observations of the interaction, might provide a three-dimensional picture of the exchanges.

The focus on teachers as street-level bureaucrats suggests two further areas in which it would be appropriate to collect data. If the frequency and direction of various *bureaucratic* interactions are the primary dependent variables, as students of bureaucracy we should also collect data on the (1) incentive systems in which teachers work; and, relatedly, (2) recruitment and maintenance of employees within the school systems.

On incentives, we should ask what kinds of behaviors are rewarded and what kinds are negatively sanctioned with the systems? What is the nature and the extent of the "zone of indifference" of school administrators, in terms of which teachers may exercise discretion? What is the relationship between work-load strains (such as class size) and administrative demands in determining teacher role behavior?

With regard to recruitment and maintenance, we must know what kinds of individuals comprise teaching staffs. As in the study of any organization, we should know what kinds of people are recruited to the organization, and what kinds of people are induced to continue in employment. The study of school incentive systems should help explain the answers to these questions. In turn, the profiles of school personnel will facilitate explanation of variations in teacher-client interactions—our primary concern.

These are a few of the areas of concentration which are suggested by the focus on teachers as street-level bureaucrats. There are two directions in which the development of the theory of street-level bureaucracy will proceed. On the one hand, we may look forward to refining the theory and developing a better understanding of its utility in studying teacher-client interactions. At the same time that research may be guided by this perspective, future research findings may be illuminated by the introduction of a coherent perspective from which to link the results of disparate investigations undertaken so often without theoretical guidance.

## Notes

1. Social scientists have recently urged attention to such research. See, e.g., Wilson, *Varieties of Police Behavior*, pp. lff; Peter M. Blau and W. Richard Scott, *Formal Organizations*, p. 74; Peter Rossi, Richard Berk, David Boesel, Bettye Eidson, and W. Eugene Groves, "Between White and Black, The faces of American Institutions in the Ghetto," in *Supplemental Studies for the National Advisory Commission on Civil Disorders* (Washington, D.C.: U.S. Government, 1968); Herbert Jacob and Michael Lipsky, "Outputs, Structure, and Power: An Assessment of Changes in the Study of State and Local Politics," *Journal of Politics* 30 (1968), 538.

2. Robert Rosenthal and Lenore Jacobson, *Pygmalion in the Classroom* (New York: Holt, Rinehart and Winston, 1968).

3. For a critique and summary of decentralization proposals, see Alan Altshuler, *Community Control: The Black Demand for Participation In American Cities* (New York: Western Publishing Co., 1970).

4. See David Rogers, *110 Livingston Street* (New York, Random House, 1968).

5. For a more thorough development of the concept than is possible here, see my paper, "Toward a Theory of Street-level Bureaucracy," revised after original presentation at the Annual Meeting of the American Political Science Association, September, 1969, New York, N.Y. This paper is scheduled to appear in Willis Hawley and Michael Lipsky (eds.), *Theoretical Perspectives in Urban Politics* (tentative title), forthcoming.

6. See Theodore Sarbin and Vernon Allen, "Role Theory," in Gardner Lindsey and Elliot Aronson (eds.), *The Handbook of Social Psychology*, 2nd ed. (Reading, Mass.: Addison-Wesley, 1968), pp. 488-567.

7. On tracking, see the decision of Judge Skelly Wright in *Hobson v. Hanson*, June 19, 1967, 269 F. Supp. 401 (1-67). Also see Howard Becker, "Social Class and Teacher-Pupil Relationships," in Blaine Mercer and Edwin Carr (eds.), *Education and the Social Order* (New York, Rinehart, 1957).

8. Bernard Kelner, *How to Teach in Elementary School* (New York: McGraw-Hill, 1958), p. 19.

9. See Becker, previously cited.

10. Jerome Skolnick, *Justice without Trial* (New York: John Wiley, 1967), p. 105.

11. See Kenneth Clark, *Dark Ghetto* (New York: Harper and Row, 1965), pp. 125ff.; Rossi, et al., p. 136; and Becker, pp. 281-282.

12. See Rogers, and Wilson, both previously cited.

13. Albert Reiss, "Police Brutality—Answers to Key Questions," *Trans-action* (July-August, 1968), pp. 10-19.

# 14 The Politics of Education: Some Thoughts on Research Direction

J.P. CRECINE

In many respects a research program focusing on the "politics of education" or "political variables in the educational process" would be concerned with the wrong set of questions. The reason we are interested in political variables per se (or rather the reason we *should* be interested in political variables) is due to a logically prior interest in the outcomes of certain formal educational processes. It seems more appropriate to first look at the processes which generate these outcomes. If "political variables" turn out to be important determinants of educational outcomes all to the good. If not, that should not particularly disturb us. Naturally there is every reason to include "political variables" and "political processes" in an a priori check list of things to look for when investigating educational processes, but if we are truly interested in education and educational outcomes, "political" phenomena are relevant only with respect to those outcomes and hence should be examined in that context.

## How Do Educational Processes Work?:
## A Prior Question

To examine and better understand processes that generate educational outcomes, one must first focus on specific outcomes of particular interest. E.g., average annual income of ex-students after five years, etc. By choosing a particular set of outcomes one partially defines the processes to be examined. A logically prior decision, therefore, is to determine which set of outcomes one is attempting to explain, predict, control or improve on. In that context two kinds of processes seem of crucial interest in the area of education and worthy of examination.

In my judgment the most important kind of investigation to conduct is one that might be labeled "uncovering educational production functions." What we would really like to know first is what inputs in the actual educational process we would like to change in order to get what *predictable* changes in a particular set of outputs. The answers to these questions define the political and administrative problems of relevance and hence partially determine the range of research questions dealing strictly with political and administrative phenomena. We need to know in some detail the existing technology of producing educational out-

213

comes or, ideally, the details of a better technology. Such knowledge defines the appropriate context for an examination of "political variables" in educational research. Political research should be relevant and relevant to educational outcomes.

In view of our ignorance of what actually produces different outcomes, examination of the existing technology(s) is probably an appropriate starting point. Recent attempts to assess the long run impacts of federal educational programs aimed at racial minority (Head Start, grants to inner-city school districts, etc.) and economically deprived groups have failed to identify *any* significant effects. In a re-analysis of data from the Coleman report and a detailed analysis of data drawn from a large school system in California, Eric Hanushek has shown that even though school administrators assume the level of education of teachers is positively related to educational outcomes (an M.A. is better than a B.A.), smaller class sizes are better and years of teaching experience is positively related to educational outcomes, the data suggest that these relationships are weak or non-existent.[1] His data further suggest that even though administrators are willing to pay more for certain teacher and classroom characteristics, increased resource inputs do not lead to an improvement in outputs. Hanushek's results also indicate that the nature of the educational process is quite different for whites and minority groups. The Coleman report suggests that peer-group influences are much more important than teacher influences. A study conducted by Richard Morgenstern also gives no evidence to support the common assumption that more resources generate better education.[2] His data, like Hanushek's, support the notion that there are several different production functions for education; the differences between the South and the rest of the country are dramatic. Once one controls for this regional effect, per capita expenditures on education seem to have little, if any, positive influence on results (per capita expenditures per pupil do not seem to positively affect later earnings of students). There are two points; we have evidence that there are at least several ways of producing educational outcomes and we know very little if anything about the characteristics of these production functions.

At the very least the preponderance of the studies aimed at trying to estimate some kind of production function for education at the elementary and secondary level suggests we know very, very little about the technology of producing educational outcomes. Given this ignorance it is difficult to see where detailed knowledge of the existing process of financing and delivering educational services could be very useful. E.g., what good does it do us to know the factors that determine per-capita-expenditures-per-pupil if per-capita-expenditures-per-pupil do not seem to be very important in terms of effect on pupils? Who, aside from members of the academic community and other school administrators really cares if we know that school administrators have all the behavioral characteristics of a big city mayor?

The state of our knowledge of the educational process should make thoughtful men suspicious of proposals for changes in the process. It would seem reasonable to find out how and why the current educational mechanisms work before tinkering further.

If we identify the a priori determinants of educational outputs for a given student, $i$, at any time, $t$, $(E_{i,t})$ the list might look as follows:

1. Cumulative effects of family input to the education and life experience of the student at time, $t$. $(F_{i,t})$.
2. Cumulative effects of peer group influences to the educational outputs of the student at time, $t$. $(P_{i,t})$.
3. The set of innate endowments available to the student (native ability) $(A_i)$.
4. The cumulative effects of school or educational system inputs on the student to time $t$. $(S_{i,t})$

$$E_{i,t} = f(F_{i,t}, P_{i,t}, A_i, S_{i,t})$$

To summarize our above discussion, we do not know what the relationship between the inputs, $f$, is. We do "know" that there are many different educational production functions or f's, that there are probably important interrelationships between the inputs,[a] and that we probably have not included the proper set of inputs. From this formulation it is clear that the primary "political" effects are through the inputs of the school or educational system. If one is interested in the primary outcomes of this educational system $(E_{i,t})$ and if the above formulation of the problem is even approximately correct, it would seem important with respect to those outputs we are interested in. The amazing thing is there is no strong evidence that formal educational inputs are important in significant ways, independent from the others. Until we can show that the formal educational system is indeed important in its own right, is it not premature to study political factors just because they are "political"?

There are some important reasons why the current educational production function studies are inadequate and have yet to show clear results. The primary reason, of course, is that the data are generally cross-sectional. We are less concerned with identifying structural differences over the nation than with uncovering the characteristics of *dynamic*, ongoing educational *processes*. Most sensible observers would emphasize the *cumulative* effects of the four classes of input mentioned above and the importance of the interactions between these inputs *over time*; are three of the four inputs all acting in one direction?; do they reinforce one another? Briefly, two kinds of research are called for to uncover and identify these kinds of dynamic relationships. To uncover existing educational technologies requires panel data over a long period of time with a sufficiently

---

[a]In the language of econometrics, there is *probably* a multiplicative relationship among the input variables; formal schooling $(S_{i,t})$ must be supported by family and life experience $(F_{i,t})$ in order for either factor to effectively influence outcomes $(E_{i,t})$. E.g., $E_{i,t} = g\left[(S_{i,t})(F_{i,t})\right]$ is probably more significant than $E_{i,t} = h(S_{i,t}, F_{i,t})$.

large sample to estimate parameters and to detect different technologies among different groupings of the producers (teachers, classrooms, schools and school systems, regions of the country) and consumers (population groups—minorities—among students). It would certainly be advisable to monitor existing and possible policy variables (educational preparation of teacher, size of classes, per capita expenditure on school equipment, racial and economic composition of in-class peer groups, years teaching experience for teachers, etc.) in order to insure these studies are useful to practitioners. One thing seems clear, however. It is possible to conduct research of this type without explicitly considering "politics of education" questions. Where politics of education questions seem important is after we have decided to change the existing system, educational technology, etc. in particular ways. How might we implement these changes?

A second branch of research on educational production functions seems called for as well. In particular we would like some clues as to what better technologies might resemble (programed learning and teaching machines, mixed individual and mass instruction, Head Start programs, etc.). This, of course, suggests a series of well-designed and monitored long-run experiments. Even recognizing the intellectual difficulties involved (Hawthorne effect, expense, generalizability, etc.), the potential benefits would seem to far outweigh the cost.

**An Important Administrative and Political Process**

More to the point of the research-in-the-politics-of-education question, one of the first kinds of processes worth investigating in greater detail would be the determinants of the level and allocation of expenditures for education. Almost any outcome one would care to examine, almost any change in the educational system one would care to consider includes financial resources, either as an important constraint or as an important input. The outcomes of the resource allocation process form the context of most of the outcome-determining processes further down in the educational system; e.g., what students learn to enable them to survive economically. If, as the result of research suggested above, one knows why and in what sense one is interested in an "educational production" process then the resource allocation process becomes of prime importance. Resource allocation is important in its own right as a focal point of political and administrative decision-making as well. Research in this area is clearly possible; it involves repetitive processes and metric variables. It provides the researcher with the chance to uncover the underlying dynamics of systematic elements of decision processes. Once the systematic elements are uncovered the remaining (or unexplained) events are explicitly identified as interesting or unique in their own right and perhaps deserving of detailed case study (analysis of residuals).

I would argue that most research to date on the determinants of the level and allocation of educational expenditures is inherently misleading with regard to process; partly because most researchers to date have ignored bureaucratic and political processes and have assumed that decision-makers in the educational system were merely passive translators of well-defined and unambiguous public taste with regard to education. If we wish to implement changes in the system, detailed knowledge of process is essential. Components-of-variance and other results seldom suggest or illuminate implementation strategies.

Let us confine our attention to elementary and secondary school systems. If one looks at the process by which expenditure and allocation decisions get made in school systems, it is clear that an important determinant of outcomes concerns total revenues from local taxes—for the most part federal and state contributions are out of the control of the local district. Local taxes equals tax rate times yields, summed over tax bases. It is clear that general economic well-being and local assessment practices explain the bulk of the variance in per capita expenditure levels between districts because of their systematic influence on yields. Political factors in processes, the constitutional tax structure of the school district and tax burdens imposed by other units of government (which share the property tax with the district) in the area are important determinants of rates. To the extent that rates are determined by community referenda the process is inherently political. The relation of "public response to school tax proposals" to the "need and demands for quality and quantity of education" in a district is largely an unknown quantity.

Most school districts divide their budget into capital and operating budgets. The decision processes within the school system for these two kinds of budgets are drastically different. We know very little about capital budgets except for a suspicion that various concepts of neighborhood schools, maximum walking time to elementary schools, etc., are important policies with respect to capital decisions. We know a great deal more about the *process* of determining resource allocations within the operating budget. The works of Gerwin and Decker are particularly revealing.[3,4] My own work on governmental budgeting in cities and the Department of Defense would seem relevant as well.[5]

One of the most important resource allocation decisions made by local school boards concerns salary schedules for teachers. Gerwin has shown in a rather convincing way that this is largely a market phenomenon. School districts compete with a limited set of other school districts for teachers and when either teacher organizations force increases, or a district is unable to hire teachers to fill authorized slots, or the school district starting salary levels fall to the bottom of the set of reference group school districts, a salary increase occurs. Quite different heuristics for allocating the remainder of the budget exist. Whether these decision rules are consistent across school districts is another question.

On an a priori basis, a study of budgeting in school districts should be more interesting and productive than studies of budgeting in units of general government. With more general sets of functions there is no feasible way to make rational trade-offs between the many incommensurable functions of government. In a school district setting, however, the units among which the pie must be allocated are much more comparable. There exist widely agreed upon, objective measures of quality (even though little evidence exists that these are really relevant to *educational* quality) such as student-teacher ratios, classroom size, hours per day of instruction or days per school year, per capita expenditures, per pupil expenditures, test score averages per pupil, percent graduates continuing on to higher education, etc. Exactly how these measures do or could enter the resource allocation process seems to be an extremely important question. These measures are important especially as they relate or do not relate to the results of research on educational production functions; i.e., can one substitute more relevant measures for the existing ones in the allocation process? What changes in the political and bureaucratic system would be necessary to make these substitutions: Detailed knowledge of the existing political and administrative allocation *process* is necessary to properly design social change strategies.

Research into the characteristics of the processes that determine total revenues per school district, the resource allocation process in the capital budget, the allocation process in the operating budget all requires time series data on one or more educational units or school districts, assumptions about the degree of change in the process during the period examined, and some assumptions about the generalizability of findings between school districts (similarity of processes). The professionalization of teachers and educators gives some cause for optimism concerning process stability over time and between school districts. Similarity in revenue structures (property taxes, state contributions and federal funds), school boards, the existence of comparative data on teachers' salaries, per capita expenditures (or *per pupil*, for capital and operating costs), promotional criteria, output measures (exam performance or dropout ratios) give some cause for hope that there are a reasonably small set of educational production processes currently employed that are different in any fundamental sense. This gives additional hope that findings concerning characteristics of a process are likely to be generalizable.

It is relatively easy to define a priori conditions *suggesting* causes for differences in process, both over time and currently. For example: Morgenstern's data suggest the South is different. Different reference school districts or determinants of teachers' salaries suggest different structures of external stimuli and the like. To identify "similar processes," perhaps school districts should be grouped by city size and tax structure, by community wealth—and education? —by different city political structures (cities where education performed by city rather than independent), formal linkages between city and school revenues, machine politics vs. nonpartisan, etc.

In summary, research on the politics of education should focus on those processes that allocate resources in the formal educational system, viewed as the political and administrative control mechanisms for educational production functions and processes. Design of appropriate control processes requires detailed knowledge of the (educational) processes being controlled and detailed knowledge of existing control processes. Knowledge of the latter is useless without knowledge of the former.

**Notes**

1. Eric Hanushek, "The Production of Education, Teacher Quality and Efficiency," *Do Teachers Make Difference?* U.S. Office of Education Report, OE-58042 (Bureau of Educational Personnel Development, 1970).

2. Richard Morgenstern, *The Returns to Improved Quality of Elementary and Secondary Education*, Unpublished Ph.D. dissertation, University of Michigan, 1970.

3. Donald Gerwin, *Budgeting Public Funds: The Decision Process in an Urban School District* (University of Wisconsin Press, 1969).

4. Michael Decker, "Representing the Educational Policy-Making Process," *Education and Urban Society*, Vol. 1, No. 3 (May 1969), 266-288.

5. J.P. Crecine, *Government Problem Solving: A Computer Simulation of Municipal Budgeting* (Rand McNally, 1969); *Defense Budgeting: Organizational Adaptations to External Constraints*, RM-6121-PR (The Rand Corporation, 1970).

# Part 4: An Analysis of the Conference Discussion

# An Analysis of the
# Conference Discussion

MICHAEL KIRST and DAVID GROSSMAN

What was distinctive about the research concerns of Cluster I (Part 1 in this volume), as opposed to those of the two remaining Clusters, was a general reaction against the paradigms commonly used in the study of the relationship between politics and education, and beyond that, for some of the participants at least (e.g. Wolin, Greenberg), a reaction against those paradigms used in the discipline of political science generally. While, in the main, Cluster II (Part 2 in this volume) dealt with the interface between political and educational processes, and Cluster III (Part 3 in this volume) with the outputs of educational and political systems, Cluster I challenged the processes and outputs themselves *and their underlying assumptions.* Rejecting such well-known modes of analysis as systems "theory," political socialization theory, or production function models, this group instead focused on the search for new goals for the study of politics and education.

As might have been expected from the nature of the task they accepted, Cluster I became, at once, both the least defined and the most controversial of the three Clusters, and the intragroup conflict was only surpassed by the arguments at the meetings of the whole. Still, certain common themes did appear, or can be extrapolated from the participants' papers, their discussions, and their final report. These themes should bear on the formulation of future research questions in the study of the politics of education.

## Research Guidelines: Cluster I

As suggested by Bailey in this Cluster's final report to the Conference, the concerns of Cluster I fell basically into four areas:

1. *broad speculative questions about norms* – including questions of what kind of world/society do we want, and what does the educational system have to do with getting us there;
2. *questions of assumptions* – about nature, man, society, etc.; here emphasis was also placed on the question of the nature and direction of the relationship between politics and education, i.e., the question of the dependent versus independent variable in the relationship between politics and education raised in Heinz Eulau's paper, and repeated in the introductory section of this volume.

3. *descriptive and analytic questions of how views/values/goals* are formed in the educational system; and
4. *a series of instrumental questions* dealing with possible alternative goal formations, including questions of what is researchable, and questions of how do we get from here to a more desirable there.

As broad, encompassing, and open-ended as these four areas of speculation may seem to be at first glance, the actual discussion of these issues in Cluster I was framed within a particular context. That context was provided by Sheldon Wolin's conference paper, "Politics, Education, and Theory." In his paper, Wolin offers us a tentative outline of an alternative paradigm (in particular vehement opposition to "systems theory") which he hopes will form the beginnings of a new theory of the politics of education. While it is not possible or useful to completely recount Wolin's proposal here, some discussion of it is necessary to provide a basis for understanding Cluster I's proposals.

In brief, Wolin offers us a new paradigm for the study of politics and education, that of "technological society" or more broadly, "technological culture." As Wolin himself explains,

Today there is scarcely a sphere of society or a major aspect of human activity which is not infected by a technological component. There is daily confirmation that contemporary politics is mostly about the future imperatives and past consequences of technology; that education is increasingly affected by it; that, in short, our society can be most accurately described as technological. Neither politics nor education, nor any combination of the two, can be properly understood apart from the technological society. (See Wolin, p. 19.)

In his paper Wolin proceeds to enumerate some of the possible characteristics which his paradigm, or incipient theory, of the technological society might include. In harshly abbreviated form these concepts are as follows:

1. Like all previous societies, technological society constitutes an *order*, but of a distinctive kind.
2. Although many previous societies have accorded a high place to the pursuit of *knowledge* and to the value of "useful" knowledge (and have supported the institutions of knowledge), technological society is not only deeply dependent on knowledge, but particularly reliant upon knowledge which is systematic and interlocked.
3. Technological society is not classless; the destruction of work and the ever-changing demands of technology (e.g., new complex skills) threaten the lower classes with permanent subjugation.
4. Technological society accentuates *concentrations of power and influence*.
5. In technological society it becomes increasingly difficult to alter or significantly modify the society by means of political action.

Much of the early argument in Cluster I focused on Wolin's conception of the "technological society" and its implications for the goals and processes of educational institutions. As Salisbury summarized these implications in Cluster I's final report:

First is the rapidity of changes in environment, in work roles, and in nearly every aspect of one's physical and social circumstances. Secondly, there is the steady shrinkage in the social requirements for physical labor in the production of goods. Third is the probable drive for increased efficiency and/or stability in the allocations of resources with the result that pressures will mount to close out deviant or dissonant activities and groups.

While it must be said that not all of Cluster I (much less the whole conference group) could agree on the validity, relevance, and usefulness of Wolin's model and its implications, there was wider agreement on the model's ability to generate broad major questions often neglected in the pursuit of empirical political data. Three of these major questions were formulated and expressed as follows:

1. What shapes might a future society take?
2. Given these futures, what role might education take?
3. How might alternative futures be changed and at what price? — including the question of how the relationship between politics and education might change in the future.

In answer to those, particularly in the meetings of all conference participants, who challenged such formulations as illegitimate, arrogant, or unanswerable, Heinz Eulau argued that indeed the construction of futuristic models was a legitimate task of political science (*a la* Lasswell), especially when linked to and used to shed light on the present. On the other hand, Professor Eulau criticized Wolin's model for failing to provide the requisite connections between his hypothesized future and a past and present. Wolin, it was argued, failed to present an empirical basis for his model either in the form of trend lines based on present empirical data or selected empirical indicators for the future society he was attempting to describe. Eulau further criticized Wolin's model for failing to vide these same linkages in terms of measurable *political* variables, such as the composition and behavior of elites. In any case, as was indicated above, many conference participants were willing to accept the validity of questions of alternative futures as research pursuits, while taking exception to the validity of Wolin's particular model.

A second and related phase of the discussion of the research concerns of Cluster I focused on Wolin's notion that because of the implications of his notion of the technological society, that the role of education in the future might be constructed to be "counter-political." Because of the inchoate nature of his theoretical conceptions, Wolin neither could nor would specify the nature of his concept of "counter-politics," but it was clear that the notion was neither "antipolitical" nor "nonpolitical" in substance. Rather what was implied here is that once the characteristics of the technological society (or at least some of the concepts therein) are accepted, one must then distinguish between its fortuitous and its destructive aspects. According to Wolin's conceptualization, inherent in certain tendencies of the technological society, such as the growth of interlocking control and the demand for increased efficiency, are clear and present threats to both human and democratic values, and these threats have become increasingly manifest in contemporary America. (It became clear during the conference that Wolin's paradigm was largely one of "incipient evil," —evil derived from the imminent values of the technological society.)

It was in the context of these destructive tendencies of the technological society that Wolin prescribed educational institutions that were to be "counter-political"—that is, counter to the destructive thrusts of the technological society. The role of the educational system in his formulation thus becomes to teach people to question, if not resist, many of the societal forces acting upon them. This was not, Wolin argued, a defense of traditional liberal arts or humanistic curricula as it questioned the rational objectivist values which lay at the base of such curricula. A "counter-political" educational system would, in contrast, value personal expression and subjectivity. However, Wolin's "counter-culture" is not the privatized withdrawal from society. His concern is rather to assure that educational programs will not serve only the manifest requirements of efficient technology, even on the consumer side of that technology. A counter-system education would build into the curriculum the direct examination of the society's assumptions and practices so that *within the system* a critical dialog could be maintained and support a dialectic of social change.

Objections to Wolin's formulation of a "counter-political" educational system came rapidly and heavily, particularly when presented to the entire group of conference participants. In general, those who objected fell into three categories: (a) those who were willing to accept Wolin's notion of education as "counter-political," or at least to allow education the role of critic and innovator, but who had serious doubts about the ability of a society to tolerate such deviant institutions; (b) those who wondered if such a counter-cultural role could be institutionalized and still survive, e.g., could the state actually fund a "counter-political" university without compromising the thrust of its counter-politics. Here it was suggested that in order to be truly "counter-political" a movement, group, or institution would almost by definition have to stay outside of established systems; and (c) those who thought it was beyond the jurisdiction of political scientists to prescribe the context and structure of educational institutions.

The final phase of the discussion of Cluster I's research concerns centered on the implications of the questions raised for research designs in the study of politics and education. Because of the broad and assumptive nature of the issues raised in Cluster I, the proposals for research scattered in various directions and were expressed at various levels of generality. No concrete list of research proposals emerged in Cluster I's final report, nor was a specific list of priorities proposed. (In fairness, it should be added that the topic faced by Cluster I was not amenable to the completion of such tasks in a week's time.) Instead we are forced to present our own distillation of research proposals, based on the conference papers, discussions, and Cluster I's final report.

The broadest of the proposals made by Cluster I was by Wolin himself, who advocated that a small number of political "theorists" or "thinkers," (who would be "relatively easily identifiable" in the field) be subsidized for one or two years for the development of new paradigms for the study of politics and education. Whether these paradigms would turn out to be those of the technological society or not would make little difference. The important task would be the identification of a *range of alternative futures.* Or as Norton Long put it, the task would be to develop ways of thinking about our society's problems in a way that solutions are not inhibited. In short, it was proposed to support people who are judged to be good bets for critical insights into societal patterns and institutional linkages and their implications. Here capacity for critical thought and willingness to give sustained, disciplined attention to broad problems would be more important than fully elaborated research designs.

The remaining, and more specific, proposals for research generally fell into two categories: (a) those that emphasized education, educational institutions, or the educational system as independent variable(s) with impact on the individual as the dependent variable; and (b) those that used the political system, or sets of political variables, as the dependent variable in the study. No typology is ever completely satisfactory, but this one adequately represents the two major thrusts of suggested research designs.

In the former category were basically four proposals:

1. A study of what makes individuals adaptive to change, and what role education might play in such a process. The concern here was that if technology creates a rapidly changing environment, then education should strive to produce individuals capable of dealing with change. At one level the rapidity of technology induced change might lead us to study an educational program that stressed modes of inquiry and "learning about learning" rather than conveying a particular body of knowledge or set of skills. At another level, how does one teach a child so as to induce adaptive openness toward change? It is a matter for research to establish (a) what images of time and of the flow of events through time people hold, (b) how and when these are acquired, (c) what consequences these images have for adaptiveness and for other basic social postures and predispositions, and (d) how alternative educational processes might alter these images of social and historical time.
2. A study of how in a consumption culture, "connoiseurship," or the ability to

discriminate with taste might be taught. In the technological society, the student grows up to be a consumer. What are the implications of this for education? How might education prepare students for this role?

3. A study of how primary and secondary education might be made less monolithic, i.e., more responsive to differing types of individuals. In the technological society, for example, the large comprehensive high school has become the norm. Is it this kind of standardization and size we want in our educational institutions? Can we provide alternatives and options for various kinds of individuals? Two studies that were suggested by conference participants focussed on the politics of (a) alternative and/or "free" schools, and (b) of the tuition voucher system. The former proposal would involve such questions as the political use of state regulations to close down alternative and/or "free" schools. The latter would involve examination of experimental uses of the voucher system (as in Christopher Jencks' program), in terms of various political variables.

4. A study of how structural changes produce changes in values and value orientations. Here the focus was on researchable questions of what happens to individuals in schools, and how schools might be changed to produce different value structures in individuals. Again it was proposed to study the impact of alternative structures and changes in existing structures of education.

In the latter category of the research proposals of Cluster I come a set of suggestions in five areas:

1. A study of the future orientation of educational elites. As Salisbury explains, opinion research has too seldom tapped the projective side of the ways people look at the world. To draw out and articulate what are now half-formed and inarticulate preferences might reveal, among other things, a greater range of political alternatives than we now believe exists.

2. A study of change in professions to assess both the effect on the authority structure of the profession and on the behavior of the professionals in the public order. Has there been any change in the professions—law, medicine, engineering, etc.? If so, in what areas, and what impact has it had on the authority structure of the profession, and the behavior of the professionals? For example, what is the meaning of such phenomena as community clinics run by medical students, or community legal services donated by law students?

3. An examination of the cost factor of alternatives both within and outside the present educational system. Here the basic issue is incremental change within system versus changing the system itself. To what extent can desired changes be carried out within the present educational system? Or, as Wolin has suggested, have we reached a point where significant alternations will only occur outside the present system? Which direction is more costly? Here "costs" referred to *both* political and economic costs.

4. A study of what strategies produce structural changes in the educational system. If one assumes that significant changes can be induced within the present educational system, how are such changes to be introduced? Is it possible to get beyond those traditional case studies in the education literature, e.g., "how bond issue X was passed in County Y," into a new theoretical area of political strategies in education? and

5. A study of how a new set of orientations becomes a political paradigm. On the one hand, it was suggested that there be studies of the development of political paradigms in textbooks and curriculum materials (e.g., see Greenberg's paper), or those paradigms held by elites (e.g., see Salisbury's paper). On the other hand, studies of how ideological symbols get into schools and become legitimate were proposed. Here the suggested pattern of studies was to investigate how schools and school systems deal with such phenomena as (a) elections, (b) the presidency, (c) the draft, (d) the Vietnam War, and (e) the legal system and legal rights. The need for longitudinal as well as cross-sectional studies in this area was stressed.

This list gives us little in the way of clues as to where to start, for Cluster I never attempted to assign definitive research priorities. However, Sheldon Wolin did give us a clue as to his own set of priorities. According to Wolin, the basic problem in our society, as well as our educational and political systems, is change. Citing the case of the university in the past five years, Wolin argued that often by the time we study a system, it's gone in the form we knew it. The great priority, Wolin continued, is for future study in the area of politics and education to be more projective.

But, lest it be underestimated, Wolin's argument for priorities should be examined in the light of a new and prominent branch of research (largely funded by USOE) in the study of politics and education, that of "alternative future histories." Groups like the Educational Policy Research Center of the Stanford Research Institute (Menlo Park, California) and Johnson Research Associates (Santa Barbara, California) have constructed as many as forty future histories *for the purpose of investigating their educational policy implications.* In a report based on their work EPRC/SRI and Johnson Associates, report that there are very few plausible future histories which avoid some period of serious trouble between now and 2050. The few that do, moreover, seem to require "a dramatic shift of values and perceptions with regard to what we come to term the 'world macroproblem.' " As the report further explains,

This macroproblem will be the predominant concern of the foreseeable future for all the alternative paths. It is the composite of all the problems that have been brought about by a combination of rampant technology application and industrial development, together with high population levels (in turn, a consequence of technology-reduced mortality rate). These fall mainly into three groups: problems of the ecosystem; technological threats of various kinds; and an intrinsically expanding "have—have-not" gap (increasingly seen as unjust exploitation of the have-nots). It is so named since the problems are mutually exacerbating and since there appears to be high likelihood that they can be solved only in systematic fashion and not piecemeal. Further, it appears that although various aspects of the world macroproblem may be ameliorated or postponed by certain technological achievements, its nexus is intrinsic in the basic operative premises of the present Western industrialized culture. If this is correct, then it follows that *education toward changing those premises, directly or indirectly, is the paramount educational task for the United States and for the world.* This means that education should be directed toward responsible stewardship of life on earth with the associated changes in values and premises that are necessary for this shift.[1]

It is just the kind of priority suggested by this report that the members of Cluster I were concerned with. However, as political scientists, we would suggest that residual questions remain which are of particular relevance to our discipline. First of all, there is a clear implication in the passage cited above that the key independent variable in long range systemic change is the education system while the political system is the dependent variable—an assumption which, as Professor Eulau points out in his paper, is open to serious question. Secondly, the authors of the cited passage, and rightly so given their concerns, concentrate on the shape of the educational system. Yet the question remains, given the kind of concerns expressed, what *should a future-oriented political system look like.*

Therefore, given the nature of these residual questions, we would suggest (using some poetic license) that the kind of priorities that Cluster I would finally propose would be as follows: First, that research attention should be devoted to the construction and explication of futuristic *model(s) of the political system* which allow for the solution of such "macro-problems" as might be facing our society, and which at the same time delineate both the nature and direction of the relationship between political and educational institutions; *secondly,* that the construction and existence of such models be validated by studies of past and present trends in the political system, e.g., that Wolin's assertion that technological society accentuates concentration of power and influence by empirically demonstrated, and *at a third level of priority,* case studies of structural changes in both the educational and political systems in terms of the kind of values and value orientations they produce (i.e., do they provide the kind of value orientations that allow for the solution of these "macro-problems"). This last level would include experimental and quasi-experimental research into alternative institutional arrangements.

In conclusion, it might be said again that Cluster I's lack of closure was largely due to the nature of the task. When a group's basic task is to examine the normative assumptions behind the goals and objectives of the study of politics and education, a few days of discussion, however intensive, will hardly suffice. In the long-run, however, and especially if Professor Wolin and others are right, it may prove to have been the most crucial topic.

## Research Guidelines: Cluster II

As the title of this Cluster indicates (i.e., "The Political Education of Youth: New Directions in Research on Political Socialization Including Cross-Cultural Studies"), the participants, in contrast to Cluster I, took as their starting point a relatively well-defined and prominent branch of research in the study of politics and education (although a recent one), that of political socialization research. Here the issue became one of defining what directions this branch of research should take in the 1970s and beyond. Once more, this problem was confronted both in intra-societal and comparative terms.

To the extent that a trend has been identifiable, political socialization research on education has commonly focused on what is learned about the political system in schools. Moreover, the prototype studies in the field (e.g., those of Hess and Easton) tended to concentrate on what political norms were learned in school and the degree to which these norms contributed to the stability of the political system. Yet, as the late 1960s approached, these cross-sectional studies of the late 1950s and early 1960s seemed less and less explanatory of the empirical data on school disruption, student alienation, and the general trend toward increased student activism on political issues. Without examining in detail all aspects of the early models of political socialization, suffice it to say that their emphasis on the transmission of adult political norms, knowledge, beliefs, and orientations to pre-adults was faced by an increasing number of anomalies in the schools of the late 1960s.

It is against this kind of conceptualization of the political socialization process that the members of Cluster II were reacting, albeit in a positive sense. For example, Robert Hess himself sent a provocative memo to the conference participants in which the following points were made:

The contemporary scene is obviously quite different and it is difficult to explain it by applying traditional models of socialization to political attitudes and especially to political behavior in young people. . . It seemed to me a couple of years ago that a model of political learning which made allowance for acquiring political attitudes and behavior from peers was more realistic than a model which conceptualized socialization as the transmission of belief systems and behavior patterns from the adults to the pre-adults. I found the notion of political learning more comfortable than political socialization in attempting to understand anti-establishment feelings and activities on the part of students and other minority groups. It was not completely satisfactory, but it helped me move out of a too-rigid way of thinking about the growth of citizen-type behavior.

It was in this spirit, one critical of previous models and designs in the field of political socialization research on schools, that the discussion and final report of Cluster II were framed. In an effort to overcome the conceptual limitations of previous models, Cluster II stressed two criteria which they felt should be invoked in researching the political effects on youth of schools and schooling.

First of all, they argued that research questions in this field should *represent a clear point of connection between political learning and the schooling experience*. Here an attempt was clearly made to separate the concerns of Cluster I from conventional political socialization designs. As was indicated above, the conventional design incorporates political data *in* schools, but very little data relevant to the *nexus between politics and schooling*. For example, it is not only necessary to collect surveys of political attitudes found in school children, but also investigate how and to what extent the authority structure of the school and/or classroom shapes attitudes which are transferred to the political system. It is this kind of connectedness between education and politics that merits research attention, according to Cluster II. The implication here is that research should focus on phenomena which are simultaneously affected by educational *and* political processes. It is also implied that findings should enrich theory-building about both schooling *and* political life.

Secondly, the members of Cluster II maintained that *research should not separate the learner, the learning, and the learned from the structures of society*. This criterion implies more than the conventional injunction that students should not, for purposes of research, be lifted from their learning environment (though the importance of this injunction is acknowledged). Here the thrust, as in the case of the first criterion, is toward a widening of conceptualization of the political learning process which, in turn, it is hoped will increase the explanatory power of theory in this area. *The emphasis in this context is on a research program which investigates political learning by also investigating social and political stratification, the criteria of political and social differentiation, and the conditions of access and influence*. (For examples of such research designs, see the papers of Meyer and Prewitt.) Schooling, it is argued, is socially chartered to direct students toward adult social and political status positions, and through credentialing activities, schools define these positions as well as legitimate the assignment of differentially educated people to them. In so doing schools are affected by and affect the structures of society.

While in isolation these ideas might seem somewhat commonplace, in the context of political socialization they could mark a significant shift of emphasis. As Kenneth Prewitt put it at the conference, it is time to realize that there is a politics of learning as well as a learning of politics. In other words, what is learned in schools is determined to some extent by certain political and social variables (in turn traceable to other structures in the society). What these variables are is not altogether clear at this point, but Cluster II could delineate certain areas for investigations as possible independent variables in the case of political learning in the schooling process.

Of course, the teaching and learning process is the arena in which political norms and behavior are transmitted to students. The formal curriculum has obvious effects on students which must be investigated. In large measure, they result from, and affect, the expectations which students and others have about schooling. *However, the expectations of school and political leaders themselves influence and are influenced by attributes of teaching and learning contexts—attributes that may reinforce, negate, or have no influence on the social and citizenship norms and behavior which are acquired.* Thus, in any investigation of the political meaning of the schooling process, the kind of independent variables we would have to consider would be as follows:

1. Students have *expectations about education*; in particular its methods for judging their social and citizenship accomplishments. Parents, peers, and teachers all influence the individual directly and through their expectations about the life chances and roles which schools control, and what they are supposed to do in sorting out students among the political and economic strata of society. Agencies of schooling, such as testing and curriculum, produce these effects. It is imperative to know how these expectations of school and student influence the political attitudes and actions the young adopt as they become functional members of the polity and the economy.
2. *If the schools are expected to operate in major ways to differentiate political elites and followers, then these expectations and their structural reality are themselves an important source of school effects.* Schools exist in a larger structural context than that of teacher-classroom-student; the elements of which play crucial roles in defining the schools' right to train, influence, and allocate students. Civil service rules, the orientations of political elites, occupational gatekeepers, and dominant myths about the social and political nature of schooling affect the political expectations and activities which schools create in their students.
3. *The academic core of teaching and learning is a critical, and often neglected source of political learning.* Expectations of academic performance by students and elites importantly shape the extent to which groups regard education as an agency to influence the allocation of political and economic resources, the distribution of those resources, and the creation of norms and experiences designed to attain the objectives in mind. In particular, the political significance of learning, credentials, and grading needs to be seen as a source of other citizenship and social outcomes we have stressed.
4. *The social context of education in the schools contains elements of conflict and participation designed to influence the distribution of rewards and sanctions and future sorting into the political and economic domains.* Once more it is imperative to understand the expectations of students and those who govern the schools about the scope and qualities of participation. Moreover, expectations and behavior in response to political conflict about the assignment of citizenship rights and duties need to be investigated as sources of political socialization.

Thus, in this set of variables, Cluster II has attempted, consistent with the criteria it set, to get at the nexus between politics and schooling, while at the same time connecting these processes to the larger structures of the society. In this context what was stressed was that persons who control educational resources, and thereby shape educational institutions, have assumptions about society. Moreover, they have assumptions about how children should be prepared for membership in the society. *These assumptions serve as reference points during times of choice regarding the allocation of resources.* However implicitly held and however variable across the relevant population, these assumptions become translated into legitimate and authoritative curricula, teacher training and selection, testing procedures, extracurricular programs, and so forth. Providing a socially sanctioned and institutional setting for the political learning of children reflects an attempt, albeit a clumsy one, to prepare children for membership in the civil and commercial adult society, and to define such membership.

Using this mode of analysis, the members of Cluster II concluded that in important ways the experience of being "educated" is to be sorted into groups which vary widely in cognitive development, relevant skills and talents, self-esteem, access and influence, social status, cultural norms, and so forth. This grouping process in part assigns students to different political and social statuses. Moreover, persons not currently in schools recognize the connection between differential education and the different groupings, and thus the impact of the school is to be traced into populations other than students.

Given the nature of these observations, Cluster II was led to an emphasis on specific types of dependent variables, particularly variables linked to the ambiguities and expectations associated with political citizenship, and variables linked to the privileges and penalties associated with different levels of social status. The bulk of the discussion in Cluster II was spent on the development of these dependent variables, as it was felt, with justification, that the range of variables in previous political socialization research has been limited and confining (e.g., see Weiler's paper). While it would be impossible to recount their discussion of these variables, let us present their own summary of these variables from their final report. The dependent variables were divided into four areas:

1. Political systems are characterized by significant, if varying, degrees of conflict over both specific policy issues and more fundamental normative assumptions about the goals to be achieved through the system's operation. While some political norms are shared by the members of the system, others are controversial and become subject to more or less polarized opinions and beliefs. The citizen's role comprises both agreement and disagreement, both consent and dissent, both acceptance and rejection of others' beliefs and behaviors. His socialization into the world of politics will have to be conceived in such a way as to reflect the condition of conflict under which his role is performed. Whether as a result of deliberate direction or not, the various processes of learning about politics result in the acquisition of cognitive and

evaluative orientations towards diversity, dissent, and conflict. *Thus, measuring the degree to which, and the conditions under which dissenting individuals and groups in the system are tolerated in the attitudes and practical behavior of socializees becomes an important further dimension in the study of political socialization.*

2. Both the assumptions guiding the role of the school in the process of political learning, and its actual effect on the results of the learning process, are subject to being at variance with the expectations held by significant other groups in the system, especially under conditions of rapid change and/or substantial cleavages within the society. The resultant discontinuities and inconsistencies create situations of stress, uncertainty, and social change. The capacities for handling such situations has to be conceived as a function of certain role norms which may or may not have been acquired in the socialization process. The ability and willingness to tolerate stress and uncertainty does, therefore, become a variable directly relevant to understanding the process of change which results from the lack of congruence between societal expectations and socialization outcomes. At the institutional level, it is important to examine the ways social changes may follow from incongruities between training expectations and principles of social allocation built into the educational system (and those held in the wider society).

3. Schools both create political attitudes, and quite independently affect the *actual political activity* of their products. A causal chain leads from schools through their immediate consequences on students to these students' ultimate participation in the political order. But there is a more direct effect. Schools are chartered with the right to allocate students into the various differentiated parts of the political order. This authority operates to socially locate students and to affect their roles and activity quite apart from any immediate effects it may have (perhaps operating through anticipatory socialization) on their attitudes. And because the authority of schools to allocate students into social and political positions occurs over long periods of time, their effects must be examined by long-term longitudinal research. School effects will appear quite different, and operate through different mechanisms if we study their products much later than if we study them while they are still students.

   Further, if schools have the social authority to lead their students in actual political participation during the educational process itself, they greatly affect the present and later participation of these students. Student groups in many societies are participating political elites, as the social boundaries of the educational system are extended to include parts of the political system itself. Through such processes attitudes may be affected, but activity is directly created by the institutional structure.

4. School structures provide an important means of legitimating a whole system of inequalities, both in the eyes of students or graduates, and in the view of

large sectors of the adult population. The chartering of a given set of schools with the authority to allocate present rights and future roles to students may have crucial effects on many parts of the society—quite beyond the student population being socialized. School structures, and the charters or rights of allocation on which they are based, provide a basis for many myths about equality, the rights of citizens, and the rights of elites. Is it not surprising that we rely so much, in modern societies, on the specialized competences of professionals who we *privately* may suspect of having training of dubious utility? And is it not surprising that we place the ultimate powers in the hands of ordinary citizens whose every idea we suspect? Clearly we explain and justify these extraordinary concessions partly by referring to the charter and presumed effects of the various parts of the educational system. These institutions, if they do nothing else, provide comforting and stabilizing justifications of our dependence on both elite and citizen. Whether or not an educational system improves the political competence of these parties, it helps to provide a legitimization of their "proper" participant roles.

It is necessary to investigate the consequences of the development of educational systems, and the expansion or contraction of their authority over political instruction and allocation; for all sorts of groups in the political system, not only the students themselves.

As valuable as this discussion of dependent variables is in terms of broad insights into the impact of the schooling process on political learning, it is hardly specific enough to provide us with a clear set of research priorities in the field of politics and education. Yet Cluster II did attempt to briefly define four areas which they thought were essential to the variables they emphasized and the kind of social reality they were attempting to describe. This is as close as Cluster II came to setting research priorities and indicating specific research designs (beyond those developed in their individual conference papers). These are the areas Cluster II considered most significant for further exploration:

1. In order to trace the development of political norms and styles of political activity among adults and to understand the unfolding of the social sorting and selecting process, some indicators must be collected longitudinally. Such effects can be traced to characteristics of schools and schooling only (if at all!) through longitudinal research in which those who are subjected to different schooling patterns are observed as they progress through later life.

2. Identification of schooling patterns which are likely to make a difference in later political life and their isolation in quasi-experimental designs using "field experiments" will conserve research funds and simplify data analysis. We can stage experiments (as Professor Litt suggests) or take advantage of the

wide variations which already exist in the schooling patterns in this country and abroad.

3. The use of field experiments implies the preservation of contextual elements of the data. Concepts like conflict, consensus, status allocation, or docility must be operationalized in ways which have meaning for the contexts in which they are observed. If, for example, we posit different results from schoolings provided blacks and whites in American schools, we must be certain that the concepts have valid meaning in both contexts even if that requires that we use somewhat different measures of the concept for each social group. Expectations about the consequences of schooling may not only be different among several social groups or geographical area but they may also exist along different dimensions.

4. In order to obtain data about expectations and the cognitive maps of the educational process from students and nonstudents, individuals must be approached as *informants* as well as *respondents*. The picture of reality that individuals perceive are evoked by quite unstructured interviews while responses to particular attitudinal and behavioral stimuli provide data about norms and role perceptions in situations that are highly structured by the researcher. How individuals see the effects of schooling is as important (or more so) as the roles and norms that are evoked by the researcher's structured inquiries.

In summary, the members of Cluster II, given the nature of their stated interests, would probably suggest the following kind of priority for the further study of the political education of youth. Cluster II, it seems, would choose to direct research into the *"nexus" between politics and schooling.* They would emphasize the study of certain phenomena in the schooling experience which are simultaneously affected by educational and political processes. To use Kenneth Prewitt's phrase again, it is time to recognize that there is a "politics of learning" as well as a learning of politics in school.

In this context, Cluster II calls for the use of a set of independent variables in future studies which will place political learning in a wider social context. To what extent, it is asked, is what is learned in the schools traceable to other structures in the society (and, in particular to the patterns and criteria for political and social differentiation)? At another level, Cluster II would call for the expansion of the kind of dependent variables used in studies of the political education of youth. Can we ascertain, it is asked, the different kinds of political learning that result from variance in the school experiences of youth? In approaching such questions, Cluster II suggests a wide variety of research designs (depending on the scope of the question), including survey, longitudinal, experimental and quasi-experimental designs.

## Research Guidelines: Cluster III

*Major Areas of Consideration: General*
*Research Guidelines*

In a meeting where ideas are many but the focus is uncertain, some scatteration follows in any presentation of the outcome. Several themes appeared. These are statements of what this cluster ("the governance of public education") believed it is important to study in understanding the politics of education. Among these themes will be found ideas in many of the papers offered under Cluster III; additions arose out of the group sessions. At the present time, we cannot rank order the specific research suggestions discussed below. We began with some general considerations and then moved to some proposed thrusts.

1.  Given the great variety of American school systems, how can we generalize about their politics? Whether the element of these systems we wish to understand is, in Eastonian terms of environment, needs and demands, policy conversion, or outputs, we must work toward classificatory schemes which emphasize comparative analysis. This theme had several, oft-repeated insistences. The case study alone, selected randomly or fortuitously, is obviously inadequate to this task. Macroanalysis provides more answers, of course, but it alone often masks important political variables and is also insufficient. Much was heard about the need to match macroanalytic survey results with identification of deviant cases (e.g., high achieving slum schools, free schools) for the illumination they provide of the norm from which they deviate. In short, typologies are useful as long as they are exposed to aggregate data for the distributional or development lessons they may provide.
2.  Whether the focus of policy research should be upon the total process in which policy is born, authorized, and administered, or whether the focus should be upon one level with a range of policies operating, is a query of some disagreement. But most participants stressed the former, insisting upon the need to understand policy primarily by following it vertically through all levels of government from the federal government to classroom units. This permits developmental analysis for a given policy, demonstrates all the operative forces at work, and encourages theory building about the life histories— or pathologies—of policy. Yet horizontal focus upon one unit of decision-making—Washington's Office of Education or the East Hogsville, Arkansas School District—enables us to see what is happening to an array of policies (curriculum, integration, teacher retraining, etc.) in the conversion-output-outcome chain. In this way we can build toward general theory that spans sub-system decisional structures.

Note, however, two aspects of either analytical framework. Each partakes of the case study, whether it is a single policy studied through vertical layers of decisional apparatuses or a single layer through which an array of policies are viewed. Second, little of either kind of study exists in the literature. More typically, studies consist of one phase and substantive focus of the policy process, e.g., policy conversion alone (Congress makes a law, the school board finally votes to accept sex education courses). Or, there may be a review of a few policy decisions at one level, but certainly not the full range which commands the energies and other resources of the local school system. The absence of research fitting either of the two alternative approaches may well be an indication of the difficulty and expense of execution each involves. In light of the paucity of research via either alternative, the resolution of the methodological debate awaits more research along both lines. Regardless of which option is pursued, more will certainly be assembled than we presently have.

*Two Specific Research Projects*

The subject of innovation or educational change enjoyed considerable importance, to judge from the time spent on dissecting its phases for future analysis. There were suggestions about uncovering peer clusters, and information circuits as one way of finding how new ideas might get effectively to policy-makers.[a] Curriculum innovation as a specific policy study was urged, particularly in light of the disappointing evaluation methods presently employed to urge or continue such new notions. Strategies for achieving innovation were urged as highly useful information for policy-makers, particularly given the capacity of the school bureaucracy to absorb or deflect innovative thrusts into their territory.

The basic framework of analysis underlying these suggestions seems to run as follows. There is imputed a chain of innovation which theoretically underlies the adoption of any new policy into a closed system. Thus, how do ideas enter a system (what are the communication chains which filter novelty to powerful people so that they perceive it?). Next, how does the perceived innovation differentially affect actors so as to cause them to use their resources to oppose or defend it? Finally, once accepted in policy form, how does it affect the school system? The payoff for acquiring such knowledge of the innovation process is a wiser use of resources by those wishing to introduce innovation. Note that basic to all this is the assumption that innovation means improvement, namely, that the difference between present and desired conditions can be narrowed by a new policy. This is not the only place where normative judgments were brought to bear upon empirical propositions.

The special independent force exerted by the quality of leadership upon policy decisions appeared in several forms. One specific proposal suggested viewing superintendents in some typological fashion (Heroes and Bums) to see what

[a]One study was specifically cited that found certain leading lighthouse superintendents and school districts that many of their neighbors followed.

differences in policy outcomes were associated with each. Such categorization of leaders matched with policy differences appeared in less conceptual terms in numerous anecdotes of what specific superintendents did under given circumstances with what consequences. Or, given the constraints which are imposed upon policy by structural characteristics of place (which may be inferred from some macroanalysis), how much independent effect exists for personal leadership under what kind of conditions (e.g., at what level can a hero make a difference)? How much of this independent personal force is diluted by decisions made outside the jurisdiction of the leader, e.g., USOE guidelines, court orders, professional certification requirements?

Such a general inquiry was widely discussed and approved, but one countersuggestion should be noted. If one finds the difference which personal leadership qualities can make, but these are absent in given locales, maybe then we need systemic explanations for policy change. Knowing these it would be possible in the absence of leadership to gauge better what can be done.

*What is the Dependent Variable?*

A theme of constant recurrence was dissatisfaction over the kind of dependent variables to be studied. There was little enthusiasm for studying the political process *only* (such as board elections as an end in itself). All agreed that it was imperative to focus upon policy or outputs that are "important" (e.g., who benefits). Possible benefits ranged from financial inputs to changes in achievement test scores or self-concept. But without agreement otherwise upon what "important" means, studying policy should not be studying only conversion and leaving out the more vital question—what difference does the conversion make for the society in which it takes place? The search for such notions of significant outcomes against which to measure results was inherent in every theme outlined above. Classification in the sense of morphology is not sufficient; what difference in policy outcome is associated with differences, in forms, structures, processes, personalities, etc.? Whether studying the vertical or horizontal policy process, the payoff will be what difference the process or the level makes for the real world in which it operates—and that means an evaluation of effects upon important outcomes. Innovation is not important either, unless we know what the desired end it is we have in view, and hence wish to achieve by policy change. Obviously an evaluation of the effect of leadership must proceed within the framework of knowing the answer to the question: leadership for what ends?

Various suggestions floated in the air about what the important dependent variables were. "Docility" and educational achievement had its numerous champions; "accountability" and institutionalization of a counter culture were offered; and at the plenary session pleas for "being free" or "happy" will be recalled. But the free-floating anxiety about this problem never focused. One participant noted that uncertainty about the dependent variable gave an air of unreality to discussion about methodology and research strategies. Yet others noted that the public was becoming increasingly concerned about productivity in their schools, although what that meant at times, one suggested and others supported, was a docile, controlled student body. Part of our inability to identify dependent variables was caused by the lack of learning theory and inconclusiveness of studies like the Coleman report.

## Other Themes

Although most of the discussion was conducted loosely within the input-conversion-output framework, certain types of research which do not fall clearly within these categories were felt by some to be of value as well. First, Easton himself would emphasize that analysis of value allocation may be no more important than analysis of the way in which political structures seek to maintain their legitimacy. The crisis in contemporary education may not be simply (or even primarily) an allocative crisis. It is quite possible the crisis centers over the symbol of legitimacy. The way in which systems respond (or fail to respond) to the demands articulated by new social forces, and the consequences of these processes for the legitimacy of the system itself was felt to be a significant area of inquiry. Looked at from this perspective, the study of who governs may not simply be acting as a court chronicler to a King, but a matter as critically significant as the examination of the consequences of their governing.

Secondly, the tools of political analysis might also be applied to the evaluation of current policy proposals, such as state-wide bargaining between teachers and the authorities, the movement towards community control, and changes in state aid formulae. The political consequences of these proposals need to be considered systematically before hasty adoption. For instance, on the one hand we see a movement for centralized control through such devices as Program Planning Budgeting Systems and teacher accountability. On the other, we see movements for community control, free schools, and storefront academies. What are the changes in the locus of political influence under these alternatives? Do school professionals still dominate?

Thirdly, it was suggested that macroanalyses of the contours of the American educational system and its relation to American politics and society more generally might clarify the parameters of the system within which variations in the policy-making process occur. As mentioned in the general sessions, such macroanalysis might be profitably undertaken from an international comparative perspective, such a study would demonstrate that the values parameters take in the American context are not universal constants.

Fourthly, in any analysis of policy the distinction between policy adoption and policy implementation is critical. The character of the organization responsible for "actualizing" policies becomes such a crucial aspect of the policy process that it deserves special attention. Little is known about administrative politics and the way this affects educational policy. Likewise, little is known about intra-district variations in educational practice and results—what goes on within individual schools and classrooms. Does the bureaucracy form a barrier (as conventionally defined) and educational outcomes? Do educational administrators shape the agenda of decision-making so that crucial questions are kept solely within their purview?

A related issue stressed by Professor LaNoue of Columbia Teachers College is the political aspects of teacher accountability. If the development of objective criteria for teaching performance (e.g., achievement tests) may take too long and require too much emphasis on "knowledge bits," perhaps there is some value in examining the method of peer group standards that are used in higher education to achieve quality control to see if any of it is transferable to public education. The implementation of the higher education model, however, would be impeded by the tendency for collective bargaining agreements to dictate the outcome of many policy issues. Increasingly, decisions like student discipline, compensatory opportunities, and ethnic studies are made through collective bargaining. Consequently, political scientists need to investigate these collective bargaining trends and their implications for accountability. Neither research into peer group processes nor collective bargaining takes us very far into the problem of accountability for socialization. One way to further accountability is to research the nature and intensity of the public's value preferences regarding education. A follow-up study could collect information on how the school system had responded to the value choices expressed by its citizens.

*Summary of Cluster III Discussion*

There was general agreement that any proposed research project in this cluster should be comparative and work toward classificatory schemes which assist us in generalizing about the great variety of American schools. Within this overall guideline two thrusts were viewed as most important: (1) following a policy through all levels of government from the federal government to classroom units; (2) exploration of a wide array of substantive policies at any one unit and level of decision-making.

A high priority for the first thrust would be to explore the chain of innovation around some important policy area such as curriculum. The second thrust could be implemented with great potential through a focus on the special independent force exerted by the quality of local school superintendent's leadership.

Other areas that deserve urgent consideration for research support are the political legitimacy of contemporary educational institutions, and accountability.

## Concluding Comments

This report has attempted to accurately synthesize and interpret the outcome of a five day conference. The individual papers were only summarized briefly and contained many good ideas for further research. The major theme in most of the papers was discussed and is reflected to some degree in this report. However, the treatment here could not convey the full argument of analysis in most papers. Consequently, the reader is urged to review each of the papers individually.

The conference was successful in bringing out many new ideas and good research projects in educational politics. The priorities are inherent in the major areas of concentration in the discussion and the conclusions of each cluster. An analysis of gaps was not difficult given the paucity of past research. In short, the research projects and approaches included in this report all deal with gap areas. We have attempted at the end of each cluster to tackle the questions of which individual projects should be undertaken first because they would contribute most to later projects.

We were not successful in defining the specific limits or nature of the interest of politics of education. We could not rank order proposed research endeavors or some scale of utility. We could not do this because the state of the art, empirical base, and theoretical frameworks in political science and education are not sufficiently developed. The difficulty in specifying dependent variables discussed by every cluster is a good example of the above limitations. The problems in establishing a dependent variable for Clusters I and II stems primarily from the lack of political theory and data. For Cluster III the dependent variable problem is basically caused by the inability of practicing educators and educational researchers to agree on the most important "goals" of schools (achievement versus other outcomes) and to discover education production functions.

It would have been extremely helpful if theories could be borrowed from political science to guide priority setting and to explore the boundaries between education and politics. As Landau pointed out, however, this discipline is marked by a "high information level and low theoretic yield."[2] Unfortunately politics of education is not one of the areas where the discipline has chosen to focus or develop a high information level. Consequently, a decision on which of the research endeavors discussed here should come first is difficult to answer from the standpoint of theory but relatively simple if one looks at unexplored substantive areas.

In sum, the conference and the papers were replete with specific suggestions for urgently needed research in politics of education. The conferences felt each of the specific research thrusts could be grouped under one of three different clusters of interests and fact. There was no logical way to decide which of the three clusters deserves highest priority. Within each cluster, however, there was substantial agreement on the desirability of using specific new paradigms. The relative importance of certain research projects in each cluster is covered in the reports of the proceedings.

It is difficult in a report of this nature to convey the tone of the conference that political research should receive sufficient support to begin work soon on the agenda described herein. The concepts of "crisis" and "turning point" were used frequently to describe the current politics of education. There was also a general sense that the conferees had agreed on some very different conceptual approaches, that had higher potential for yielding important results and were more powerful in an analytic sense.

## Notes

1. Quoted from W.W. Harman, O.W. Markley, and Russell Rhyne, "The Forecasting of Plausible Alternative Future Histories: A Progress Report of Methods, Tentative Results, and Educational Policy Implications," Stanford Research Institute, abstract, p. 6.

2. Martin Landau, "On the Use of Functional Analysis in American Political Science," *Social Research* 35 48-75; 1968.

**Part 5: American Schools
as a Political System:
A Bibliographic Essay**

# American Schools as a Political System: A Bibliographic Essay

FREDERICK M. WIRT

## Introduction

By a mutual but unspoken and longstanding agreement, both American citizens and scholars have decided that the world of education is unrelated to the world of politics. But while election and referendum might be judged "political" for other policies, in education, Americans have proceeded on the assumption of magic that one can change an object's quality by giving it a different name. Yet not all have been deceived. Over a decade ago, Eliot demonstrated to political scientists how education was political, while also urging research along many lines.[1] His agenda of research is still valuable because so few scholars have dealt with his suggestions.

But recent signs suggest that the rivulet of research on the politics of education which we knew in the 1960s will in the next decade become a flood. The reason for this is that perspectives on education have changed as a consequence of strained local resources and new national policies. The point is not that the school system suddenly became politicized. Rather it is that more have become aware of this political quality because of publicity over state-local demands for financial assistance, the passage and administration of massive and growing federal aid programs, national efforts to eliminate racial imbalance, and increasingly bitter contests locally to wrest school control into the hands of groups aroused over these policies.

Our purpose in this paper is not to argue why education should be viewed politically.[2] Rather it is to explore the need for more useful theoretical orientation of the research movement now getting under way and, in the process, to indicate some of the knowledge gaps which research might fill. Iannaccone has explained why much needs to be done in such research.[3] When education is a "closed system," its leaders, by maintaining an isolation from politics, free themselves from external control and, by controlling their own environment, reduce change within the system. Such effort is clearly functional for professional educators, freeing them from the plurality of external constraints and unsettling de-

The author wishes to express his appreciation for assistance in developing this article to David Easton, James Guthrie, and Michael Kirst, although responsibility for the final work is the author's alone. Financial assistance was provided by the Institute of Governmental Studies and the School of Education at Berkeley. An earlier version of this appeared in the *Australian Journal of Educational Administration,* May, 1970.

mands of internal change which characterize other social institutions touching the political. But in the past, so skilled were educators that they moved the community to adopt ostensibly nonpolitical concepts and terms to apply to their work. As Eliot noted, a successful superintendent was one adept in "community relations," but "Why not say frankly that he must be a good politician?"[4] As for political scientists, they unquestioningly accepted the closed system definition of the educators. Only recently have they begun to see here similarities to other policies; "Rosy O'Grady and the Colonel's lady are sisters under the skin."

The objectives of research into politics and education are those of any research interest: description, explanation, prescription and evaluation. Educational journals are filled with *descriptions* of pieces of reality—of the operations of school systems and subsystems, of their actors and agents, and of their laws and regulations. Further, this description of reality is invariably accompanied by normative *evaluations*, that is, statements of preference, often accompanied by recommendations to change or retain the observed reality. Further, description and evaluation merge undefinably into *prescription*—recommendations on how to change reality so as to achieve normative objectives, how to close the gap between the real and the ideal. What is least found is *explanation*—suppositions and supporting evidence about the causes, consequences and interrelationships of that which is found in reality. In the scholarship of education, causal theory of this kind is found a great deal in the psychology of education, to some degree in the sociology of education, and very little in educational administration.[5]

However, when we ask how much of these four research objectives are found in the study of the politics of education, whether case studies or aggregate analysis, the answer must be, "very little." The reasons for such omissions lie in the myth of nonpolitical education, in the mass of data to be studied, and in the lack of a directing empirical theory. Less is found about educational politics than about politics of almost any other widespread policy in American life because, in part, of the belief that one has satisfactorily described reality by saying education is "above" politics. Under the mantle of such thinking, descriptive research is regarded as misguided, and consequently it becomes impossible to test theoretical statements. Further, there is a vast array of data to be dealt with: in 1962 there were almost 35,000 school districts in the United States, constituting the most numerous elected units (38%) despite their sharp reduction during the 1950s, although by 1970 the number was down to about 19,000[6]; these districts are holding board elections every year or so; and there are thousands of annual school referenda. Further, this pool of data is swollen even more by the profusion of school policies among states and districts.

But if one pierces the screen of "unpolitical schools" and wishes to work with such data, he finds highly inadequate theory and methodology for his employ. As Kirst and Mosher have shown, there is no single theory, simple or complex, which presently guides this work, nor is there agreement on the appropriate methodology.[7] Political scientists are severely split between traditional studies of institutional and legal analysis and studies of political behavior which utilize statistical and other empirical methods. What one finds in a review of the literature, then, is a grab bag of both theory and method. While this is a typical condition in the early stages of scholarship on any subject, such consolation makes it no less frustrating for those concerned to make some order out of the confusion. This is certainly no discipline for those who define scholarship as the explication of established truths, but it will be exciting to those who prefer to innovate and develop theory and hypotheses.

## A Sketch of Systems Theory

Much of this uncertainty can be seen in the application of "systems theory" to the politics of education. This theoretical formulation provides what its author, David Easton, has termed *A Framework for Political Analysis*.[8] We would like to demonstrate such a framework and its limitations by showing how the available research relates to it and by noting what it does not do.

Easton visualizes the *political system*—which provides in every state an "authoritative allocation of values"—as the focus of societal stresses which create *inputs*—in the form of *demands* and *supports*—which the political system may *convert* into *outputs* or public policies, which in turn *feeds back* values or resources into the society whence the process began. The major concepts here— system, stress, input, conversion, output, and feedback—are thought to be interrelated in a dynamic and ongoing fashion. We can see each of these major concepts as a useful way of categorizing the research of educational politics, but a somewhat fuller explanation might be helpful.

Inputs arise out of other systems in society—economic, for example—which generate stress over value concerns. That is, stress, generated by differing claims for scarce resources, produces organized activities directed toward the political system, seeking to satisfy these claims. These inputs to the political system take the form broadly of demands or supports. Demands we associate most often with the private pressures upon public government, the claims for justice or help, for reward or recognition. These demands mobilize resources in order to affect other private groups and to influence the disposition of the political system. The particular kinds of issues which develop and the particular form in which the attendant demands make their way into the political system vary with different cultures, economies, and political systems. As for the input of support, a steady flow is necessary if any political system is long to maintain its legitimacy, that is, the generally accepted sense that the system has the right to do what it is doing. Indeed, so vital is this input that all societies indoctrinate their young to support the system, a function in which the schools have a dominant, although not exclusive, role.

The political system, the object of such inputs, is defined as the mechanism for converting inputs into outputs, demands and supports into policy. Clearly, however, not all demands are so converted, and this differentiation is a function of values dominant in the conversion machinery and personnel as well as in the larger society. The conversion is seen in its machinery—elections, referenda, boards, legislatures, all carefully authorized by some charter or constitution—as well as in its personnel—executive, legislative, judicial. The personnel constantly interact in the conversion process, either with those outside or inside the political system, and their behavior stems from role definitions imposed by that system. Indeed, such interaction generates inside the system certain pressures which also shape the conversion process, what Easton termed *withinputs*.

Finally, the outputs of public policy, although varying with culture and over time, tell us much about the values of those who have power and privilege in the system. The administration of this policy upon the larger community always has differential impact. Any administration must enhance the safety, income, and deference of some while restricting that of others. Such impact constitutes feedback; that is, it differentially affects groups, other systems and, inevitably, future inputs which will be fed back into the political system itself.

The preceding résumé is unfortunately an oversimplification of extremely complex institutions and processes which Easton has sought to integrate into a comprehensive description and explanation; for the educational scholar for whom this is new it is highly recommended that Easton's original work be examined. Such a theory has two broad uses in the study of educational politics. First, like any good theory, it should generate hypotheses amenable to operationalizing for research purposes, the results of which can test the theory. Theory in this form is directed toward explanation and predictions by means of "a set of . . . related propositions, which include among them some lawlike generalizations, and which can be assigned specific truth value via empirical tests. . . ."[9]

We would like to set aside that purpose for now, however, to consider a second use of general theory, which is its *heuristic* value. That is, theory may not be so much a predictive scheme as one which analytically separates and categorizes items in experience. Systems theory enables us at least to order or arrange existing knowledge and thereby determine what portions of the theory are clearly untenable, what have at least some empirical support, and what totally lack previous research. Heuristic theory provides a "framework for a political analysis," as Easton clearly claims for his own work.[10] He describes it as a "conceptual framework," a "preliminary" to theory development, a way of raising "appropriate questions" and finding "appropriate ways for seeking answers." Indeed, he entitles one of his writings, "Categories for the Systems Analysis of Politics."

In this view, then, systems theory can enable us to see in a more or less connected way what the phenomena of educational politics are and where research is needed. The rest of this chapter relates available research findings to Easton's categories as a brush clearing necessary before describing our research needs.

## Review of Research

*Macroanalysis*

The environment in which the political system operates has consequences for its operation and output. Easton conceives of the political system as "analytically separate from all other systems," but realizes that these others create influences across such putative boundaries; he refers to these as "exchanges or transactions [by which] each is coupled to the other in some way, however slight it may be."[11] Thus stress within these other systems influences inputs flowing into the political system. For example, the structure of the economic system should be such a powerful influence. Our reference here is not merely to the fact that a school is a commercial institution or that it is the object of commercial pressures.[12] More importantly, variations in economic resources from district to district should be associated with variations in life-styles and hence with inputs of demands about the resources and outputs of the schools.

This concept has given rise in the last decade to much use of the technique of macroanalysis to test such a relationship. Essentially this involves testing sets of socioeconomic indicators for their relationship to other sets of policy indicators by the use of multivariate analysis. Dye, in his extensive work on state and city policy outcomes,[13] uses such a model to test whether the economic or the political system is more related to school outcomes. These concepts of "development," "political system," and "outcomes" are operationalized by the selection of purportedly appropriate variables. Then we are ready to ask, in Dye's words: "Do political system characteristics mediate between socio-economic inputs and educational outcomes . . . or are policy outcomes determined by socio-economic variables without regard to system characteristics. . . .?"[14]

From the pioneering work of James onwards, the repeated answer has been: if educational output is measured in expenditure terms, socioeconomic variables are more important than the political in shaping the policy outcomes. Further, the measures of wealth are directly and strongly associated with size of educational expenditures, holding all other considerations constant.[15]

This primacy of the economic in policy outcomes is a finding not without normative and methodological debate. Some, regarding political variables as more significant in affecting state policies, deny that for creating a good life the reputed values of the democratic political process are less important than a given stage of economic development. The rebuttal has also taken the form of questioning the appropriateness of the statistical techniques and variables used to indicate inputs and outputs. By the end of the 1960s, the best reading of the research would be that (1) different models of economic and political interaction are associated with different policies, and (2) the statistically unwary should tread carefully when he enters this field.[16]

Expenditures are not the only measure of educational policy, of course. Polit-

2

52

ical scientists have traced the factors associated with the output of educational innovation[17] and school segregation.[18] Yet others have turned from standard economic and political input variables to determine the influence upon educational expenditures of other inputs—religion, metropolitanism, and city-suburban life styles.[19] The sophistication of such macroanalysis studies is impressive, and the use of comparative data contributes much to extending the generalizations they test. At the very least, we have learned more in recent years about the factors underlying the variability of public policy in the American states than was possible earlier where arithmetical means were about as far as political statisticians went.

*Community Power Structure*

One environmental context contributing inputs to the political system is the configuration of power—social, economic, or other—within which the political system operates. More simply, what inputs do or do not enter the political system for conversion into policy and how the conversion process itself operates may be shaped by those not in the political system but who nevertheless control it. One can conceive of nations or communities dominated by a particular subsystem—the military, the clergy, the wealthy, the aristocratic—which in turn dominates that political system. Indeed, much of the literature of political science from Athens to the present concerns itself with whether such subsystems do or should dominate.

One aspect of this consideration in the study of educational politics is the American fascination with "community power structures." A voluminous research and polemical literature exists, often pitting sociologists against political scientists, debating whether the structure of local power in America is hierarchical and elitist or whether it is segmented or pluralist. There is debate over the methods for detecting the powerful and over the implications of these findings for our democratic society. Such research has in the most recent years leaned increasingly toward comparative studies.[20]

The community level is of course the site of schools, so this debate has some consequences for school administrators. If a community were "run" by an "elite," as earlier studies by sociologists found, professional schoolmen could only operate as a dependent of that clique. If on the other hand, as political scientists later said, power tended to rest in a number of hands, being more specialized to a given policy area, then the administrator might not be so constrained. Further, regardless of the particular structure of power in the community, it is important for the administrator to detect the real power holders and not be misled by reputations for influence.

During the 1960s, we can trace a transference of this scholarly interest from the social sciences to educational administration. Bloomberg and Sunshine in 1963, as part of the excellent series by Syracuse University on the politics of education, showed the relevance of community power studies in four suburbs.[21] But the work having greatest impact among students of educational administration was that by Kimbrough; his study of the way in which the school policies of four Southern counties were sharply affected by differing power structures was the first by an educationalist to transmit word of this research to his fellows.[22] Also in 1964, a collection of essays stressing the research potential of this analytic context brought together both political scientists and school administrators.[23]

Much of this work has consisted of showing educators how to be better administrators, but this prescriptive air has yielded to more empirical work. McCarty suggested how community power structures influenced administrative tenure; Gregg showed the relevancy of community power studies to educational leadership; Minar found in a study of several score suburbs some factors differentially affecting conflict in school systems; Crain studied the relationship between power structures and segregation in eight major cities; while others have suggested an interdisciplinary framework for community study.[24]

### Gatekeepers of Demand Inputs

If demands originate outside the political system, what do we know about them? Appearing as "a social want, preference, hope expectation, or desire," some of these become political demands when they "are voiced as proposals for decision and action on the part of the authority."[25] What enters the political system is determined partly by cultural restraints against some wants; thus gangsters have little overt access to this system. Also affecting entry are what Easton terms "gatekeepers," positions in the social and political structure which can control the demands—interest groups, party groups, opinion leaders or the mass media. What gets in the system then, as well as what gets out, reflects these gatekeepers' preferences and power. However, the system undergoes considerable stress if its outputs do not meet insistent and persistent demands and/or if the volume of demands exceed the system's capacity to handle the inputs.

Because in a democratic polity public preferences play some role in the system's outputs, the detection of these demands and the determination of the conditions under which they are heard and made effective have been questions of concern to educational administrators long before the recent interest in the politics of education. Given the probably unique condition among nations in which our citizens vote upon school policy and its makers, it is not surprising that such officials have long sought to detect and defend themselves against such control. Such concern in past decades was concealed under the rubric of "community relations," a literature much preoccupied with methods of selling professional views to the public. But little of this rested upon empirically researched propositions. Often it was, and to some degrees still is, anecdotal in form, a nice little story about how a bond issue was maneuvered to success in some town. But by the end of World War II, such validation was appearing in the literature, as in the report by Hamlin on tested techniques for increasing citizen participation in school decisions.[26]

Because such analysis focused upon gatekeepers who shaped public inputs, only occasionally did research turn to the reverse question, how did the demands shape the gatekeepers' position and policy? Thus, Walden has traced the relationship between school board members' defeats and consequent superintendent turnover, reflective of a syndrome of voters' discontent with school policies.[27] Only a few have examined the relationship between referendum decisions and other policies; despite the widespread nature of such data, they are nowhere centrally collected for convenient access. Masotti has traced biracial differences in referendum participation and support in one city for a five year period, while Willis has analyzed voter response to school financial issues.[28] It is conceptually possible that the referendum device can make for conflict between school board and public over a given policy; it has been empirically validated in efforts at school desegregation and district reorganization.[29] However, when there is public satisfaction with schools, as there generally is in the more affluent districts,[30] there is less conflict expressed through the referendum. But that consensus shatters when gatekeepers and citizens diverge; currently across the nation such a schism appears in the increasing refusal of citizens to support local bond issues.[31]

Intermediate between citizens and officials are the special interest groups of educational concern. As early as 1958, Gross showed how, among the major forces affecting school policy, were groups exerting pressures to split the board and weaken financial support.[32] Concern over curriculum (discussed later), teacher qualifications, tax increases, and school decentralization seems recently to have proliferated educational pressure groups across America.

Educators themselves use pressure tactics to secure a larger allocation of resources, although as the comparative study of Masters and others shows, they have been timid in some states[33]; at the national level, educators were long active in seeking federal money.[34] In the latter 1960s, teachers became more aggressive in demanding not merely better salary and working conditions but also control over the education process itself. From 1956 to 1968, those teachers believing they should be free to work in partisan elections rose from 23 percent to over 75 percent. The two major national groups—National Education Association and American Federation of Teachers—are presently showing increasing signs of merging, if not organizationally, at least in their issues and tactics.[35]

## The Nature of Support Inputs

Inputs consist not merely of demands but also of supports—for specific policies, for the regime, or for the constitutional order. Decline of support for the total political system is always dangerous to those in power and so must be strengthened. Strengthening can occur by changing system structure of processes. But it occurs less radically and more frequently by generating what Easton terms "sentiments of legitimacy, recognition of the general welfare, and a sense of political community" through the usual processes of political socialization.[36] Finally, flagging support can be checked by providing inputs to the system which meet a particular dissatisfaction, a form of *quid pro quo*. Research here has concentrated upon political socialization. How nations socialize their members to political norms of belief and behavior has captured the attention of many political scientists during the 1960s. Consequently a voluminous amount of such work has evolved, treating the perceptions, attitudes, and knowledge of the young and the means by which these come into being.[37] Essentially two questions are involved: what support do citizens provide the schools and what support does the political system seek of citizens through the schools?

Evidence of citizen support for schools is ambivalent. On the one hand education is very highly regarded; as the earliest observers of America noted, we believe that "Education Is a Good Thing." Its financial support is regarded more vital than that for other major policies, even though the citizen often has very little knowledge of his own schools and much criticism of specific policies. Research on this subject conducted at Stanford University in the late 1950s represents the most comprehensive effort to understand this ambivalence; covering all the states, it surveyed community leaders, several thousand voters, hundreds of school administrators, and many elections.[38] A decade later the Field Poll of Californians reported their high regard for schooling but their belief that they could do little to improve it and their willingness to leave it to the professionals. This is certainly not the case, however, on specific issues.[39]

When we reverse the question, however, and ask what supports the political system seeks of citizens, one finds wide belief that schools are a vital tool for transmitting basic political system values. Easton has provided theoretical statements and major empirical analysis of the proposition that a primary function of schools lies in its political socialization which contributes to—or may undermine—the support of the constitutional system and the wider political community.[40] The reinforcing role is not new, of course, but little research examines the possibility that some schools may undermine the system. Thus, do schools in black ghettos today add to or detract from the level of support for policies, the regime, or the constitutional order?

Whatever the reality of this supportive process, there is a popular expectation that teachers and the curriculum will support the political system. While such constraint might offend those who associate it with authoritarian nations, studies of the freedom of American teachers and the rigidity of the civics curriculum consistently point to their constraints. Almost thirty-five years ago, Beale found in a national survey that American teachers were not free, as he defined it; thirty years later Spitz could still castigate teachers for their conformity to community pressures.[41] Yet because of such pressures or teachers' own beliefs, recent research demonstrates that they, much like their students, have little knowledge of, or attachment to, the values of civil rights or other aspects of the democratic theory.[42] They also stand in sharp distinction from other findings that the strongest support of civil liberty exists among the most educated.[43]

Inculcation of system support is also seen in the familiar ethnocentrism of each nation's curriculum. Certainly in America the fifty states control the instructional courses, some of which are imbedded in state constitutions, and all of which show considerable variety.[44] Litt has shown that different models of civics courses—the usual conduit for system support—are at work in political socialization.[45] Their professional level tends to be very low; teachers, poorly trained in concepts and methods of political science, emphasize idealized description with little relevance to reality. During the 1960s, some political scientists began to develop curriculum and training programs to overcome these defects.[46] The need for such remedies stems from lack of evidence that these courses were actually effective in their socialization.[47] An unexplored possibility is that unreal instruction in system operations, when acted upon, may contribute to cynicism about—if not alienation from—that system and its values.

Whatever its shortcomings, however, efforts to move the curriculum away from this formalized support precipitates a fierce counterattack from what Lunstrum has called "curriculum evangelism,"[48] thereby weakening efforts to apply professional standards of curriculum theory.[49] Curriculum and textbook which speak well, or even at all, about the United Nations or established welfare policies have in some regions precipitated tremendous pressures upon administrators and teachers, with the latter essentially helpless.[50] Elsewhere, any textbook treatment of America's diverse minorities which ignores or insults them also precipitates complaints and even Congressional hearings.[51] Ironically, little such pressure arises in support of the original Americans, the Indians, who may be the most poorly educated of all our minorities.[52] Under pressure from the right and left, the teachers lack independent power to resist, particularly when their loyalty is questioned.[53] Although increasingly militant on other aspects of school life, on support matters they are not masters in their own house.[54]

*Conversion Process—Structures and Policies*

This mixture of demands and supports pours in upon a political system to be converted or not into outputs by the process of (in Easton's familiar definition) the "authoritative allocation of values." To Easton, the political system's conversion process is not static or its parts passive, for in:

the goal-setting, self-transforming and creatively adapted system . . . . members of the system are not passive transmitters of things taken into the system, digesting them in some sluggish way, and sending them along as outputs . . . . They are able to regulate, control, direct, modify, and innovate with respect to all aspects and parts of the processes involved.[55]

Here, then, are the institutions and personnel of government, the offices and officials, who interact with their environment to convert private preferences into public policy.

At the local level, the thousands of school districts can be viewed as a myriad of miniature political systems. There is, of course, a uniform pattern in this profusion: voters elect a school board which develops and oversees policy administered by the superintendent whom the board appoints.[56] But within this common rubric, political conflict can rage, as in the recent demands of urban blacks for community control and decentralization of their children's schools.[57] Another example of the political variety in school policies arises from the seemingly prosaic budgetary process. Budget decisions in any district combine not only economic and technical but also political criteria; considerations of political and social benefit are thus as important as measures of economic efficiency. How board members and superintendents differentially evaluate these input components provides one analytical scheme for understanding some influences upon educational policy.[58] Patterns of school board and principal relationships may be viewed conceptually in other ways. Research has shown how elections and superintendents are reciprocally related,[59] how the boards are functionally related to inputs from their community,[60] and how community, board, and administration can interrelate in different fashions.[61] Or, in more normative terms, questions may be raised about such boards' responsibility and responsiveness to community demands.[62]

Then, too, one might approach this conversion process by focusing upon a specific level of government, viewing each as a political system, some of whose inputs are from other systems. Some have fastened upon the suburb, in case study[63] or comparative analysis.[64] There are also studies of educational politics in the big cities of America, also in case studies[65] or comparison.[66] At a yet higher level, there are studies of the school political system at the state level, and again there is case study[67] and comparative analysis.[68] Most recently we find interstate coalitions developing to coordinate planning on common problems and to confront federal educational policy.[69]

Climaxing decades of public debate, Washington from the mid-1950s onward became a major participant in local education through policies of regulation and subsidy. Regulatory policy stemmed originally from the decisions of the Supreme Court overturning local actions deemed repugnant to the Constitution, e.g., public support of religious schools. When in the last decade it struck down the widespread practices of school prayers and Bible reading, resistance developed that moved Congress close to amending the Constitution to permit what the Court had banned.[70] In another regulatory area—racial balance—the Court's decision of 1954[71] did not find Congressional support until the Civil Rights Act of 1964. Directed first against Southern segregation, by 1970 the effort involved Court, Congress, and president in striking, albeit turbulent, improvements. Segregation in the North, however, is just beginning to be attacked, a prospect which has unglued Congressional and presidential support.[72]

Another federal involvement in local schools is in supportive policies, primarily financial aid. Washington has provided such aid since even before the founding of the republic, although the amounts were limited and the programs few.[73] But after World War II, increased demand for schooling strained state and local sources and generated demands for federal assistance. The subject of intense partisan debate, such laws were few during the 1950s,[74] but in the Johnson landslide of 1964, additional Congressional support, when paired with a solution of long-standing religious conflicts, produced the landmark Elementary and Secondary Education Act of 1965.[75] If it had not been known before, certainly the passage and administration of this law emphasized the strong tie between education and politics. In the cut-and-thrust of conflicting demands pouring in upon Congress and in its reaction to such pressures,[76] we can clearly see the group struggle to obtain that authoritative allocation of resources so central to Easton's notion of the political system.[77]

### The Conversion Process—Personnel

Yet the conversion process involves not merely authoritative groups—boards, legislatures, and so on. There is a very personal element in the interplay of politics in which the outcome must be judged also by the feelings and values, failures and successes, of human beings. Thus, school politics may be viewed as a struggle for power among parents, teachers, administrators, or school board members.[78] In another sense, it may be viewed as a study in leadership, the way by which a few mobilize large numbers in support of the few's judgment.[79] In this perspective, any notion that only blind blocs of men engage in the politics of education is simply insufficient in description and explanation.

The empirical literature of conversion personnel overflows with anecdotes of individuals in a given place and time. Much of this was earlier used as a source for learning how to be more effective as administrator and "community relations" expert[80]; political science literature of recent years had its case studies, also.[81] But most political scientists and educational scholars now employ more aggregate studies of key personnel which are designed to draw broader generalizations about their role in the political process. Thus, there are studies of the role of state governors and attorneys-general in the Southern desegregation conflict,[82] and of state legislators' differing evaluations of school needs.[83]

At the local level, board members, administrators, and teachers have had their personal values and perceptions explored. McCarty and Carver have studied different sets of board members to determine why they serve and how their class affects their role expectations.[84] Increasingly educators note that superintendents, particularly those in large cities,[85] perform a political role in the community, and that their leadership styles are mediated by different structures of power in the community and board.[86] The superintendent, the go-between of the polity and bureaucracy,[87] finds his politicization thrust upon him not merely by communities seemingly more contentious about school affairs but by the once docile teachers' turn to unionism.[88]

### Output and Feedback

In this interplay of groups and individuals, demands and resources, educational policy flows out from the political system. These are outputs in Easton's terms, "authoritative allocations of values for binding decisions and the actions implementing and related to them."[89] Designed to meet demands by acting, or seeming to act, to change the conditions which gave rise to the demands in the first place, such outputs serve to diminish the stress which precipitated prior demands. By this feedback the system is made to respond to environmental stress; thus, as Easton has it, "A system is able to make some effort to regulate stress by modifying or redirecting its own behavior."[90]

This process of feedback and response to output is writ large in the infrastructure of education. The effects of practices in curriculum and administration constitute "withinputs" of the profession, and the texts and journals of the profession for long have been filled with such evaluation. Often however, such withinputs radiate outwards to affect community segments who in turn transmit into the total school political system the demands for new practices. The public outcry during the 1950s over why Johnny could not read is illustrative of the school professionals generating public concern which is transformed into a political question. In that sense then, probably any professional policy has the potential for becoming a political issue, so that the syndrome of output-feedback-input is an analytic framework applicable to many school aspects. Even in other nations lacking the decentralized sovereignty of our schools, this possibility exists; one recalls the French college students' riots in 1968 over instructional practices.

While this conceptual framework may be applicable to a wide range of school policies, this chapter cannot cover them all. However, it might be useful to apply the framework to a recent policy output with great consequence for schools, namely federal aid. Such involvement has been with us since 1785; over a score of major federal policies have been or are now on the statute books.[91] In adult education policy alone there are 454 separate programs,[92] and the scope of federal involvement in other policies promises to expand immeasurably in the decades ahead. The more significant question for citizens as well as scholars, however, is the impact of these policies upon their schools. The requirement in the Elementary and Secondary Education Act of 1965 insisted on by Senator Robert Kennedy, that the programs under this act should be evaluated subsequently for their effects, provides institutionalization of feedback and response. This could be a powerful tool for reshaping future educational programs, although by 1970 there was sharp criticism that evaluation was lagging badly.[93]

Federal policy has consequences for other aspects of the school than curriculum. Thus, it can place major demands upon state and local school administrative structures, but the consequences of this are not yet clear. Campbell has recently urged that the ESEA of 1965 generates such a demand upon state educational departments,[94] and that this reaches even down to the school boards.[95] Even without federal laws, it is likely that the penetrating influence of other national forces develops mutual interests which creates standardizing inputs on school systems.[96] Further, Osman has shown that federal financial aid stimulated considerably all state-local expenditures for education; for every $1.00 contributed federally, there was $4.11 increase in state-local outlay.[97] Given the presently strained support of local levies and the sweet taste of federal money, the most likely consequence of federal aid will be a feedback demand for more, despite the fears of the ideological opponents. It is certainly true that the state policy output has consequences for the local level. As Guthrie et al. have recently shown for Michigan, the traditional distribution of state funds has created schools with rigidly unequal resources and pitifully unequal student achievement.[98]

In the administration of major federal policies, the value orientation of representatives of different levels in the system are not always the same, a differentiating factor which affects the outcome in ways which have had little research. A Congressional report on a sample survey of state-local officials suggests some of this variety. Along a continuum, the polar extremes "Orthodox States Rights" and "New Nationalism" philosophies, accounted each for only a little better than 10 percent of all officials; 43 percent held a state rights philosophy but pragmatically accepted federal aid on specific issues, while another 33 percent accepted the federal aid but reflected little philosophical orientation.[99]

Certainly differential attitudes by local officials have made a difference in the administration of the Supreme Court and Congressional requirements for school desegregation in the South. Just as some Southern judges have been more reluctant to urge compliance,[100] so some Southern states have been more adaptable to this policy demand; as the reports of the U.S. Commission on Civil Rights have shown over the years, there has been more compliance in the border states than in the Deep South. Recent federal law has converted the U.S. Office of Education's primary concern from supporting local control of education to demanding equality of educational opportunities; these two values clashed sharply throughout the South in the 1950s and 1960s, and will do so in the North in the 1970s.[101] Even in an act as popular as that of ESEA of 1965, its administration has precipitated a continuous set of problems. This has resulted partly from the newness of federal-state cooperation in this field but also from the differing value orientations of the two levels. Bailey and Mosher have shown that for the first years of this act such conflict arose from the best, and sometimes mutual, motives among federal partners.[102]

## The Need for Theory, Conceptualization, and Research

*Problems in Theory*

The preceding bibliographic review misleads in one major respect by suggesting more theory, hypothesis, and research findings than actually exist. Citations are often only to a single study, a study may often treat with only a few cases, and the restricted locale and incidence of research limit the possible generalization. In this concluding section we hope to outline the dimensions yet to be pursued in the study of school politics.

That very systems theory which has provided the analytic framework for the preceding section is far from satisfactory as a theory. As Kaplan noted a decade ago:

Perhaps the first thing to be said about systems theory is that it is not a theory. It consists of a set of concepts. No propositions about the real world can be derived from infinitesimal calculus, or from the methods of science in general. Advice to a political scientist to use systems theory to solve a problem, even when it is the appropriate methodology, would advance him as far but no farther than would advice to a physicist to use the methods of science.[103]

In other recent writing, the inutility of systems theory as a *theory* has been stressed.[104] These critics' persuasive reasoning and analysis have moved the present author to use systems theory much in the manner they have suggested, as a device for "mapping the field." As such, this article is in keeping with Landau's judgment that our discipline is marked by "high information level and low theoretic yield."[105]

Yet this research review has pointed up another way to utilize theory. This alternative purpose is not prediction of what will happen but understanding of what does happen. Both theories seek to explain the interrelationships of events in experience, that is, both strive to speak of, if not explain, causation. The understanding function, however, is satisfied by far less demanding criteria of validity than the predictive function. In this chapter, we have sought to show how understanding a complex process of school politics may be sought by using a theory which simply categorizes data. In so doing, we have pointed to discrete research projects which have aimed at the predictive function, even though they are not necessarily or demonstrably generated by systems theory.

In such heuristic terms, then, systems theory seems to provide an understanding of an inter-linked policy conversion structure responding to persistent stress by achieving outputs of policy which lead to outcomes which in turn reduce the original stress. This involves not merely one system, but a mosaic of subsystems, and at different time all or part may be operating. In Figure 1, we can see some

262

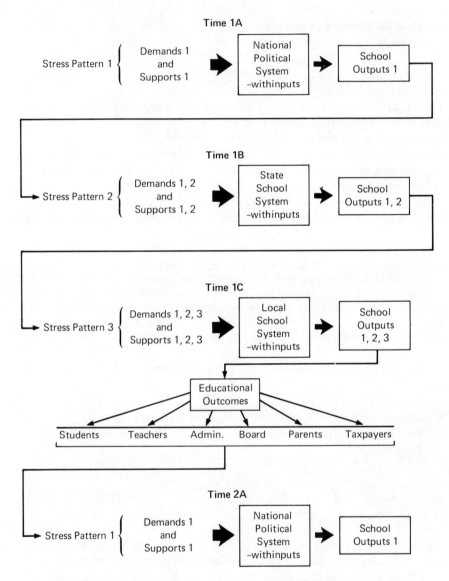

**Figure 1.** Intergovernmental Relations in a Systems Framework.

of this complexity of categories as they exist within our federal system. At a beginning point, arbitrarily labelled Time 1A, a sequence of stress-conversion-output transpires upon and through the national political system. The School Outputs 1 refers to the policy set which results and which is transmitted for administration at Time 1B to the State School System, forming a somewhat different Stress Pattern 2 (the difference indicated by the 1, 2 designation of Demands and Supports). The result here is the set of School Outputs 1,2, the numerals indicating that the national policy has been transmuted by state inputs and withinputs into a somewhat different form from that which emerged at the national level.

At Time 1C, such outputs, when administered upon the Local School System from the State System (direct federal-local system relations can exist also), constitute yet another Stress Pattern (3) and another combination of transmuted demands and supports (1,2,3). These interact with the Local School System to achieve yet another modification noted in School Outputs 1,2,3. These may be decisions on curriculum, attendance zoning, salary improvements, racial composition of teachers, budget allocations, etc. This policy set is then administered so as to achieve some kind of Educational Outcome for those who interact with Local Schools—Students, Teachers, etc. The outcome may involve no change or it may constitute some degree of change in the educational stress which precipitated the policy-making process originally. Thus, does the output of federal aid, when it finally gets down to those it is designed to affect, actually achieve the desired outcome, e.g., more qualified teachers of science or language, or students better prepared to start school or express their ideas? These outcomes may in turn generate yet another set of stresses, e.g., defects in administrative techniques, insufficient resources being employed, or unattainable goals. As a consequence of such feedback, then, at some future time (Time 2A) the whole process is recycled.

While such system analysis contributes to our understanding of a complex process, its utility does not end there. If sufficient data can be provided to describe what happens for many of the jurisdictions symbolized in Figure 1, it may then become possible to develop some predictive theoretical statements for testing. For example, it is quite certain that on the federal aid policy, differential results will be observed as outcomes across the sweep of 19,000 school districts for even one phase of that policy, while differential patterns will likely develop across several policy phases. That outcome is more than speculative, given the power of diffusion in the prism of a federal system. If so, what theoretical explanations less sweeping than the federal structure are there for such variety of outcomes? Is it possible to predict the conditions under which local compliance with national or state outputs is high and when low? Is the key variable the structure of the community in which the policy operates or is it attributable to the skills and other qualities of actors on the local scene? Macroanalysis studies, which emphasize the primacy of wealth as the best indicator of system performance, undermine severely the scope left to actors to affect the system. Yet another set of queries might seek to determine the explanatory power of the presence of the state system in the process. Does funneling policy administration through the state facilitate or inhibit local systems' achievement of national goals? If the answer is variable, what factors account for—and thus possibly predict—occasions when either facilitation or inhibition take place?

This merely suggests the fashion in which one may move from heuristic theory through categorization of data to the development of true general theory and hypotheses. The theoretic yield is highly promising despite the critical condition of general empirical theory at the present. Yet, if misery loves company, we might note that this current theoretic poverty is possibly no less than that of education itself in its other aspects; according to Smith, education currently lacks that theory which would give structure to its body of knowledge.[106]

It is certain that this application of systems theory does not bypass the perspectives of social science which are being increasingly brought to bear as explanations of the behavior of the educational system.[107] There is a whole new world of models and paradigms now being focused upon educational administration.[108] Of considerable utility are concepts of organizational behavior and research, some of which Bogue has shown to have direct application for educational administration.[109] There is a similar body of knowledge on decision-making which can have utility[110]; we have shown earlier its use for understanding community decision-making but which may also be of value within school administration.[111]

Yet we should not exaggerate the availability of general theory; much of those we have described are of limited range, at best middle range. One sign of the inadequacy of general theory is the paucity of research in comparative politics of education. While there is considerable literature in the field of comparative or public administration,[112] little of it deals with educational politics in a number of nations. Coombs, it is true, has recently brought a systems analysis to bear upon "the world educational crisis," but we agree with Sroufe that the relationship between the theory and the crisis is not clearly established.[113] Lacking guiding theory, scholars have provided mainly special studies of educational politics in a given country, such as the USSR, Canada, and England.[114] It may well be that the scholarly perspective of the schools as being political (as distinguished from Marx's political perspective, in whose view everything is political) originated in America because of local control of education through the ballot box. But an appropriate general theory of educational politics should encompass the variety of experience, of which the American is but one.[115] Accordingly, developing such theory cannot proceed when scholars fail to look elsewhere for educational politics.

One essential element of such general theory must treat with the origins, operations, and consequences of *social change*. Systems theory has been criticized for its emphasis upon the system's efforts to maintain stability and to fend off stress; Easton himself is aware of this criticism but regards it as inaccurate. He focuses upon the "persistence" of some kind of system for authoritatively allocating values, even though the regime (political structure plus political values) may change or remain stable. The allocation system can persist regardless of the change or stability of the regime. Easton insists he has nowhere postulated "either stability or change as a necessary condition, a goal, or even as a useful theoretical tool for analyzing the . . . . regime."[116]

What we urge, however, is a concern for a theory which explains, and predicts, the origin and acceptance of innovation. The role of social change is emphasized here because it offers a chance of explaining differences in the many aspects of systems theory seen earlier. What is required is a theoretical explanation of the origin, acceptance, or rejection of change.[117] Clearly there are available different models of how such innovation arises and is accepted,[118] in which some officials such as educators may be "agents of change"[119] working against the inertia of bureaucracy.[120]

*Problems in Methodology*

Nor is this policy area without needs in methodology, both simple and complex. At the simplest level, there are questions of whether we can obtain some data; thus, there is resistance by many Americans to studies of their children's politicization.[121] More broad, however, are the problems of the kinds of data gathered and the method of doing so. Kerlinger has criticized the "mythology" of educational research for its overemphasis upon methods and descriptions and its failure to ask proper questions for which data can be gathered.[122] Such problems are not unknown in political science, of course.

Possibly we can best indicate the needs in methodology in more summary fashion.[123] It is clear that one can go just so far in understanding general behavior through the use of case studies. While a philosopher has noted that one can understand the universe by reflection upon a pebble, few of us are philosophers and even less have the perspicacity to perform that task. We need to know the relationship between the many pebbles, the pebbles and the shore, the wind and waves, and indeed the total ecology of pebbles. Further, we need better integration of case and aggregate analysis studies, and the knowledge when to do which. Clearly also, aggregate analysis techniques have problems of validation and reliability, that is, whether the grossness of the measure aggregated encompasses the important but subtle aspects of the relationship studied. Thus, if one measures school output only by educational expenditures, he is not measuring whether the system will make the child happy or inculcates belief in democratic values. Similarly, we need to determine better the range of inputs operating in a given policy decision, for it seems unlikely that the totality of demands on school boards is encompassed within the records of official minutes.

We believe that the recent work of Salisbury considerably advances the specifying of such input-output variables and the theorizing about conditions under which the conversion process operates.[124] Expanding upon Lowi's distinctions among distributive, redistributive, and regulatory policies,[125] Salisbury adds the self-regulation type and then suggests how such outputs may vary as a function of differential demands and differential costs of policy production. Thus, he hypothesizes that as there is an increase both in the aggregate demand and the cost of meeting that demand, one set of policies is more likely to be the output than when demand and costs are low. Assuming that empirical indicators of such input components as "demand" and "cost" can be devised, this strategy provides clearer notions of inputs and outputs, particularly applicable to a policy world more colored in plaid than in dun. We recommend Salisbury's ideas about concept and method as an illustration of how the two interrelate and what direction we need to move in operationalizing the components of general theory.

*Some Research Suggestions*

These needs in theory and methodology are equally matched by the needs for research in special topics. In a general sense, there is a need for replication of almost any topic cited in this article, for very often the empirical underpinning of a statement we have made rests upon no more than one or two studies. There is also need for more longitudinal studies; much of the work cited here covers only the last fifteen years, which means that we have no way of knowing whether the finding can be extended back into the past. Too, there is clearly more need for aggregate studies and less of case research. While use of the latter is more characteristic of the early stages of research in any discipline, if any systematic statements about the field are to be made, however, there comes a time when comparative studies must be undertaken.

In reviewing the literature in the main section, some specific suggestions have arisen about where research might be fruitfully directed. How do we know that our input and output analysis is related to "stress," that it is this phenomenon which activates the political system? Given the variety of American communities,[126] we need to know more about how the variety of community power structure is relevant to education administration; one innovative approach is the development of a permanent community sample with resident investigators who can be used for comparative study about the origin of and conflict over a particular policy.[127] We need more studies of educational policy demand—why are some educational pressure groups effective and others not in engendering support for school programs, under what kind of demand conditions is a school referendum accepted or rejected, and what role do forces *outside* the community play in generating *local* demand?

Also, is the pattern of school support found as the 1960s opened[128] the same as that known in the 1940s or 1970s? Thus, are younger school teachers as supportive of the regime as may have been true earlier, and if not, is their political socialization effect upon the young as monolithic as it once was? What difference in socialization content arises from those male teachers deferred from the draft, those who have military service, and those never affected by the problem? Or in another dimension, is opposition to school policies diffuse or concentrated in the population? Do some oppose many school policies consistently while others oppose only one issue and support the schools otherwise? Are the political values transmitted covertly as well as overtly to the very young? The shifting nature of the issue agenda of education makes judgments drawn from an earlier day of limited utility.

Research needs in the studies of the conversion process are numerous. There is great room for aggregate studies of the relationship among superintendent styles, school board roles, community demands, and policy output. There is need to know the way in which the conversion machinery is affected by state and national policy requirements. Curiously, there exists no single case study showing the interrelationship of state, national, and local policies in a single school district as the diagram of Figure 1 implies. One may find an inventory of such policies existing in a given district, but their interrelationships and their impact upon school operations and educational policy are not provided.[a] As for the conversion personnel, many research questions are raised by existing literature and others need be asked. Why are some teachers militant, others not, and what accounts for their change; how does the professional training in administration affect leadership qualities, if at all; is the institutionalization of the administrative profession functional for the whole school system or just for the profession; what are the conditions maximizing community support for administrative innovation; in newly developing nations can the teacher or school administrator be an agent of change independently of the dominant political system?

As to the research on the feedback process, we can do no better than raise the various inquiries about this process put by Easton himself.

We would need to know, for example, what kind of information typically returns to the authorities along the feedback loop and the extent to which it is accurate, false, or distorted. To what degree do time leaves and lags, the number of feedback channels, the length of these as transmission belts and their variety, influence the type of information fed back? To what extent is accuracy dependent upon the perceptual apparatus of the authorities and the way in which it may be influenced by ideology, prejudice, indifference, or lack of ability to obtain and interpret information?. . . . We would also need to inquire into the decision rules guiding the retrieval of information from the collective memory banks in which past experience is stored.[129]

The preceding paragraphs have provided an agenda for a decade of research at least. It suggests we have made but limited advances from the agenda set by Eliot

---

[a]I am obliged to Michael Kirst for bringing this omission to my attention.

as the 1960s opened with his call to political science. But as Kirst and Mosher have shown recently, the development of this scholarship during the 1960s has been curiously uneven and biased (for example, emphasizing input rather than output analysis), but major forces as the decade closed have begun to move students of school politics more in the direction suggested by the present article.[130] When the 1970s end with many of the research questions raised above more nearly answered, it will be a particularly difficult task, for the contours of American education will be constantly altering under the increased federal and state finances.[131] Certainly the task will be easier if more students of education and political science enter this field, rich in theoretical and empirical innovation. Possibly by that time we will have begun to meet the criticisms of Goldhammer in 1965 in reviewing books on school politics:

All the books appear to waver between a sort of missionary zeal to help the educational administrator become a more adept politician and a concern to found exhortations upon a more respectable knowledge base than is currently available. . . . Until there is a more general theory developed, descriptive data are likely to appear merely as curiosa, interesting facts of little value in suggesting further research or in providing assistance in guidance of practical affairs.[132]

The change required, then, is from the use of "a knowledge base" for "exhortation" purposes to its use in developing a systematic explanation of the causes, processes, and consequences of school politics. Such a requirement is not without its challenge to the best of scholarly thinking. At its worst it may do no more than correct "the schoolmen's political myopia"[133] that they are magically blind to and unseen by the political process. At its best we may be able to make a major contribution toward developing a general field theory of political behavior in its broadest sense.

## Notes

1. Thomas H. Eliot, "Toward an Understanding of Public School Politics," *American Political Science Review*, 53 (1950), 1032-51.

2. The theme may be traced in part to Nelson B. Henry and Jerome G. Kerwin, *Schools and City Government* (Chicago: University of Chicago Press, 1938). Statements on this theme in the last fifteen years are found in Eliot, op. cit.; Roald F. Campbell, "The Folklore of Local School Control," *School Review*, 67 (1959), 1-16; Richard J. Brown, "Party Platforms and Public Education," *Social Studies*, November, 1961, 206-10; Roscoe Martin, *Government and the Suburban School* (Syracuse: Syracuse University Press, 1962); Vincent Ostrom, "The Interrelationship of Politics and Education," *National Elementary Principal*, 43 (1964), 6-11; Essay review, "The Politics of Education," *Educational Administration Quarterly*, (1965), 54-76; George R. LaNoue, "Henry and

Kerwin and Politics and Educational Policy," *School Review*, 75 (1967), 76-92; Michael Decker and Louis H. Masotti, "Determining the Quality of Education: A Political Process," in Henry J. Schmandt and Warner Bloomberg, Jr. (eds.), *The Quality of Urban Life* (Beverly Hills: Sage Publications, 1969), Ch. 13.

3. Laurence Iannaccone, *Politics in Education* (New York: Center for Applied Research in Education, 1967).

4. Eliot, loc. cit.

5. Fred N. Kerlinger, "The Mythology of Educational Research: The Descriptive Approach," *School and Society*, 93 (1965), 222-25.

6. See the comparative statistics in Charles R. Adrian and Charles Press, *Governing Urban America*, 3d ed. (New York: McGraw-Hill, 1968), 268.

7. For an excellent review of this problem, see Michael W. Kirst and Edith K. Mosher, "The Politics of Public Education: A Research Review," *Review of Educational Research*, 39 (1969).

8. The major source is David Easton, *The Political System* (New York: Knopf, 1953), and *A Framework for Political Analysis* (New York: Prentice-Hall, 1965). The latter volume is used for major references hereafter, referred to as *FFPA*. A brief version is found in "An Approach to the Analysis of Political Systems," *World Politics*, 9 (1957), 383-400.

9. A. James Gregor, "Political Science and the Uses of Functional Analysis," *American Political Science Review*, 62 (1968), 425.

10. Ibid., 435. On Easton's understanding of the developmental nature of his thought, see the preface to *FFPA*. See also, his "Categories for the Systems Analysis of Politics," Easton (ed.) *Varieties of Political Theory* (New York: Prentice-Hall, 1966), 1.

11. *FFPA*, 108-09.

12. Roy A. Larmee, "Commercial Pressures and the Local Schools," *Theory into Practice*, 4 (1965), 178-80, and Meno Lovenstein, "The School as a Commercial Institution," ibid., 172-75.

13. Thomas R. Dye, "Politics, Economics, and Educational Outcomes in the States," *Educational Administration Quarterly*, 3 (1967), 30. Dye's major study is *Politics, Economics, and the Public* (Chicago: Rand McNally, 1966). For other of his works with application to educational policy, see "Governmental Structure, Urban Environment and Educational Policy," *Midwest Journal of Political Science*, 11 (1967), 353-80, and "Executive Power and Public Policy in the States," *Western Political Quarterly*, 22 (1969), 926-39.

14. Dye, *Politics, Economics, and the Public*, 40.

15. H. Thomas James, *Wealth, Expenditures, and Decision-Making for Education* (Stanford: Stanford University Press, 1963), and James et al., *The Determinants of Educational Expenditures in Large Cities of the United States* (Stanford: Stanford University Press, 1966). See also, Seymour Sacks and William F. Hellmuth, *Financing Government in a Metropolitan Area* (New York: Free Press, 1961); Werner Z. Hirsch, "Determinants of Public Education Expenditures,"

*National Tax Journal*, 13 (1960), 24-40; Jerry Miner, *Social and Economic Factors in Spending for Public Education* (Syracuse: Syracuse University Press, 1963); Richard E. Dawson and James A. Robinson, "Inter-Party Competition, Economic Variables, and Welfare Policies in the American States," *Journal of Politics*, 25 (1963), 265-89; Seymour Sacks and David C. Ranney, "Suburban Education: A Fiscal Analysis," *Urban Affairs Quarterly*, 2 (1966), 103-119; Y.H. Cho, "Effect of Local Governmental Systems on Local Policy Outcomes in the United States," *Public Administration Review*, 27 (1967), 31-38; Glenn W. Fisher, "Interstate Variation in State and Local Government Expenditures," *National Tax Journal*, 17 (1964), 57-74.

16. To review the dispute, see articles in *American Political Science Review*, 63 (1969), by Charles F. Cnudde and Donald J. McCrone, "Party Competition and Welfare Policies in the American States," by Ira Sharkansky and Richard I. Hofferbert, "Dimensions of State Politics, Economics, and Public Policy," and by James W. Clarke, "Environment, Process, and Policy: A Reconsideration."

17. On this dimension, see Harmon Zeigler and Karl Johnson, "Educational Innovation and Political-Economic Systems," *Education and Urban Society*, 1 (1969), 161-76, and Jack L. Walker, "The Diffusion of Innovations among the American States," *American Political Science Review*, 63 (1969), 880-99.

18. Dan W. Dodson, "School Administration, Control and Public Policy Concerning Integration," *Journal of Negro Education*, 34 (1965), 249-57; Thomas R. Dye, "Urban School Segregation: A Comparative Analysis," *Urban Affairs Quarterly*, 4 (1968), 141-65; B.E. Vanfossen, "Variables Related to Resistance to Desegregation in the South," *Social Forces*, 47 (1968), 39-44.

19. Marvin C. Aklin, "Religious Factors in the Determination of Educational Expenditures," *Educational Administration Quarterly*, 2 (1966), 123-32; Dye, "City-Suburban Social Distance and Public Policy," *Social Forces*, 44 (1965), 100-06; David C. Ranney, "The Impact of Metropolitanism on Central City Education," *Educational Administration Quarterly*, 4 (1968), 39-44.

20. For a review of this debate, see Willis D. Hawley and Frederick M. Wirt, *The Search for Community Power* (Englewood Cliffs, N.J.: Prentice-Hall, 1969). For illustrations of the level of analytical thinking, see Terry N. Clark (ed.), *Community Structure and Decision-Making: Comparative Analyses* (San Francisco: Chandler, 1968); for an illustration of comparative research, see Clark, "Community Structure, Decision-Making, Budget Expenditures, and Urban Renewal in 51 Communities," *American Sociological Review*, 33 (1968), 576-93. See also, Frederick M. Wirt (ed.), *Future Directions in Community Power Research* (University of California, Berkeley: Institute of Governmental Studies, 1971).

21. Warner Bloomberg, Jr., and Morris Sunshine, *Suburban Power Structures and Public Education* (Syracuse: Syracuse University Press, 1963); the Syracuse studies are integrated in Jesse Burkhead, *Public School Finance: Economics and Politics* (Syracuse: Syracuse University Press, 1964).

22. Ralph B. Kimbrough, *Political Power and Educational Decision-Making* (Chicago: Rand McNally, 1964). For a multi-city study in a political sociology framework, see Robert R. Alford, *Bureaucracy and Participation: Political Cultures in Four Wisconsin Cities* (Chicago: Rand McNally, 1969).

23. Robert S. Cahill and Stephen P. Hencley, *The Politics of Education in the Local Community* (Danville, Ill.: Interstate Printers & Publishers, 1964).

24. Donald J. McCarty, "How Community Power Structures Influence Administrative Tenure," *American School Board Journal* 148 (1964), 11-13; John H. Bunzel, "Pressure Groups in Politics and Education," *National Elementary Principal*, 43 (1964), 12-16; Russell T. Gregg, "Political Dimensions of Educational Leadership," *Teachers College Record*, 67 (1965), 118-25; David W. Minar, "Community Basis of Conflict in School System Politics," *American Sociological Review*, 31 (1966), 822-35 [Errata, 32 (1967), 637]; Robert L. Crain, *The Politics of School Desegregation* (Chicago: Aldine, 1968); Fred D. Carver and Donald O. Crowe, "An Interdisciplinary Framework for the Study of Community Power," *Educational Administration Quarterly*, 5 (1969), 50-64.

25. *FFPA*, 122.

26. H.M. Hamlin, "Organized Citizen Participation in the Public Schools," *Review of Educational Research*, 23 (1953), 346-52. Compare this study fifteen years later with Otis A. Crosby, "How to Prepare Winning Bond Issues," *Nation's Schools*, 81 (1968), 81-84.

27. John C. Walden, "School Board Changes and Superintendent Turnover," *Administrator's Notebook,* 15 (1967).

28. Louis H. Masotti, "Patterns of White and Nonwhite School Referenda Participation and Support: Cleveland, 1960-1964," in Marilyn Gittell (ed.), *Educating an Urban Population* (Beverly Hills: Sage Publications, 1967); C.L. Willis, "Analysis of Voter Response to School Financial Proposals," *Public Opinion Quarterly*, 31 (1967-68), 648-51.

29. As illustrated in Bertram Swanson, "Subcommunity Response to City-Wide School Policies: Measuring White-Parent Decisions of School Pairing," *School Review*, 73 (1965), 392-409; Basil G. Zimmer and Amos H. Hawley, *Metropolitan Area Schools* (Beverly Hills: Sage Publications, 1968) and by same authors, "Opinions on School District Reorganization in Metropolitan Areas: A Comparative Analysis of the Views of Citizens and Officials in Central City and Suburban Areas," *Southwestern Social Science Quarterly*, 48 (1967), 311-24; Crain, loc. cit.

30. See Minar in note 24.

31. According to *U.S. News & World Report*, Oct. 20, 1969, citing U.S. Office of Education sources, from 1965-1969, the proportion of local bond issues rejected increased from 25 percent to 43 percent.

32. Neal Gross, *Who Runs Our Schools?* (New York: Wiley, (1958).

33. Nicholas A. Masters et al., *State Politics and the Public Schools* (New York: Knopf, 1964).

34. On aid to local education, see Fenno and others cited in notes 73-76 below. On aid to universities, see Harland Boland, "National Associations and the Shaping of Federal Higher Education Policy," *Sociology of Education*, 41 (1968), 156-78.

35. For one study of such militancy, see Martin Mayer, *The Teachers Strike, New York, 1968* (New York: Harper & Row, 1969). The poll is an NEA press release, Oct. 18, 1968, cited in Michael W. Kirst, "Strategies for Research: The Politics of Education," paper of the American Educational Research Assn. Convention, 1970.

36. *FFPA*, 124-25.

37. A seminal work is Herbert H. Hyman, *Political Socialization* (New York: Free Press, 1959). Extensive nationwide projects are reported in Robert D. Hess and Judith V. Torney, *The Development of Political Attitudes in Children* (Chicago: Aldine, 1967), and David Easton and Jack Dennis, *Children in the Political System* (New York: McGraw-Hill, 1969). For an urban study, see Fred I. Greenstein, *Children and Politics* (New Haven: Yale University Press, 1965). A relevant methodological survey is M. Kent Jennings and Lawrence E. Fox, "The Conduct of Socio-Political Research in Schools: Strategies and Problems of Access," *School Review*, 76 (1968), 428-44.

38. Richard F. Carter and John Sutthoff, *Voters and Their Schools* (Stanford: Stanford University Press, 1960); Carter, "Voters and Their Schools," *Phi Delta Kappan*, 42 (1961), 244-49.

39. For an earlier study of this relationship, see Chilton R. Bush and Paul J. Deutschman, *The Inter-relationship of Attitudes toward Schools and Voting Behavior in a School Bond Election* (Stanford: Stanford University Press, 1955).

40. David Easton, "The Function of Formal Education in a Political System," *School Review*, (1957), 304-16, and "The Theoretical Relevance of Political Socialization," *Canadian Journal of Political Science*, 1 (1968), 125-46. See also, J. Steinrager, "Poltical Socialization and Political Theory," *Social Research*, 35 (1968), 111-29; Dean Jaros and Bradley C. Canon, "Transmitting Basic Political Values: The Role of the Educational System," *School Review*, 77 (1969), 94-107.

41. Howard K. Beale, *Are American Teachers Free?* (New York: Scribner's Sons, 1936); David Spitz, "Politics, Patriotism, and the Teacher," *National Elementary Principal*, 43 (1964), 17-22.

42. John C. Weiser and James E. Hayes, "Democratic Attitudes of Teachers and Prospective Teachers," *Phi Delta Kappan*, 47 (1966), 476-81; Merlyn M. Gubser, "Anti-Democratic Attitudes of American Educators," *School and Community*, 54 (1967), 14-16.

43. Samuel Stouffer, *Communism, Conformity and Civil Liberties* (New York: Doubleday, 1955); Herbert McClosky, "Consensus and Ideology in American Politics," *American Political Science Review*, 58 (1964), 361-82.

44. George D. Marconnit, "State Legislatures and the School Curriculum." *Phi Delta Kappan*, 49 (1968), 269-72, lists for all states the required courses.

45. Edgar Litt, "Education and Political Enlightenment in America," *Annals of the American Academy of Political and Social Science*, 361 (1965), 32-39. Forty years ago Charles E. Merriam and others were interested in the function of such civic instruction; for a comparative study, see his *The Making of Citizens* (Chicago: University of Chicago Press, 1931), as well as Bessie L. Pierce, *Civic Attitudes in American School Textbooks* (Chicago: University of Chicago Press, 1930).

46. For example, see the occasional papers of the High School Curriculum Center in Government at Indiana University, under Director Howard Mehlinger.

47. K.P. Langton and M. Kent Jennings, "Political Socialization and the High School Civics Curriculum in the United States," *American Political Science Review*, 62 (1968), 852-67, with rejoinder by Edgar Litt, 63 (1969), 172-73. For such data in another site, see Frederick M. Wirt, et al., *Introductory Problems in Political Research* (Englewood Cliffs, N.J.: Prentice-Hall, 1970), Ch. 3.

48. John P. Lunstrum, "The Treatment of Controversial Issues in Social Studies Instruction," *High School Journal*, 49 (1965), 13-21.

49. N.H. Campbell, "Conceptual Models of the Curriculum," *Australian Journal of Education*, 13 (1969), 47-62; John S. Mann, "A Discipline of Curriculum Theory," *School Review*, 76 (1968), 359-78.

50. For examples of such attacks, see Joseph Maloney, *"The Lonesome Train" in Levittown* (University, Ala.: Inter-University Case Program, 1958); Donald W. Robinson, "The Teachers Take a Birching," *Phi Delta Kappan*, 43 (1962), 182-88; Mary Anne Raywid, *The Axe-Grinders: Critics of Our Public Schools* (New York: Macmillan, 1962); Jack Nelson and Gene Roberts, Jr., *The Censors and the Schools* (Boston: Little, Brown, 1963).

51. Lloyd Marcus, *The Treatment of Minorities in Secondary School Textbooks* (New York: Anti-Defamation League of B'nai B'rith, 1961); Sol M. Elkins, "Minorities in Textbooks: The Latest Chapter," *Teachers College Record*, 66 (1965), 502-08; U.S. Congress, Committee on Education & Labor, Ad Hoc Subcommittee on De Facto School Segregation, *Books for Schools and the Treatment of Minorities* (Washington: Govt. Printing Office, 1966); John Brademas, "Don't Censor Textbooks—But Let's Keep Out Biased or Inaccurate Information," *Nation's Schools*, 79 (1967), 38-52.

52. Virgil J. Vogel, "The Indian in American History," *Integrated Education*, 6 (1968), 16-32; U.S. Congress, Senate Committee on Labor & Public Welfare, Special Subcommittee on Indian Education, *The Education of American Indians: A Survey of the Literature* (Washington: Govt. Printing Office, 1969).

53. Probably the most publicized evidence of this, affecting college faculty, is analyzed in David P. Gardner, *The California Oath Controversy* (Berkeley: University of California Press, 1967).

54. Harmon Zeigler, *The Political World of the High School Teacher*

(Eugene: Center for the Advanced Study of Educational Administration, University of Oregon, 1966), and *The Political Life of American Teachers* (Englewood Cliffs, N.J.: Prentice-Hall, 1967).

55. *FFPA*, 132-33.

56. Alpheus L. White, *Local School Boards: Organization and Practices* (Washington: Govt. Printing Office, 1962), Office of Education report.

57. E.g., see Mayer in note 35. For some new thinking on the subject, see Milton Kotler, *Neighborhood Government: The Local Foundations of Political Life* (Indianapolis: Bobbs-Merrill, 1969).

58. A review of what is involved would include J. Alan Thomas, "Educational Decision-Making and the School Budget," *Administrator's Notebook*, 11 (1963); Otto A. Davis, "Empirical Evidence of Political Influence upon the Expenditure Policies of Public Schools," in Julius Margolis (ed.), *The Public Economy of Urban Communities* (Baltimore: Johns Hopkins, 1965); Aaron Wildavsky, "The Political Economy of Efficiency: Cost-Benefit Analyses, Systems Analysis, and Program Budgeting," *Public Administration Review*, 26 (1966), 292-310; Ralph Huitt, "Political Feasibility," from Austin Ranney (ed.), *Political Science and Public Policy* (Chicago: Markham, 1968), 263-75. For an example of the specification of inputs, see Michael Decker, "Representing the Educational Policy-Making Process: A Problem-Solving Approach," *Education and Urban Society*, 1 (1969), 265-86.

59. Joseph M. Cronin, "The Politics of School Board Elections," *Phi Delta Kappan*, 46 (1965), 505-09.

60. Jay D. Scribner, "A Functional-Systems Framework for Analyzing School Board Action," *Educational Administration Quarterly*, 2 (1966), 204-15.

61. Norman D. Kerr, "The School Board as an Agency of Legitimation," *Sociology of Education*, 38 (1964), 34-59.

62. Donald R. Thomas, "Urban School Boards: The Need for Accountability," *Education and Urban Society*, 1 (1969), 289-94.

63. Louis H. Masotti, *Education and Politics in Suburbia: The New Trier Experience* (Cleveland: Western Reserve University Press, 1967).

64. See the articles by David Minar: "School, Community, and Politics in Suburban Areas," in B.J. Chandler et al. (eds.), *Education in an Urban Society* (New York: Dodd, Mead, 1962), 91-102; "Community Politics and School Boards," *American School Board Journal*, 154 (1967), 33-38; and the source cited in note 24.

65. On New York City, see David Rogers, *110 Livingston Street* (New York: Random House, 1968) and Marilyn Gittell, *Participants and Participation* (New York: Praeger, 1967). On Chicago, see Joseph Pois, *The School Board Crisis* (Chicago: Aldine, 1964). On Boston, see Peter Schrag, *Village School Downtown* (Boston: Beacon, 1967).

66. Joseph M. Cronin, "The Selection of School Board Members in Great Cities," *Administrator's Notebook*, 14 (1966); Alan K. Campbell, "Educational

Policy-Making Studied in Large Cities," *American School Board Journal*, 154 (1967), 18-27; David Minar, "The Politics of Education in Large Cities," Marilyn Gittell (ed.), *Educating an Urban Population*, 308-20; Robert Salisbury, "Schools and Politics in the Big City," *Harvard Educational Review*, 37 (1967), 408-24; Marilyn Gittell and T. Edward Hollander, *Six Urban School Districts: A Comparative Study of Institutional Response* (New York: Praeger, 1968).

67. Michael D. Usdan, *The Political Power of Education in New York State* (New York: Institute of Administrative Research, Teachers College, Columbia University, 1963).

68. Sources cited in notes 3 and 33 above; Stephen K. Bailey, *Schoolmen and Politics* (Syracuse: Syracuse University Press, 1962); James B. Conant, *Shaping Educational Policy* (New York: McGraw-Hill, 1964), Ch. 4; B. Dean Bowles, "The Power Structure in State Education Politics," *Phi Delta Kappan*, 49 (1968), 337-40; G. Alan Hickrod and Ben C. Hubbard, "Social Stratification, Educational Opportunity, and the Role of State Departments of Education," *Educational Administration Quarterly*, 5 (1969), 81-96; LeRoy C. Ferguson, *How State Legislators View the Problem of School Needs* (Washington: Govt. Printing Office, 1960), Office of Education Report, reprinted in Robert C. Crew, Jr. (ed.), *State Politics* (Belmont, Cal.: Wadsworth, 1968), 479-500.

69. Allan M. Cartter, "The Shaping of the Compact for Education," *Educational Record* (Washington: American Council on Education, 1966), reprinted in Daniel Elazar et al., (ed.), *Cooperation and Conflict* (Itasca, Ill.: F.E. Peacock, 1969), 389-402; Michael D. Usdan, "The Role and Future of State Educational Coalitions," *Educational Administration Quarterly*, 5 (1969), 26-42.

70. For some research studies on such compliance, see William M. Beaney and Edward N. Reiser, "Prayer and Politics: The Impact of Engel and Schempp on the Political Process," *Journal of Public Law* 13 (1964), 475-503; Robert H. Birkby, "The Supreme Court and the Bible Belt: Tennessee Reaction to the "Schempp" Decision," *Midwest Journal of Political Science*, 10 (1966), 304-15. Probably the earliest such analysis was Frank Souraf, "Zorach *v*. Clauson: The Impact of a Supreme Court Decision," *American Political Science Review*, 53 (1959), 777-91. For a national survey of the impact, see Frank Way, Jr., *Liberty in the Balance* (New York: McGraw-Hill, 1967), 83-84, and "Survey Research on Judicial Decisions: The Prayer and Bible Reading Cases," *Western Political Quarterly*, 21 (1968), 189-205. For comparative state studies, see two papers, Kenneth M. Dolbeare and Phillip E. Hammond, "Local Elites, The Impact of Judicial Decisions, and the Process of Change," American Political Science Assn. meeting, 1969; Donald R. Reich, "Schoolhouse Religion and the Supreme Court: A Report on Attitudes of Teachers and Principals and on School Practices in Wisconsin and Ohio," American Law Schools Assn. meeting, 1969; both have excellent bibliographies on this subject.

71. For analysis of events leading to this decision, see Daniel M. Berman, *It Is So Ordered* (New York: Norton, 1966).

72. On the South, see Gary Orfield, *The Reconstruction of Southern Education* (New York: Wiley-Interscience, 1969). On the North, see U.S. Commission on Civil Rights, *Racial Isolation in the Public Schools* (Washington: Govt. Printing Office, 1967). For further references to the desegregation struggle, see Meyer Weinberg, *School Integration: A Comprehensive, Classified Bibliography of 3100 References* (Chicago: Integrated Education Associates, 1967), and 2d ed. 1971.

73. The historical pattern is treated in Frank J. Munger and Richard F. Fenno, *National Politics and Federal Aid to Education* (Syracuse: Syracuse University Press, 1962); Sidney W. Tiedt, *The Role of the Federal Government in Education* (New York: Oxford University Press, 1966).

74. Details are provided in Richard F. Fenno, "The House of Representatives and Federal Aid to Education," in Robert L. Peabody and Nelson W. Polsby, (eds.), *New Perspectives on the House of Representatives* (Chicago: Rand McNally, 1963), 195-235; James L. Sundquist, *Politics and Policy* (Washington: Brookings Institute, 1968), Ch. 5.

75. Several major works on this subject are Eugene Eidenberg and Roy D. Morey, *An Act of Congress* (New York: Norton, 1969); Philip Meranto, *The Politics of Federal Aid to Education in 1965* (Syracuse: Syracuse University Press, 1967). For a briefer statement, see James W. Guthrie, "The 1965 ESEA: A Political Case Study," *Phi Delta Kappan*, 49 (1968), and Stephen K. Bailey, *The Office of Education and the Educational Act of 1965* (Indianapolis: Bobbs-Merrill, 1967), Inter-University Case Program No. 100.

76. Julius Menacker, "The Organizational Behavior of Congress in the Formulation of Educational Support Policy," *Phi Delta Kappan*, 47 (1966), 78-87; the article by Fenno, loc. cit.

77. Eidenberg and Morey, loc. cit., purposefully employ a systems model for explaining the passage and administration of this law.

78. Frank W. Lutz and Joseph J. Ayzarelli, *Struggle for Power in Education* (New York: Center for Applied Research in Education, 1966).

79. Edwin P. Hollander and James W. Julian, "Contemporary Trends in the Analysis of Leadership Processes," *Psychological Bulletin*, 71 (1969), 387-97.

80. William P. McLure and James E. Stone, *A Study of Leadership in School District Reorganization* (Urbana: University of Illinois, 1955).

81. For example, Edward L. Pinney and Robert S. Friedman, *Political Leadership and the School Desegregation Crisis in Louisiana* (New York: McGraw-Hill, 1963).

82. See the two studies by R.E. Cleary, "Gubernatorial Leadership and State Policy on Desegregation in Public Higher Education," *Phylon*, 27 (1966), 165-70, and "The Role of Gubernatorial Leadership in Desegregation in Public Higher Education," *Journal of Negro Education*, (1966), and earlier, Samuel Krislov, "Constituency vs. Constitutionalism: The Desegregation Issue and Tensions and Aspirations of Southern Attorneys-General," *Midwest Journal of Political Science*, 3 (1959), 75-92.

83. See Ferguson, loc. cit.

84. Donald J. McCarty, "School Board Membership: Why Do Citizens Serve?" *Administrator's Notebook*, 8 (1959), 1-4, and Fred D. Carver, "Social Class and School Board Role Expectations," *Urban Education*, 3 (1968), 143-54.

85. Michael D. Usdan, "Some Issues Confronting School Administrators in Large City School Systems," *Educational Administration Quarterly*, 3 (1967), 218-37.

86. Donald J. McCarty and Charles E. Ramsey, "Community Power, School Board Structure, and the Role of the Chief Administrator," ibid., 4 (1968), 19-33; Bruce M. Fogarty and Russell T. Gregg, "Centralization of Decision Making and Selected Characteristics of Superintendents of Schools," ibid., 2 (1960), 62-72.

87. Illustrative of this theme are E.D. Hodgson, "Decision-Making and the Politics of Education," *Canadian Education and Research Digest*, 8 (1968), 150-62; John J. Hunt, "Politics in the Role of the Superintendent," *Phi Delta Kappan*, 49 (1968), 348-50. A major statement is Roald F. Campbell et al., *The Organization and Control of American Schools* (Columbus, Ohio: Merrill, 1965).

88. This message is typically transmitted anecdotally, as in David Mitchell, "How Kentucky Teachers Won at Politics," *Phi Delta Kappan* 44 (1963), 25-27. Alan Rosenthal is the leading analyst of the new pedagogue; "Pedagogues and Power: A Descriptive Survey," *Urban Affairs Quarterly*, 2 (1966), 83-102; "Administrator-Teacher Roles: Harmony or Conflict?" *Public Administration Review*, 27 (1967), 154-61; *Pedagogues and Power: Teacher Groups in School Politics* (Syracuse: Syracuse University Press, 1969). See also Stephen Cole, "The Unionization of Teachers: Determinants of Rank-and-File Support," *Sociology of Education*, 41 (1968), 66-88.

89. *FFPA*, 126.

90. Ibid., 128.

91. These include: Ordinance of 1785; Ordinance of 1787; 1862, First Morrill Act; 1887, Hatch Act; 1890, Second Morrill Act; 1914, Smith-Lever Agricultural Extension Act; 1917, Smith-Hughes Vocational Act; 1918, Vocational Rehabilitation Act; 1933, School Lunch Program; 1935, Bankhead-Jones Act (amended Smith-Lever); 1936, George Dean Act (amended Smith-Hughes); 1937, First Public Health Fellowships granted; 1940, Vocational Education for National Defense Act; 1944, GI Bill of Rights; 1950, National Science Foundation Act; 1954, Cooperative Research Program; 1958, National Defense Education Act; 1963, Higher Educational Facilities Act; 1963, Manpower Defense Training Act; 1964, Economic Opportunities Act; 1965, Elementary & Secondary Education Act. For a review, see Congressional Quarterly Service, *Federal Role in Education*, 2d ed. (Washington: CQ Service, 1967).

92. Cyril C. Houle, "Federal Policies Concerning Adult Education," *School Review*, 76 (1968), 166-89.

93. An illustration of evaluation is U.S. Office of Education, "Project Head Start: A Research Summary," *Integrated Education*, 6 (1968), 45-54; some shaken notions are discussed in "10 Research Lessons That Are Shaking Educational Programs," *Nation's Schools*, 81, (1968), 55-64. For a severe criticism of the failure to provide effective evaluation of programs under ESEA, see *Title I of ESEA: Is It Helping Poor Children?* (Washington: Washington Research Project, 1969), 2d ed.

94. Roald F. Campbell and Donald H. Layton, "Thrust and Counterthrust in Educational Policy Making," *Phi Delta Kappan*, 49 (1968), 290-94, and Campbell et al., *Strengthening State Departments of Education* (Chicago: Midwest Administration Center, University of Chicago, 1967).

95. Roald F. Campbell, "Federal Impact on Board's Decisions," *American School Board Journal*, 154 (1967), 38-42.

96. Burton R. Clark, "Interorganizational Patterns in Education," *Administrative Science Quarterly*, 10 (1965), 224-37.

97. Jack W. Osman, "The Dual Impact of Federal Aid on State and Local Government Expenditures," *National Tax Journal*, 19 (1966), 362-72. See also, Edward F. Renshaw, "A Note on the Expenditure Effect of Aid to Education," *Journal of Political Economy*, 67 (1960), 170-74.

98. James Guthrie et al., *Schools and Inequality* (Cambridge: MIT Press, 1971).

99. U.S. Senate Committee on Government Operations, Subcommittee on Intergovernmental Relations, *The Federal System as Seen by State and Local Officials* (Washington: Govt. Printing Office, 1963), Section E. It should be noted that this sample is heavily loaded with the larger, more urban states, especially with those from large cities; see 31, 215.

100. Jack Peltason, *Fifty-Eight Lonely Men: Southern Federal Judges and School Desegregation* (New York: Harcourt, Brace & World, 1961).

101. This value conflict is drawn from Orfield, loc. cit., an excellent study of the difficulties of administering the Civil Rights Act of 1964 for school desegregation. For illustrations of the Southern resistance patterns, see U.S. Commission on Civil Rights, *Southern Schools, 1966-67* (Washington: Govt. Printing Office, 1968). A case study of the latter is found in Frederick M. Wirt, *Politics of Equality: Law and Social Change in a Mississippi County* (Chicago: Aldine, 1970), Chs. 9-11, and of the Northern problems in T. Bentley Edwards and Frederick M. Wirt, (eds.), *School Desegregation in the North* (San Francisco: Chandler, 1968), and Crain, loc. cit.

102. Stephen K. Bailey and Edith K. Mosher, *ESEA: The Office of Education Administers A Law* (Syracuse University Press, 1968); Eidenberg and Morey, op. cit., Ch. 7. Joel Berke in 1971 was directing a team of scholars in an extensive national study of ESEA administration. Compare this administrative problem with that in Sidney C. Sufrin, *Administering the National Defense Education Act* (Syracuse: Syracuse University Press, 1963).

103. Mortimer Kaplan in Gabriel Almond and James Coleman (eds.), *The Politics of Developing Areas* (Princeton: Princeton University Press, 1960), 30-31.

104. An excellent critique as it applies to educational politics is found in Gerald E. Sroufe, "Political Systems Analysis and Research in Educational Administration: Can The Emperor Be Clothed?" Paper at the annual meeting of the American Educational Research Association, 1969; Kirst and Mosher, loc. cit.

105. Martin Landau, "On the Use of Functional Analysis in American Political Science," *Social Research*, 35 (1968).

106. S.L. Smith, "The Pattern of Educational Theory," *Australian Journal of Education*, 12 (1968), 252-64.

107. Donald Tope et al., *The Social Sciences View School Administration* (Englewood Cliffs, N.J.: Prentice-Hall, 1965).

108. For a description and evaluation of some models in the field, see the issue of *Alberta Journal of Educational Research*, 12 (1966), especially the articles by D.A. MacIver and E.A. Holdaway at 163-83. For a briefer explanation, see Robert B. Norberg, "Modus Model—Some Problems about the New Jargon," *American Behavioral Scientist*, 9 (1965-66), 12-14.

109. Louis R. Pondy, "Organizational Conflict: Concepts and Models," *Administrative Science Quarterly*, 12 (1967), 296-320; James L. Price, "Design of Proof in Organizational Research," ibid., 13 (1968), 121-34; E.G. Bogue, "The Context of Organizational Behavior: A Conceptual Synthesis for the Educational Administrator," *Educational Administration Quarterly*, 5 (1969), 58-75 illustrate the point.

110. There is an extensive literature here; for an overview, see Amitai Etzioni, "Mixed Scanning: A 'Third' Approach to Decision-Making," *Public Administration Review*, 27 (1967), 385-92.

111. For example, see Lawrence J. Clarke, "Decision Models for Personnel Selection and Assignment," *Personnel Administration*, 32 (1969), 48-56.

112. For a review, see Robert H. Jackson, "An Analysis of the Comparative Public Administration Movement," *Canadian Public Administration*, 9 (1966), 108-30.

113. Philip H. Coombs, *The World Educational Crisis: A System Analysis* (New York: Oxford University Press, 1968), and the critique by Sroufe, loc. cit., 104.

114. George Z.F. Bereday and Jaan Pennar (eds.), *The Politics of Soviet Education* (New York: Praeger, 1960). Frank Mackinnon, *The Politics of Education: A Study of the Political Administration of the Public Schools* (Toronto: University of Toronto Press, 1960); Ronald Manzer, "Selective Inducements and the Development of Pressure Groups: The Case of Canadian Teachers' Association," *Canadian Journal of Political Science*, 2 (1969), 103-17. Note also R. Saran, "Decision-Making by a Local Educational Authority," *Public Administration*, 45 (1967), 387-402, about community input to local schools in Great Britain, and

Theodore L. Reller, "The Greater London Council and the Education Service," *Educational Administration Quarterly*, 4 (1968), 5-18.

115. Such an approach is suggested in Hans Weiler, "Education and Political Development," *Review of Educational Research*, 38 (1968), 231-42.

116. David Easton, "The New Revolution in Political Science," *American Political Science Review*, 63 (1969), 1051-61, notes the major criticisms of behavioralism and his own work, suggesting that some are quite valid; his point on social change is at 1057. The Easton and Dennis volume (at note 37) defends his theory against such criticism; the citation is from a letter from Easton.

117. There is an extensive literature in one aspect; see the review in Elihu Katz et al., "Traditions of Research on the Diffusion of Innovation," *American Sociological Review*, 28 (1963), 237-52. As illustrations of some useful thinking, see Bryce Ryan, "The Resuscitation of Social Change," *Social Forces*, 44 (1965), 1-7; Guy Barbichon, "Social Change: Innovator or Conformity," *International Social Science Journal*, 20 (1968), 412-30. Typical of global theories of social change is Richard LaPiere, *Social Change* (New York: McGraw-Hill, 1965). An effort to work out such theory in the matter of law and social change, see Wirt in note 101, Chs. 1, 14, 15.

118. Terry N. Clark, "Institutionalization of Innovations in Higher Education: Four Models," *Administrative Science Quarterly*, 13 (1968), 1-25.

119. Samuel Moore and Kujoto Mizuba, "Innovation Diffusion: A Study in Credibility," *Educational Forum*, 33 (1969), 181-85; Guy Benveniste and Warren F. Ilchman (eds.), *Agents of Change: Professionals in Developing Countries* (New York: Praeger, 1969).

120. A. Ross Thomas, "Innovation within a Bureaucratic Education System," *Journal of Educational Administration*, 6 (1968), 116-31, reviews the research; see also Stephen P. Hencley, "Innovation and School Policy," *Educational Leadership*, 25 (1968), 308-11.

121. See Jennings and Fox, loc. cit.

122. See note 5; a fuller treatment appears in his *Foundations of Behavioral Research* (New York: Holt, Rinehart & Winston, 1964).

123. An excellent review of this subject is Kirst and Mosher, loc. cit.

124. Robert H. Salisbury, "The Analysis of Public Policy: A Search for Theories and Rules," in Austin Ranney (ed.), *Political Science and Public Policy* (Chicago: Markham, 1968); and with John P. Heinz, "A Theory of Policy Analysis and Some Preliminary Applications," in Ira Sharkansky (ed.), *Policy Analysis in Political Science* (Chicago: Markham, 1970), Ch. 3.

125. Theodore Lowi, "American Business, Public Policy, Case-Studies, and Political Science," *World Politics*, (1964), 677-715.

126. For the various meanings of "community" and the resulting real-world variety, see David Minar and Scott Greer, *The Concept of Community* (Chicago: Aldine, 1969).

127. Peter H. Rossi and Robert L. Crain, "The NORC Permanent Community Sample," *Public Opinion Quarterly*, 32 (1968), 261-72.

128. See note 38 above.

129. *FFPA*, 130.

130. See note 104, and Iannaccone, in note 3.

131. Nicholas A. Masters and Lawrence K. Pettit, "Some Changing Patterns in Educational Policy Making," *Educational Administration Quarterly*, 2 (1966), 81-100. For case studies of such changes as a result of recent federal poverty programs, see Masters et al., *Politics, Poverty and Education: An Analysis of Decision-Making Structures* (University Park: Institute of Public Administration, Pennsylvania State University, 1968), OEO Report.

132. Keith Goldhammer, book review in *Educational Administration Quarterly*, 1 (1965), p. 69.

133. Wallace S. Sayre, "The Politics of Education," *Teachers College Record* (1963), pp. 178-183.

## About the Editor

**Michael W. Kirst** is currently Director of the Joint Program in Educational Administration at Stanford University where he is also Assistant Professor of Education and Business Administration. He did his undergraduate work at Dartmouth College, graduating in 1961 as an Alfred P. Sloan Fellow. He subsequently earned both masters and doctoral degrees from Harvard University. He has been both Staff Director of the Senate Subcommittee on Manpower, Employment, and Poverty, and Director of Program Planning and Evaluation at the Bureau of Elementary and Secondary Education of the Office of Education. Prior to that he held a number of positions in various departments of the federal government. He is a member of both the American Political Science Association and the American Educational Research Association. He is the coauthor of *The Political Web of American Schools* (Little Brown, 1965) and of many articles and papers.